Praise for *Christ Brings All Newness*

"Theology today can seem surprisingly rudderless, as if the acquisitions of the last century's return *ad fontes* had been casually mislaid. It is a tonic to find a theologian whose mind is both disciplined and open, who interprets the signs of the times as such—as significant, not as oracles—in the light of a life-giving tradition. Not easily labelled as 'conservative' or 'liberal,' he manages to span wide expanses, a balancing act he performs with surefooted elegance still, well past his threescore and ten. This volume by Robert Imbelli, a learned man of the Church, is a treasure."

—**Bishop Erik Varden**, OCSO, author of *The Shattering of Loneliness: On Christian Remembrance*

"In the realm of literature, it has long been recognized that there are some great masters who excel especially in the short story format. In the field of modern theology, there is no one, in my judgment, who surpasses Robert Imbelli's mastery of the form of the short theological essay. The essays in this volume are profound, inspired, and perspicacious meditations on the deepest and most central theological themes—above all the perennial newness of Christ. They are filled with the light of Christ and the fervor of the Spirit and will communicate this light and warmth to the attentive reader."

—**Khaled Anatolios**, John A. O'Brien Professor of Theology, University of Notre Dame

"When Hans Urs von Balthasar concluded that the theological guild needs people 'who devote their lives to the glory of theology, that fierce fire burning in the dark night of adoration and obedience,' it is unlikely that he had Fr. Robert Imbelli specifically in mind; *Christ Brings All Newness* suggests, however, that he well could have. In winsome, sometimes ecstatic prose, our author joyfully embraces both the seriousness of the theological task and the eternal freshness of Christian life and practice. This book, indelibly marked by a lifetime of contemplative reading, spiritual reflection, preaching, and pastoral ministry, invites its readers not only into the circle of Imbelli's dear friends—Irenaeus, Augustine, Fra Angelico, Bach, Newman, Ratzinger, Dante, and a plentitude of others—but also and more urgently to friendship with Jesus Christ, who makes all things new."

—**Jennifer Newsome Martin**, Associate Professor, University of Notre Dame

"Robert Imbelli is a theologian who might rightly be described as both 'Irenaean' and 'irenic.' Like Christianity's first great systematic thinker, Irenaeus of Lyons, Imbelli finds the coherence of Christian thought—indeed of all human history and culture—in the person of Jesus Christ, and Christ serves for him at the criterion by which he judges all human achievements. Yet this judgment is always rendered in an irenic spirit that seeks common ground in Christ even as he frankly acknowledges disagreements. This volume gathers essays, reviews, and reflections on a wide range of topics, figures, and forms of theological expression, yet it possesses a remarkable coherence because of Imbelli's determination to take every thought captive for Christ."

—**Frederick C. Bauerschmidt**, Professor of Theology, Loyola
    University Maryland

"Father Robert Imbelli's pellucid, luminous collection renews our faith in Christ's promise that he will remain with us always. We come away from this book more vibrantly aware of the way beauty—in Scripture, liturgy, art, and Imbelli's own theological reflection—can draw us more deeply into friendship with Jesus Christ, who 'plays in ten thousand places,' and in whom all things hold together. This work is a splendid companion to *Rekindling the Christic Imagination*."

—**Paul J. Contino**, Distinguished Professor in Great Books,
    Pepperdine University

"To everyone who sees this book of Robert Imbelli's essays and reviews, I urge, 'take and read!' Here is strong medicine to heal reductive constrictions of spirit instilled by modern self-referentiality. These writings lead toward doing theology as 'scrutinizing in the light of faith all the truth stored up in the mystery of Christ' (*DV* 24). They stir rejuvenating movements of spirit that arise as ramifications of the Incarnation of the Son of God. Imbelli will attract you to exist in the broad frame of New Testament revelation, being thankful to God and generous to many others, moving out ever afresh from your center in the Christ-event as depicted in the letters to the Ephesians and the Colossians."

—**Jared Wicks**, SJ, Emeritus Professor of Theology of the Gregorian
    University, Rome

CHRIST

BRINGS ALL

NEWNESS

CHRIST
BRINGS ALL
NEWNESS
ESSAYS, REVIEWS, AND REFLECTIONS

ROBERT P. IMBELLI

EDITED WITH AN INTRODUCTION BY
RICHARD G. SMITH

Published by Word on Fire Academic, an imprint of
Word on Fire, Elk Grove Village, IL 60007
© 2023 by Word on Fire Catholic Ministries
Printed in the United States of America
All rights reserved.

Design and layout by Cassie Bielak and Rozann Lee

"Three Tantalizing Enigmas in Dante's Heaven of the Sun" and "Remembering
and Misremembering Vatican II" originally published in and reprinted by
permission of *Church Life Journal*, a Journal of the
McGrath Institute for Church Life.

"Until Christ Be Formed in You: Newman's Theological-Pastoral Mystagogy"
originally published in *Heart Speaks to Heart: John Henry Newman and the Call
to Holiness*, ed. Kevin O'Reilly (Leominster, UK: Gracewing, 2021).
Reprinted by permission.

"He Is Head of the Body, the Church: Salvation as Incorporation into Christ"
originally published in and reprinted by permission of
Communio: International Catholic Review.

"Resurrection and Real Presence" © 1990 Commonweal Foundation;
"From Homer, to Picasso, to Piaf, to God" © 1989 Commonweal Foundation;
"No Glib Gospel" © 2016 Commonweal Foundation;
"Our True Identity" © 2022 Commonweal Foundation. Reprinted with
permission. For more information, visit www.commonwealmagazine.org.

All other essays have been used under fair use, or if not, all efforts have been
made to contact copyright holders for permission.

ISBN: 978-1-68578-090-6
Library of Congress Control Number: 2023944296

For Michael, More than Brother—Friend

"Omnem novitatem attulit, semetipsum afferens"

"Christ brought all newness in bringing himself"

—Irenaeus of Lyons

Contents

Preface

Sursum Corda!

As will be abundantly clear from the writings that follow, all my priestly-theological ministry has been shaped and nurtured by the event and the documents of the Second Vatican Council. I was privileged to live and study in Rome during the four sessions of the council. I followed the slow and careful elaboration of the documents and have continued to draw guidance and sustenance from them during my more than fifty-five years of preaching and teaching.

If there is a golden thread that links the essays, reviews, and reflections of this volume, it is the conviction that underlying the diverse writings of the New Testament (and of the Tradition of the Church that unfolds those original witnesses of the faith) is a foundational "logic" or "depth grammar." I call it the logic of "*novum*/transformation." In many and diverse ways, it celebrates and proclaims the absolute newness of Jesus Christ and the radical transformation to which Jesus Christ summons believers. Hence the title of this volume, drawn from Saint Irenaeus: *Christ Brings All Newness.*

Vatican II recovered that logic and liberated it from the scholastic encrustations which had dimmed its revelatory luster. Moreover, it presented that salvific Good News in a more experiential and personalist key, rather than in the more abstract and conceptual style of previous councils. It drew inspiration from a renewed and contemplative reading of the Scriptures and the Fathers of the Church: it heralded *ressourcement*. But, as I insist, this *ressourcement* is, at its deepest, a re-Sourcement: a return to the unique Source who is Jesus Christ himself.

From my perspective, the many evident failures (at times painfully scandalous) of the postconciliar Church are not due to the council's teaching but to our failure to appropriate whole-heartedly its Christic depth and joyfully to bear witness and proclaim it to others. Too often the council's "universal call to holiness," to radical transformation of heart and mind, has been ignored or betrayed by human self-preoccupation and sin—as has, of course, been the case throughout history.

Apostasy, turning from Christ, assumes myriad practical and theoretical manifestations. Far too frequently Christians act and judge as though Jesus Christ were not present and acting in the world. Thus, the council's endorsement of *aggiornamento* (bring-ing the Gospel to the contemporary world in intelligible terms) has too easily slipped into an accommodation to the values of a secular age or even, in some quarters, a complete capitulation to the day's fashions. Theology thereby risks being reduced to soci-ology, and the salt of the Gospel loses its savor. Then discernment in the Spirit of Christ degenerates into the distribution of surveys and the taking of opinion polls.

It will be apparent that, among the theological authors to whom I am especially beholden, John Henry Newman, Joseph Ratzinger, and Robert Barron stand out. Newman, because he so clearly anticipated the council in many of its main themes and concerns. Ratzinger, because as theologian and pope, he faith-fully interpreted its teaching. Barron, because he is creatively communicating its evangelical imperative in a postmodern (yet often still searching) American cultural context. In their writings the logic of *novum*/transformation is conspicuously present and determinative.

A further conviction that characterizes all three is that there can be no separation between confession of Christ and transfor-mation of life, between Christian thinking and Christian living, between theology and spirituality. Intimately connected with this is another important sensibility that unites them. It is their persuasion of the crucial importance of the aesthetic in making real, in embodying and appropriating, the truths of the faith. Each of them draws on images and art, not merely to illustrate but to incarnate the life-giving truths they expound.

So renewing the Catholic vision and imagination must be the task of many minds and hearts, poets and artists very much in the forefront. In this regard, I have often told students that among the great doctors of the Church must be counted Dante Alighieri and Johann Sebastian Bach. To ponder the *Divine Comedy* or plunge into the Mass in B Minor is to be moved to one's depth, where affection and thought take root in the heart, where beauty and truth embrace.

Others will surely identify artistic works that decisively shape and guide their own faith journey. Many may join me in according especial esteem to the great mosaic of the cross as the Tree of Life in Rome's Basilica of San Clemente, which graces the cover of this volume. The vision of the cross as the recapitulation in Christ of all humanity and all creation (Eph. 1:10) continues to rekindle the Catholic imagination of multitudes after almost a thousand years. For Christ, being lifted up from the earth, indeed draws all to himself (John 12:32).

My particular offering in this book is to present three dimensions of the mystery of Christ that can illuminate our ongoing quest. They are the Ascension, the Eucharist, and the Transfiguration. For each there is an artistic representation in the book (the *via pulchritudinis* strongly encouraged by John Paul II, Benedict XVI, and Francis), accompanied by a quote from the New Testament that provides a point of entry into meditation upon the mystery. In the essays and reflections that follow, I seek to explicate and expand upon the choice of these three facets of the Christic mystery. Suffice it to suggest here that there is dynamic interrelation and mutual penetration among them. The risen-ascending Christ is working the transfiguration of believers by incorporating them into his Body in preeminent fashion through the Eucharist, the sacrament of sacraments. Years ago, Henri de Lubac reminded us that the mystery of Christ's embodiment comprises three inseparable dimensions: the risen-ascended body of the Lord, his Eucharistic Body, and his ecclesial Body. The Word of God continues to take flesh and to dwell in us and in our world.

I have long insisted that the richest theological event which we experience is the celebration of the Eucharist on the Lord's Day. It is the matrix of all our Christian living and Christian thinking. At the beginning of the most solemn part of that celebration, the priest admonishes the congregation: "*Sursum corda!*"—"Lift up your hearts!" Lift them up to the Lord who is both present and ever coming. And, lifting them up, let us widen them further by giving thanks to the Lord our God. Thanks, because all we have is gift. The gift of our very being. The gift of our redemption in Christ. The gift of everlasting life that is the communion of holy ones rejoicing in the vivifying presence of the Triune God—indeed, truly partaking in God's glory.

Meanwhile, still *in via*, my gratitude abounds for all who have accompanied me on the journey of faith. Teachers from grammar school through doctoral studies. Colleagues and students at St. Joseph's Seminary (Dunwoodie), Maryknoll School of Theology, and Boston College. Friends too numerous to name, but very present in thoughts and prayers.

At risk of omitting others let me single out a few whose friendship has been at once challenge and support: Cardinal Timothy Dolan, Bishop James Massa; Monsignors Thomas Guarino, Michael Heintz, and Thomas Derivan; Fathers Khaled Anatolios, Anthony Andreassi, Samuel Bellafiore, John Cush, Giuseppe Fazio, Mauro Gagliardi, Joseph Komonchak, Joseph McLafferty, Louis Masi, Aaron Pidel, SJ, Vincent Strand, SJ, Thomas Joseph White, OP, and Jared Wicks, SJ; and Professors Angela Franks,

Andrew Meszaros, Christopher Ruddy, Andrew Salzmann, and George Weigel.

Professor Matthew Levering and Father Richard Smith were instrumental in the volume's genesis. Jason Paone, David Augustine, and Andrew Tolkmith of Word on Fire Academic have my thanks for their professional and patient assistance.

Years ago, I came upon this musing by the French author Antoine de Saint-Exupéry which still resonates deeply with me: *"L'homme n'est qu'un noeud de relations. Les relations comptent seules pour l'homme"*—"Man is but a web of relations; relations alone count for man."

Those already mentioned certainly bear witness to—indeed, give substance to—that realization. Even more so did my parents, Julia and Frank, the human *fons et origo* of my life's journey—not merely biologically, but spiritually. As do those who continue to nourish that journey in ways beyond telling: my sister-in-law, Lillian; my niece, Julia; and my nephews, Charles and Nicholas. And, of course, my brother, Michael, to whom this book is dedicated.

Lifting up my heart to the Lord, I bear them up with me, and with them continuously give thanks to the Lord our God.

Robert P. Imbelli
Solemnity of the Annunciation of the Lord, 2023

Introduction

The Heart of the Matter

RICHARD G. SMITH

The true preaching of the Gospel is to preach Christ.
—St. John Henry Newman, *Lectures on Justification*

. . . what love sees is true;
That the world's fullness is not made but found.
—Richard Wilbur, *A Wedding Toast*

I

The following essays, reviews, and reflections had various beginnings—several were prepared for scholarly journals, collections, or conferences, others for more popular magazines, still others for internet sites intended for a wide general audience, and one for a Sunday Mass congregation. What makes the varied parts a whole is a thorough and vibrant *Christocentrism*. Such a Christocentrism, most systematically articulated in his *Rekindling the Christic Imagination*,[1] is the distinctive characteristic of Fr. Imbelli's theological project. The diminishment and near-total loss of the "Christic center" in widespread currents of Christian theology, spirituality, and life represents a genuine crisis and a profound impoverishment threatening to distort and even destroy the very heart of Christian faith. Fr. Imbelli retrieves and highlights the Christocentrism that has marked and enlivened Christian

---

1. Robert P. Imbelli, *Rekindling the Christic Imagination: Theological Meditations for the New Evangelization* (Collegeville, MN: Liturgical, 2014).

thought and life, beginning with St. Paul and the Fathers of the Church, as a way forward. St. Ignatius of Antioch, writing in the early second century to the Church in Tralles on his way to be martyred in Rome, provides a powerful witness to the vibrant Christocentrism of the early Church:

> Be deaf, therefore, whenever anyone speaks to you apart from Jesus Christ, who was of the family of David, who was the son of Mary; who *really* was born, who both ate and drank; who *really* was persecuted under Pontius Pilate, who *really* was crucified and died while those in heaven and on earth looked on; who, moreover, *really* was raised from the dead when his Father raised him up. In the same way his Father will likewise also raise up in Christ Jesus us who believe in him. *Apart from him we have no true life.*[2]

Christians are to tolerate nothing "apart from Jesus Christ": that is to say, in the context of Ignatius's world, nothing from those who would diminish or call into question the centrality of Christ, or those who disdain matter as evil and then retreat into a world of ideas, rejecting especially the Incarnation. Jesus Christ, as Ignatius describes him, is not an abstract idea or theory or proposition to be discussed and debated, or a universal symbol of human potential or wisdom, or a dead man of passing historical interest. He is a living person, a *real* person who, Ignatius emphatically insists, *really* (*alēthōs*) was born, ate, drank, suffered, died, and was raised from the dead. Most importantly, it is *only* in relation to this living person that we can have true/real (*alēthinon*) life. His life *is* our life (Augustine cries out in his *Confessions*, "O Life of my life!"). If, without Jesus Christ, there is no true life at all, then *everything* depends upon coming into relationship with him.

---

2. Ignatius of Antioch, *Letter to the Trallians* 9, in *The Apostolic Fathers*, trans. Michael W. Holmes (Grand Rapids, MI: Baker Academic, 2007), 221 (emphasis added).

As Fr. Imbelli puts it below, "Intimate friendship with Jesus is the very heart of the matter" (page 237).

II

Pope Benedict XVI's conviction that intimate friendship with Christ is indeed the "heart of the matter," and his discernment that the possibility of such a friendship was being undermined by certain strains of biblical exegesis, provided the impetus for his three-volume *Jesus of Nazareth* series. Fr. Imbelli cites Pope Benedict on precisely this point in several of the present essays. The pope writes,

> [We are given] the impression that we have very little certain knowledge of Jesus and that only at a later stage did faith in his divinity shape the image we have of him. This impression has by now penetrated deeply into the minds of the Christian people at large. This is a dramatic situation for faith, because its point of reference is being placed in doubt: Intimate friendship with Jesus, on which everything depends, is in danger of clutching into thin air.[3]

Like Ignatius, Pope Benedict presents in his *Jesus of Nazareth* volumes a living person, a *real* person, rather than an abstract idea or memory of a person. A Christian comes to Scripture not with the intent of gaining more information or satisfying curiosity but in order to meet a person, to meet Christ. This means that Scripture is not only about past events but about present realities in the life of the baptized Christian disciple. Speaking to a group of American seminarians in 1984, then-Cardinal Ratzinger described the power of a particular Gospel passage: "It speaks so directly to us

---

3. Pope Benedict XVI, foreword to *Jesus of Nazareth: From the Baptism in the Jordan to the Transfiguration*, trans. Adrian J. Walker (New York: Doubleday, 2007), xii.

because these are not words we must laboriously drag back as it were from the far distance into our life. What is there affects us directly: it is our life."[4] What he says of one particular Gospel passage is true for all of Scripture: all of it *affects* us because all of it directly concerns our Life.

Scripture *affects* us; that is, Scripture touches the affections, it touches the *heart* and not only the intellect, inviting us and leading us not merely to know *about* Jesus but to know *Jesus* and so then to love Jesus and to believe in Jesus. Fr. Imbelli frequently quotes the First Letter of Peter 1:8: "Without having seen him you love him; though you do not now see him you believe in him and rejoice with unutterable and exalted joy" (RSV). In his letter, Peter is addressing a new generation of Christians, different from the first generation we meet in the Gospels. Like us, this new generation had not known Jesus during his earthly life. They only came to know him later, through the preaching and the ministry of Jesus's disciples. But that did nothing to diminish the intensity of their experience of Jesus. Peter says to them: without having seen him you *love* him and, even now, you don't see him yet you *believe* in him! The verb order is important: love *then* believe, love *leading to* belief; as Saint John Henry Newman writes, "I believe because I love!" Peter's words signify the success of the early Christians in proclaiming the Gospel, for, as Newman reminds us, "The true preaching of the Gospel is to preach Christ." They presented a person to be embraced and befriended rather than a proposition to be accepted or denied. They showed the real possibility for an intimate friendship with Jesus even for those who "do not now see him" and that this friendship would be an experience of authentic and profound joy—and, far more, that this friendship would be true life for them. At the same time, Peter's words lay out the *challenge* for every new generation of Christians: How

4. Joseph Ratzinger, *Ministers of Your Joy*, trans. Robert Nowell (London: St. Paul's, 1989), 82.

do we "preach Christ" in such a way that he is credible and attractive, so that his invitation to intimate friendship is not merely notional but real?

The distinction (not dichotomy) between notional and real, so central in the thought of John Henry Newman, is pivotal in Fr. Imbelli's writings. In terms of a friendship with Jesus, the distinction between notional and real is the difference between that which is conceptual, propositional, and abstract and that which is "concrete, vivid, enkindling affection and inspiring imitation" (page 244). This distinction in no way disparages the notional—indeed, there is a proper and important place for the notional in Christian faith. But a real apprehension of Christ is *essential* for Christian faith, life, and discipleship since it is the real, Newman suggests, that moves us to action and to make a response. Christ is preached in a real way precisely when affection for him is enkindled and imitation of him inspired.

Once again, the example of Peter is instructive. The new generation of Christians whom Peter addressed in his first letter came to know and then love and then believe in Jesus Christ primarily through the witness and *personal influence* of those who had known Jesus during his earthly life and who were eyewitnesses to his Resurrection and Ascension, including Peter himself. The next generation, in their turn, preached Christ by *their* witness to what they had seen and heard and by their personal influence, and so on, and so on. This witness and personal influence also eventually came to be extended and exerted through Christian art, music, literature, theology, spiritual writings, and sermons. Christians early on discovered the power of art to awaken the human heart, mind, and imagination to God in such a way as to enkindle affection and inspire imitation.

Most importantly, Christians came to appreciate the Church's liturgy as *the* privileged place where Christ is "preached" in a real way, so as to establish and nourish intimate friendship. In the liturgy, the living Christ is present in a way that can be seen and heard and touched and even tasted, present in a way that is both "concrete" and "vivid," inspiring a real apprehension of Jesus. Liturgy is a profoundly *incarnational* (embodied) experience, and so a remedy for the Gnostic divorce of body and spirit that has never entirely gone away, even from the time of Ignatius of Antioch. Fr. Imbelli uses Charles Taylor's evocative term "excarnational" to describe the contemporary manifestation of Gnosticism in Western thought and culture: "Many men and women today are suspicious of history and tradition, hesitant to form binding relations, prone to use others as objects to satisfy fleeting emotions as they practice death avoidance and denial. These are manifest symptoms of excarnation—a profound unease with and alienation from our bodily reality" (page 135).

Pope Benedict described a deeply personal moment of real apprehension of Jesus Christ as an intimate friend that occurred for him within the context of the Church's liturgy. Preaching at the ordination of several bishops in the Vatican Basilica in 2011, on the anniversary of his own priestly ordination, Pope Benedict said,

> Sixty years on from the day of my priestly ordination, I hear once again deep within me these words of Jesus that were addressed to us new priests at the end of the ordination ceremony by the Archbishop, Cardinal Faulhaber, in his slightly frail yet firm voice. According to the liturgical practice of that time, these words conferred on the newly-ordained priests the authority to forgive sins. "No longer servants, but friends": at that moment I knew deep down that these words were no mere formality, nor were they simply a quotation from Scripture. I knew that, at that moment, the Lord himself was speaking to me in a very *personal* way.[5]

5. Benedict XVI, "Homily for the Imposition of the Sacred Pallium on Metropolitan Archbishops," June 29, 2011, vatican.va (emphasis added).

That such a *personal* experience of Christ's invitation to friendship would come as an unexpected gift in the context of the Church's liturgy is telling: in personalist terms, the intimate friendship with Jesus to which we are invited is an I-Thou relationship (page 68). In both private and corporate prayer, Christians address God as "Thou"—and it is especially in the liturgy where this "Thou" becomes most concrete and vivid, *incarnational*, precisely because the liturgy touches mind and heart, senses and affections. In the liturgy, Christians address and meet and respond to a real, and not merely notional, "Thou." The liturgy of his priestly ordination enabled Joseph Ratzinger to hear the words of Scripture not as "mere formality" or "simply a quotation" or something laboriously dragged back "from the far distance," but as a living voice, a Thou calling him "friend."

III

The "intimate friendship with Jesus" that Christians are invited to embrace is a friendship that *recreates*. This particular I-Thou relationship is the one toward which all other I-thou relationships point and find their fullness. The "Thou" here is the incarnate God—the *Christic Novum*—and so, in this intimate friendship, we are brought into the very mystery of God in a profoundly personal and transforming way. Fr. Imbelli emphatically and frequently reminds his readers of Saint Irenaeus's words in the *Adversus Haereses*: *Omnem novitatem attulit, semetipsum afferens*— Christ brought all newness in bringing himself. At the heart of Christian faith, life, and discipleship is not a moralism, or a mere imitation of Christ, but *participation* in Christ. And this participation in Christ does not make us merely *better* people but *new* people. Christ brings all newness in bringing himself: in Christ, we experience a new creation, the birth of a new self, a new communion (the I-Thou is also a We-Thou in the communion of the Church). The Christian truly participates in the *Novum* of the Incarnation, the Cross, the Resurrection, and the Ascension. The fourteenth-century Byzantine theologian Nicholas Cabasilas puts it succinctly: "Union with Christ, then, belongs to those who have undergone all that the Saviour has undergone, and have experienced and become all that he has."[6] The Christian realizes, in Newman's strong sense of the word, the mystery of Christ's Life, Death, Resurrection, and Ascension in his or her person, so that his life really *is* our life, a new life that is "inexhaustible and unending" (page 295)—truly, *apart from him we have no true life*! When the Christian can fully *realize* this new life and say with Paul, "For to me, life is Christ" (Phil 1:21), then the newness Christ brings permeates everything, and one can *really* speak of a "new creation" in which he or she lives.

The participation of a Christian in Christ Jesus is frequently called *theosis* or *deification*. Fr. Imbelli uses the word *Christification* to make explicit and draw attention to the Christic center of this transformation/transfiguration of divine filiation in which "we stand where Jesus stands" in relation to the Father.[7] This participation begins at Baptism, but what follows is a "costly transfiguration" as "the seed planted there must be nourished so that the plant may grow sturdy. And then it must be further pruned and strengthened to withstand the 'wickedness and snares' of the world, flesh, and devil. . . . Growth in friendship with Christ entails an ever more generous embrace of his Cross" (page 238). Indeed,

the whole of the Christian life . . . is the appropriation of what has already transpired in our Baptism, but now must be

6. Nicholas Cabasilas, *The Life in Christ*, trans. Carmino J. deCatanzaro (Crestwood, NY: St. Vladimir's, 1974), 65.

7. Rowan Williams, *Being Christian* (London: SPCK, 2014), 62. The term *Christification* is central to the theology and spirituality of Cabasilas, cited above. For an insightful introduction to Cabasilas and the implications of *Christification*, see Panayiotis Nellas, *Deification in Christ* (Crestwood, NY: St. Vladimir's, 1987), 109–39.

realized fully in each of us until together "we all attain to the
unity of faith and knowledge of the Son of God, to the one
perfected humanity, to the measure of the stature of the fullness of Christ" (Eph 4:13). . . . Unlike the egotistic withdrawal of the old Adam, anyone incorporated into the New Adam,
Jesus Christ, is fundamentally a self who lives the new life of
communion. (page 234)

This "new life of communion," communion both vertically and
horizontally, is Eucharistic. Since "*Jesus Christ's very being is to be
Eucharist* . . . the Eucharist is the privileged locus where friendship with Jesus is nourished and cultivated. To the extent that
we become present to his Real Presence, our very self becomes
Eucharistic: a living out of gratitude to the Father and generosity towards our brothers and sisters" (page 82). To borrow Pope
Benedict XVI's phrase, the life of the Christian incorporated
into Christ, transformed/transfigured into a new self in the new
creation, takes a Eucharistic form and the Christian becomes a
Eucharistic mystic. Fr. Imbelli proposes that "the Christian of the
future will be a Eucharistic mystic—one who has experienced
Someone, the living Lord—or will not be" (page 81).

IV

It is true that a thorough and vibrant *Christocentrism* makes a whole
of the various texts that follow. But they are also of a piece in the intent that they be mystagogic: that these essays, reviews, and reflections lead the reader deeper into the mystery of Christ in a personal
and real way. To that end, the aesthetic dimension of Christian
faith consistently plays a central role in Fr. Imbelli's theological project to renew the Catholic imagination. It would perhaps be more
accurate to say that Fr. Imbelli seeks to address what Charles Taylor
calls the *social imaginary*. By this, "Taylor does not intend, in the

first instance, theories or even ideas. He focuses first on the images and stories that enkindle our imaginations and shape our sensibilities, the common understandings and practices that make beliefs plausible."[8] If "for some today God is not so much incredible as unreal" (page 189), then it is exactly the social imaginary that needs to be addressed. Newman once suggested that the crisis of faith in his own time was a matter of the imagination, not the intellect, and that the "passage from the merely notional to the real is mediated by the imagination, by evocative images which captivate the heart" (page 168).

Beauty has a unique role to play in the engagement of the imagination and the expansion of the social imaginary. An encounter with beauty awakens a desire to make a response. In one of his finest poems, Austrian poet Rainer Maria Rilke imagines standing before a damaged but profoundly beautiful marble statue of a Roman god or hero and seems to hear the statue call out to him, "Du mußt dein Leben ändern!" ("You must change your life!") And more, true beauty always points toward the One "to whom and in whom," in the words of Gerard Manley Hopkins, "all beauty comes home." In the mystagogic reflections of this collection, art and music, literature and poetry, Scripture, the Fathers of the Church and liturgy appear again and again to engage the imagination and awaken love. In the most poetic of the reflections in this collection, Fr. Imbelli describes, in the pattern of the First Letter of Saint Peter, love as a way of seeing and then coming to belief (pp. 166–67). The American poet Richard Wilbur puts it memorably when he writes in his *A Wedding Toast*, "What love sees is true; / That the world's fullness is not made but found." It is only love that truly knows Christ, who loves us first. He himself is the fullness of all that is—a fullness that does not have to be laboriously created or dragged from obscurity into our lives, but that is already *given*, already present, in need only

---

8. Imbelli, *Rekindling*, xxi; for a fuller explanation of "social imaginary," see Charles Taylor, *A Secular Age* (Cambridge: Belknap, 2007), 171–76.

of a preparation of the heart and eyes of love. As Fr. Imbelli tells us, Christ's "presence [is] so real as to be palpable; yet so discreet as to demand discernment" (page 160).

A final word about the word intentionally used to mark the different sections of this collection: *soundings*. Fr. Imbelli's scholarship is consistently pastoral in the best sense of the word. His is a scholarship marked by decades not only in the classroom but at the baptismal font, the confessional, the pulpit, and, most especially, the altar—so that he can say, "I know him in whom I have believed" (2 Tim. 1:12). These collected writings are a personal witness to Jesus Christ, the fruit of a long intimate friendship, offered to make Jesus known and loved and believed—and an invitation to the reader to consider his or her personal witness to Christ and the fruits of an intimate friendship with him. In the classroom, Fr. Imbelli unfailingly showed a genuine interest in what his students thought—in fact, many students can attest to this interest as a hallmark of his teaching method. In many of his classes, students were required to submit brief weekly reflections on the assigned texts in which they articulated an insight into the material and a connection between that insight and some other area of personal interest. The use of the word *soundings* is humble, but honest. The mystery of Christ, like all mystery, is inexhaustible. The best we can do is take soundings of that mystery. There is always more to be said, more to be contemplated, more to be loved. In the following reflections, we might perceive an invitation to make our own insights and connections, to take further soundings deeper and deeper into the mystery, the Christic *Novum*, the Friend who each of us can say in an intensely personal way, "loved me and gave himself for me" (Gal. 2:20).

Christ of Vézelay

"Ascending above the heavens, he fills all things."
Ephesians 4:10

PART I

Essays

Soundings in
Vatican II's Call to
Ressourcement and
Aggiornamento

1. Remembering and Misremembering Vatican II

The Paschal Rekindling of the Catholic Imaginary

I. REMEMBERING VATICAN II

On a sunny October 11, 1962, I stood, with countless others, in the vast Saint Peter's Square, observing the last untroubled procession of the Counter-Reformation Church, as mitered prelates wended their way into the basilica for the solemn inauguration of the Second Vatican Council. I was a seminarian, recently arrived in Rome, about to begin four years of theological study at the Gregorian University. Even on the periphery of the conciliar proceedings, one was perforce caught up in the event of the council, following the daily reports avidly and attending numerous evening lectures by luminaries such as Congar, Rahner, and Chenu.

Another memorable date: November 20, 1962. On that day, the document "On the Sources of Revelation," prepared by the theological commission (led by Cardinal Ottaviani), was voted on by the council fathers. There had been considerable discussion of the document in the days preceding the vote, and it had received much criticism for its style—overly Scholastic and abstract, insufficiently biblical, historical, and ecumenical—a product of the reigning neo-Scholasticism of the time.

Summoned to vote, more than 60 percent of the bishops chose not to accept the draft. But, according to the rules of the

* This essay was originally published as "Remembering and Misremembering Vatican II," *Church Life Journal*, December 9, 2021, https://www.churchlifejournal.nd.edu.

council, it required a two-thirds negative vote to remand the document to committee.

Then, Pope John XXIII, exercising blessed common sense, intervened. He ordered that the document be recomposed and created a new commission for the task, joining Ottaviani's doctrinal commission with the Secretariat for Christian Unity headed by Cardinal Bea.

The impression created among those of us in Rome was electrifying. We sensed that we were witnessing a radical new beginning, a veritable revolution.

What emerged from the new joint commission was the epoch-making Dogmatic Constitution on Divine Revelation, *Dei Verbum*. Its biblical, personalist, and pastoral style helped set the tone for all the documents of the council.[1]

In interpreting the council, in establishing an appropriate "hermeneutic," the four constitutions play a decisive role. They are, of course, *Sacrosanctum Concilium*, *Lumen Gentium*, *Dei Verbum*, and *Gaudium et Spes*. However, in many ways it is the Dogmatic Constitution on Divine Revelation, *Dei Verbum*, which holds a primacy among them.[2]

For if God does not truly reveal himself, there is no foundation for the Church. It becomes only a human association and organization. And if God has not given himself definitively in Christ, there is no basis for liturgy. It becomes a merely human gathering, bereft of transcendent reference.

Distinctive to *Dei Verbum*'s presentation of revelation is that it is *explicitly Christocentric*. Though it celebrates God's revelation in the course of the history of the people of Israel, it confesses that

---

1. For a careful discussion of many aspects of the ecclesial and theological drama of Vatican II, see Jared Wicks, SJ, *Investigating Vatican II* (Washington, DC: The Catholic University of America Press, 2018).

2. Wicks concurs with this privileging of *Dei Verbum*. See Wicks, *Investigating Vatican II*, 223–24.

God's revelation attains its fullness in *the person of Jesus Christ*.[3] It is this Christ-centered understanding of God's revelation and promise that permeates the documents of Vatican II—prominent not only in *Sacrosanctum Concilium* and *Lumen Gentium* but also in *Gaudium et Spes*. It is this Christological "depth grammar" which belies any facile separation of "doctrinal" and "pastoral." Nor can the council be read as promoting a "pastoral paradigm" in opposition to a "doctrinal paradigm."

The distinguished Church historian John O'Malley has written of three categories that help elucidate "the dynamics of the Council." The three are *aggiornamento*, development, and *ressourcement*. And he contends, "Of the three categories, *ressourcement* was the most traditional yet potentially the most radical."[4] For it is on the basis of principles retrieved from the Church's memory that the present is normed and evaluated. Hence, "*Aggiornamento* was a consequence, not the starting point."[5] The present situation, the "signs of the times," are always discerned "in the light of the Gospel."[6]

"*Ressourcement*" is a term associated with those theologians who contributed to the movement known to their detractors as "*la Nouvelle Théologie*." They were certainly interested in retrieving the texts of the great tradition, especially those of the Fathers of the Church: *Les Sources Chrétiennes*. But their animating concern sought, through the texts, to apprehend anew the true source of the Church's faith: Jesus Christ himself. Already in 1938 Henri de Lubac wrote in *Catholicism*, "The whole Christian fact is summed up in Christ—as the Messiah who was to come—who had to be prepared for in history, just as a masterpiece is preceded by a series of sketches; but as 'the image of the invisible

---

3. Vatican Council II, *Dei Verbum* 2, in *The Word on Fire Vatican II Collection*, ed. Matthew Levering (Park Ridge, IL: Word on Fire Institute, 2021), 17–18.

4. John W. O'Malley, *What Happened at Vatican II* (Cambridge MA: Harvard University Press, 2008), 301.

5. O'Malley, *What Happened*, 301.

6. Vatican Council II, *Gaudium et Spes* 4, in *The Word on Fire Vatican II Collection*, 217.

God' and the 'firstborn of all creation,' he is the universal Exemplar."[7] And, in 1950, Yves Congar wrote this of *ressourcement*: "It is re-interrogating texts, but something more also, and more essential: it is *re-centering upon Christ in his Paschal Mystery*."[8]

For some forty years, I have insisted that Vatican II's premier accomplishment was its re-Sourcement: its new realization of Christ as the living center of its faith and life, its vision and mission.[9] In this regard I recall another date of particular significance. On September 29, 1963, Pope Paul VI opened the second session of the Vatican Council with these memorable words: "The starting point and the goal [of the council] is that here and at this very hour we should proclaim Christ to ourselves and to the world around us: Christ our beginning, Christ our life and our guide, Christ our hope and our end."[10] Paul had succeeded John XXIII the previous June, and the pressing question was whether he would reconvene the council. His decision to do so was welcomed with joy and hope. In this opening address he charted that Christocentric way that would orient and guide the council's labors.

Vatican's II's re-Sourcement sought to know Christ in a new way: to re-discover the person of Jesus Christ—not only through propositions about him but by inviting and fostering a personal encounter with him. An encounter that leads not merely to an assent of the mind but a consent of the heart and, hence, to transformation of life. And it sought to bring that renewed sense of Christ's reality and primacy into all facets of the Church's life and its relation to the world—indeed, to proclaim Christ as *lumen*

---

7. Henri de Lubac, *Catholicism: Christ and the Common Destiny of Man*, trans. Lancelot C. Sheppard and Elizabeth Englund (San Francisco: Ignatius, 1988), 173–74.

8. Yves Congar, *Vraie et Fausse Réforme dans l'Eglise* (Paris: Cerf, 1950), 336 (my translation and emphasis).

9. See Andrew Meszaros, "Christocentrism in Theology and Evangelization in the Thought of Robert P. Imbelli," in Andrew Meszaros, ed., *The Center Is Jesus Christ Himself* (Washington, DC: The Catholic University of America Press, 2021), 1–25.

10. Cited in Matthew Levering, *An Introduction to Vatican II as an Ongoing Theological Event* (Washington, DC: The Catholic University of America Press, 2017), 1.

gentium (light of the nations). For, as *Gaudium et Spes* confesses, with lyric exultation, "The Lord is the goal of human history, the point on which the desires of history and civilization turn, the center of the human race, the joy of all hearts and the fulfillment of all desires."[11]

In his study of the council, John O'Malley makes the important observation that "the universal call to holiness" weaves through the documents of the council like a golden thread. He suggests that such an emphasis is unique in the history of ecumenical councils. O'Malley writes, "Among the recurring themes of the Council expressive of its spirit, the call to holiness is particularly pervasive and particularly important. . . . It is the theme that to a large extent imbued the council with its finality."[12]

Indeed, O'Malley counts this call to holiness a crucial component in what he construes to be Vatican II's unique "style"—a pastoral, dialogical style—that distinguishes it from all previous councils of the Church.[13] However, has O'Malley's suggestive insistence on style led him to scant the Christological content of the two *dogmatic* constitutions of the council: *Dei Verbum* and *Lumen Gentium*?

Hence, I would stress, more than O'Malley does, that, for the council, the source and enabler of that call is the Holy One: Jesus Christ himself. The call to holiness has, in the mind and heart of the council, a distinctive Christological foundation. The revelation of the uniqueness of Christ is not primarily a propositional truth for our instruction but an existential summons to transformation of life according to the image of Christ: being clothed with Christ, taking on the mind of Christ, living life in

11. *Gaudium et Spes* 45. John Cavadini comments regarding *Gaudium et Spes*, "It is from this perspective of the recapitulation of man, of *homo*, of the human being, in Christ, that the Church wishes to engage in dialogue with the modern world" ("Christian Conviction Doesn't Shut Down Dialogue," *Church Life Journal*, March 17, 2021, churchlifejournal.nd.edu).

12. O'Malley, *What Happened*, 310.

13. For O'Malley's important consideration of "style" as the true "spirit" of the council, see O'Malley, 43–52 and 305–8.

Christ. Thus the council's call to holiness is an *invitatio in mysterium Christi*, an invitation to enter into the mystery of Christ, and, even more explicitly, an *invitatio ad participandum in mysterium paschale Christi*, an invitation to participate in the Paschal Mystery of Christ.

Thus, among the attributes of Vatican II's distinctive style, besides the biblical, pastoral, and dialogical characteristics, suggested by O'Malley, I would add and underscore "mystagogic." In this regard, chapters 1 and 5 of *Lumen Gentium*, "The Mystery of the Church" and "The Universal Call to Holiness in the Church," are intimately, mystagogically, linked. The call to holiness is the call to appropriate more fully and enter more deeply into the mystery of Christ who is the light of the nations.[14]

Thus, it is imperative to highlight a neglected aspect of Vatican II's achievement: its employment of the term "Paschal Mystery." The term has become so commonplace we fail to attend sufficiently to its innovative appearance and usage at the council.

In an address commemorating the fiftieth anniversary of Vatican II's Constitution on the Sacred Liturgy, *Sacrosanctum Concilium*, Abbot Jeremy Driscoll noted that Pius XII's encyclical *Mediator Dei* (1947) "did much to prepare the way for *Sacrosanctum Concilium*; yet, one of the ways of measuring the difference and the progress between the two documents is to note that 'paschal mystery' is never mentioned in *Mediator Dei*."[15] And the "progress" to which Driscoll alludes is well summed up in the title of a book by Father Dominic Langevin: *From Passion to Paschal Mystery*.[16]

---

14. Pope Francis captures this Christ-centered mystagogy of the council in *Evangelii Gaudium*. He writes, apropos the homily, "Preaching should guide the assembly, and the preacher, to a life-changing communion with Christ in the Eucharist" (138). In addition, he calls for a "kerygmatic and mystagogical catechesis," with special attention paid to the aesthetic, to the "via pulchritudinis" (163–68). For the text of *Evangelii Gaudium*, see vatican.va.

15. Jeremy Driscoll, "Reviewing and Recovering *Sacrosanctum Concilium*," *Origins* 43, no. 29 (December 19, 2013): 479–87, at 486n26.

16. Dominic M. Langevin, OP, *From Passion to Paschal Mystery* (Fribourg: Academic Press, 2015).

Langevin's book argues that in Pius XII's treatment of the sacraments, "the accent . . . remained singularly and solely upon the Passion of Christ."[17] Vatican II, however, reaped the fruits of such pioneering work as Louis Bouyer's *Le mystère pascal*[18] and François-Xavier Durrwell's *La résurrection de Jésus, mystère de salut*.[19] The result of such studies, as well as the 1955 reform under Pius XII of the Holy Week liturgies, was that "when the Fathers of the Second Vatican Council assembled, they did not find it difficult to affirm that both the Passion and the Resurrection are mutually salvific."[20]

A salient text is *Sacrosanctum Concilium* 5, where the council teaches that "the work of Christ the Lord in redeeming mankind and giving perfect glory to God" was accomplished by Christ the Lord "principally by the paschal mystery of His blessed passion, resurrection from the dead, and the glorious ascension, whereby 'dying, he destroyed our death and, rising, he restored our life.'"[21] Thus the "Paschal Mystery" is both the culmination of Jesus's life and ministry and the cause of our salvation: his dying destroyed *our* death, his rising restored *our* life.

This new realization of the decisive importance of the Paschal Mystery finds striking reflection in the new liturgical books and celebrations stemming from the council's *ressourcement*. Jeremy Driscoll asserts, "There can be no question that one of the great

17. Langevin, *Passion*, 370.

18. Louis Bouyer, *Le mystère pascal*, 2nd rev. ed., Lex Orandi 4 (Paris: Cerf, 1947). (The first edition is from 1945.) For English translation, see *The Paschal Mystery: Meditations on the Last Three Days of Holy Week*, trans. Mary Benoit, R.S.M. (London: George Allen & Unwin, 1951).

19. François-Xavier Durrwell, *La résurrection de Jésus, mystère de salut* (Paris: Mappus, 1950). For English translation, see *The Resurrection: A Biblical Study*, trans. Rosemary Sheed (New York: Sheed and Ward, 1960).

20. Langevin, *Passion*, 370.

21. Vatican Council II, *Sacrosanctum Concilium* 5, in *The Word on Fire Vatican II Collection*, 157. Louis Bouyer comments somewhat sardonically about the title of his path-breaking book: "Everyone today imagines it was a current expression among the Fathers of the Church and the Middle Ages. In fact, however, as I pointed out to no effect, while Christian Latin does have *Paschale sacramentum*, it does not have *mysterium paschale*." *The Memoirs of Louis Bouyer*, trans. John Pepino (Kettering, OH: Angelico, 2015), 156.

theological achievements of the Missal of Paul VI is the way in which the paschal mystery emerges with clarity as the center of the liturgical year and, indeed, as the center of every celebration of the Eucharist. . . . In the Missal of Paul VI the word paschal in various of its forms occurs in 120 texts, many of which are repeated numerous times. In the pre-conciliar missal of 1962 it occurs in 17 texts."[22]

By the late 1980s its appropriation had become so widespread and established that it serves as the organizing principle for the treatment of liturgy and sacraments in the *Catechism of the Catholic Church*. Chapter 1 of part 2 of the *Catechism* is entitled "The Paschal Mystery in the Age of the Church," and chapter 2 is "The Sacramental Celebration of the Paschal Mystery."

Pastorally and experientially, in the span of a lifetime, we transitioned from a solemn funeral Mass, whose tone was set by the *Dies Irae*, to a "Mass of the Resurrection" where homily and eulogy (often indistinguishable) sound suspiciously like "*Santo subito!*"

If it was characteristic of preconciliar liturgical understanding to concentrate upon the Passion and Death of the Lord, today Paschal Mystery seems often reduced to the celebration of Christ's Resurrection. Thus it is commonplace to refer simply to the "Easter Triduum," instead of the fuller "Paschal Triduum."

A further remark to which I will return in part 3. Though *Sacrosanctum Concilium* 5 helpfully exegetes "Paschal Mystery" as Christ the Lord's "blessed passion, his resurrection from the dead and his glorious ascension," in the postconciliar Church, the Ascension seems relegated to a refurbished limbo—just as the liturgical feast wanders in search of a place to lay its head.

Nonetheless, *Sacrosanctum Concilium* can still serve as a beacon as we continue to enter more deeply into the Paschal Mystery of Jesus Christ, provided we realize and insist that the *participatio*

22. Driscoll, "Reviewing," 483.

9

plena, conscia, et actuosa to which it summons has far less to do with liturgical activism, as with the challenge to transformation.[23] It calls all to a *participatio plena, conscia, et actuosa in mysterium paschale Iesu Christi.*

Concluding this section, I recall another significant date: October 11, 2012. Providentially, I was again in Saint Peter's Square for the Mass commemorating the fiftieth anniversary of the opening of Vatican II. One of the few others present, who had also been there fifty years before, was Pope Benedict XVI. In his homily Benedict stated that the council's deepest desire was "to immerse itself anew in the mystery of Christ" and "to communicate Christ to individuals and to all men and women, in the Church's pilgrimage in history." Benedict insisted that both Paul VI and John Paul II had reaffirmed the council's conviction that Jesus Christ is "the center of the cosmos and history." They advanced the council's "apostolic imperative to proclaim him to the world. . . . For the Christian believes in God whose face was revealed by Jesus Christ."[24]

II. MISREMEMBERING VATICAN II

I will abbreviate my remarks in this section, since I have elsewhere lamented and attempted to chart the loss of Vatican II's Christological re-Sourcement in many academic and pastoral circles since the council. I characterize this declension from the robust Christological vision of Vatican II as the case of "the decapitated Body."[25]

Among other symptoms of this malady I have pointed to a unitarianism of the Spirit in which the names of "Jesus" and "Father" are expurgated; the not-so-benign neglect accorded *Dei Verbum*'s affirmation of Christ as both "mediator and fullness of

---

23. *Sacrosanctum Concilium* 14.

24. Benedict XVI, "Homily for the Opening of the Year of Faith," October 11, 2012, vatican.va (translation modified).

25. Robert P. Imbelli, "No Decapitated Body," *Nova et Vetera* 18, no. 3 (2020): 757–75.

revelation";[26] the soteriological relativism that places a hesitant question mark after the council's bold confession of "no other name";[27] the widespread "liturgical horizontalism" (decried by Benedict XVI) in which almost exclusive focus is placed on the community celebrating—often expressed in the reductive slogan: "What's important is who is around the altar!"[28]

I contend that this concern about Christological amnesia has animated the theological labors of Joseph Ratzinger—from his 1968 *Introduction to Christianity*,[29] through the statement of the Congregation for the Doctrine of the Faith *Dominus Iesus* (accorded a frosty reception in many theological circles),[30] to his 2007 volume, *Jesus of Nazareth*, where he calls for a "Christological hermeneutic, which sees Jesus Christ as the key to the whole and learns from him how to understand the Bible as a unity."[31] Recently, this concern at the loss of the Christic center spurred the 2021 Lenten sermons of the Preacher of the Papal Household, Cardinal Raniero Cantalamessa. He lamented that consideration of the Church often transpires "*etsi Christus non daretur!*"[32] I leave to the reader's own discernment this diagnosis of Christological deficit in Church and theology, and the identification of further instances of its corrosive spread.[33]

---

26. *Dei Verbum* 2.

27. *Gaudium et Spes* 10.

28. For further elaboration see Andrew Meszaros, ed., *Center*, 1–25.

29. See Robert P. Imbelli, "Joseph Ratzinger's 'Spiritual Christology'," in *Gift to the Church and World: Fifty Years of Joseph Ratzinger's "Introduction to Christianity*," ed. John C. Cavadini and Donald Wallenfang (Eugene, OR: Pickwick, 2021), 189–212, at 198–99. See Essay 4 in this volume.

30. See Robert P. Imbelli, "The Reaffirmation of the Christic Center," in *Sic et Non: Encountering Dominus Iesus*, ed. Stephen J. Pope and Charles Hefling (Maryknoll, NY: Orbis, 2002), 96–106.

31. Pope Benedict XVI, *Jesus of Nazareth: From the Baptism in the Jordan to the Transfiguration*, trans. Adrian J. Walker (New York: Doubleday, 2007), xix.

32. Raniero Cantalamessa, "Can Any of You Charge Me with Sin?—Jesus Christ, A True Man—Second Lent Sermon," March 5th, 2021, http://www.cantalamessa.org.

33. For an acute study of the spread after the council, in some Catholic circles, of theological liberalism, with its reductionist Christology, see Matthew Levering, introduction and conclusion to *Newman on Doctrinal Corruption* (Park Ridge, IL: Word on Fire Academic, 2022).

III. THE PASCHAL REKINDLING OF THE CATHOLIC
IMAGINARY

In the last part of this essay, I offer some thoughts which build upon and develop what I have been arguing is crucial to the achievement of the Second Vatican Council: its return to the origin and sustaining source of the Church's life, Jesus Christ himself. I do so by accenting the importance of two pillars of Christian faith: Ascension and Transfiguration. And, borrowing from Charles Taylor's use of the notion of the "social imaginary"[34]—that complex network of symbols, images, and concepts that articulate and orient a community's understanding of reality—I suggest that the Ascension and Transfiguration are critical dimensions of a rekindled ecclesial imaginary. Poets, musicians, liturgists, even theologians must realize (in Newman's strong sense of "realize") and re-imagine these two inexhaustible mysteries of the faith. Realize by reimagining.[35]

An essential moment in such realization is to insist, with *Sacrosanctum Concilium* 5, that Christ's Paschal Mystery embraces the Ascension: "the paschal mystery of Christ's blessed passion, his resurrection from the dead and his glorious ascension." The Ascension is the very *telos* of the Incarnation. It is not a "postscript" to the life of Christ, but its salvific fulfillment. Ascending, Jesus Christ "opens the gates of heaven." Indeed, heaven is Christologically constituted. As Joseph Ratzinger wrote in *Introduction to Christianity*, "Heaven and the Ascension of Christ are indivisibly connected; it is only this connection that makes clear the Christological, personal, history-centered meaning of the Christian tidings of heaven."[36]

34. Charles Taylor, *A Secular Age* (Cambridge, MA: Belknap), 171–76.

35. For the importance of the "imagination" in Louis Bouyer's theological epistemology (as it had been for his fellow Oratorian John Henry Newman), see Keith Lemna's study *The Apocalypse of Wisdom: Louis Bouyer's Theological Recovery of the Cosmos* (Brooklyn, NY: Angelico, 2019), chapter 1: "Imagination and Wisdom."

36. Joseph Ratzinger, *Introduction to Christianity*, trans. J.R. Foster (San Francisco: Ignatius, 2004), 313.

Christ's Ascension constitutes a new redeemed order of existence, a re-configuration of space and time, centered around the person of Jesus Christ, which is the present visible order brought to transfigured fulfillment.

Moreover, contrary to an impoverished imaginary, which "pictures" the Ascension as Jesus's absence, almost as though he were on a much deserved "sabbatical," a deeper perception realizes with Benedict XVI that he "has not 'gone away,' but now and forever by God's own power, he is present with us and for us. . . . His going away is in this sense a coming, a new form of closeness, of continuing presence."[37]

This "continuing presence" of the ascended Lord is not a static presence but an active, dynamic one. Christ's presence is both transcendent and transformative. He is the Head upon whom the Body remains ever dependent for its supernatural life. As Benedict insists in his apostolic exhortation *Sacramentum Caritatis*, "Christ himself continues to be present and active in his Church, starting with her vital center which is the Eucharist. . . . For the Eucharist is Christ himself who gives himself to us and continually build us up as his body."[38] Without this sustaining, life-giving presence of its Lord, the body has no life in it. A decapitated body is only a corpse.

Paul Griffiths rightly accents this nexus between Ascension and Eucharist: "The principal condition of the possibility of the Eucharist is exactly that Jesus has ascended. . . . After the Ascension, his flesh, veiled as bread, and his blood, veiled as wine, can be touched and tasted everywhere and at once, without constraint by the metronome of time or the map grid of space."[39]

---

37. Pope Benedict XVI, *Jesus of Nazareth: Holy Week: From the Entrance into Jerusalem to the Resurrection* (San Francisco: Ignatius, 2011), 283.

38. Benedict XVI, *Sacramentum Caritatis* 12, 14, apostolic exhortation, February 22, 2007, vatican.va.

39. Paul J. Griffiths, *Christian Flesh* (Stanford, CA: Stanford University Press, 2018), 51.

And in the great tradition's vision of reality, the Ascension is the *telos* not only of the Head but of the members of his Body as well. The Collect for the Mass of the Lord's Ascension prays, "Where the Head has gone before in glory, the Body is called to follow in hope" (in the terse Latin: "*quo processit gloria capitis, eo spes vocatur et corporis*").

In the rich Catholic imaginary of a former age, Dante Alighieri launches his pilgrim into the heights of *Paradiso* by boldly announcing in the very first canto the theme of this concluding portion of his pilgrimage: "trasumanar"[40] (transformation beyond the human).[41] And the final sublime canto of the entire *Commedia* poeticizes Dante' transforming vision of the Trinity. To his astonishment the pilgrim discerns that the second of the revolving circles bears a human imprint: "*la nostra effige*."[42] The graced destiny of the pilgrim/poet's transfiguring journey is divinization. And the condition for its possibility is the Ascension of the Incarnate Word.

Seven centuries later, Charles Taylor, in a little noticed retrieval, challenges a secular age to recover a sense of *theosis*. To move beyond merely human flourishing to that "further greater transformation"[43] that breaks through the constricted and ultimately dehumanizing "immanent frame." It entails a purification of the spiritual senses that enables one to perceive, in the words of Gerard Manley Hopkins (whom Taylor invokes in his final chapter "Conversions"), that "the world is charged with the grandeur of God"[44] and that "Christ plays in ten thousand

---

40. Dante Alighieri, *Paradiso* 1.70.

41. "Trasumanar": Dante's neologism; literally to pass beyond the human.

42. Dante, *Paradiso* 33.131.

43. Taylor, *A Secular Age*, 737.

44. Gerard Manley Hopkins, "God's Grandeur," Poetry Foundation, poetryfoundation. org.

places / Lovely in limbs, and lovely in eyes not his / To the Father through the features of men's faces."[45]

Christ's Ascension has definitively broken the bounds of the "immanent frame" and inaugurated the new creation of humanity's transfiguration in the glory of God. As the Collect for the Mass of the Ascension proclaims, "The Ascension of Christ your Son is our exaltation!" The Ascension brings into bold relief the unique headship of Jesus Christ and founds the new identity of Christians as members of his Body.

In a rich and stimulating study on the theology of the Ascension, Douglas Farrow writes,

> The Ascension of Jesus is the act by which God in principle— or rather in Person—completes the formation of man and perfects his image in man. In bearing our humanity home to the Father, Jesus brings human nature as such to its true end and to its fullest potential in the Holy Spirit. He causes it to be entirely at one with God, and so become the object and (for other creatures) the mediator of God's eternal blessing.[46]

That "perfected created image" of the Triune God is not the Head alone but the Head together with the members, forming the *totus Christus*, beloved of Augustine. It is the new, supernatural order of redeemed and transfigured relations which is vividly imagined and celebrated in the final chapters of the book of Revelation.

What "interpretation of reality" is offered by an "ecclesial imaginary" that sees and confesses Christ's Ascension as integral to his Paschal Mystery and that sees transfigured humanity as a perfected image of its Creator? It is a vision of reality as *constitutively relational*, of *being as communion*. Few have realized so fully the generative and transforming power of the Paschal Mystery and its

45. Gerard Manley Hopkins, "As Kingfishers Catch Fire," Poetry Foundation, poetry-foundation.org.

46. Douglas Farrow, *Ascension Theology* (London: T&T Clark, 2011), 122.

implications for Church and theology as clearly as Louis Bouyer. In his pioneering work, *Le Mystère pascal* of 1945, Bouyer has a chapter on believers' oneness in Christ that is as bold as Augustine. Bouyer writes, "By our new and supernatural subsistence in Christ, founded upon the Incarnation and conserved in all of us by the Eucharist, we form a single new being in the body of Christ, or, more profoundly still, in the whole Christ, in the plenitude of Christ. . . . New relations are established between us, uniting us indissolubly, since henceforth we all have no longer but a single life—that of Christ in us."[47]

Allow me, in closing, to recall one final date: July 24, 1965, two months before the start of the council's last session: the day of my ordination to the priesthood—a priesthood lived in the light of Vatican II's re-Sourcement.

In preparation for ordination, I had two commemorative cards printed. The first offered a quote from the Letter to the Ephesians: "Christ gifted some to be apostles, some prophets, some evangelists, some pastors and teachers, to equip the saints for the work of ministry, for the building up of the body of Christ, until we all attain the unity of the faith and of the knowledge of the Son of God, to that perfect man [*eis andra teleion*], to the measure of the stature of the fullness [*plērōmatos*] of Christ" (Eph. 4:11–13). That perfected image of God who is the whole Christ come to fulfillment.

The second card displayed a quote from Saint Augustine's *Homilies on the First Letter of John*:

> The sons of God are the body of the unique Son of God. And since he is the head and we the members, the Son of God is one. Thus he who loves the sons of God loves the Son of God. . . . Who are the sons of God? The members of the Son

---

47. Louis Bouyer, *The Paschal Mystery*, trans. Sister Mary Benoit (Chicago: Regnery, 1950), 121.

of God. And by loving, she herself becomes a member, and through loving is joined to the body of Christ. And there shall be one Christ, loving himself.

I already intuited then, and am even more convinced now, that a rich Christological ontology is adumbrated here—a joyful and hopeful vision of reality, yearning to be more fully imagined and realized.[48]

---

48. A significant contribution is Klaus Hemmerle, *Theses Towards a Trinitarian Ontology*, trans. Stephen Churchyard (Brooklyn, NY: Angelico, 2020). Hemmerle writes concerning "substances" that they . . . "go beyond" themselves "in relation." "Substance there comes to 'transubstantiation,' to 'communion'" (44).

2. "Christ Brings All Newness"

The Irenaean Vision of *Evangelii Gaudium*

The Second Vatican Council is universally considered the most important ecclesial event of the twentieth century. And its importance has been newly highlighted by the historic canonization of two of its most significant participants: Pope Saint John XXIII and Pope Saint John Paul II. The first whose inspiration convened the council; the second who was both participant and its authoritative interpreter.

As is well known, the rhythm which governed the council's deliberations and labors was that of *ressourcement* and *aggiornamento*. The recovery of the wellsprings of Christian faith in the Sacred Scriptures and in the theological witness of the Fathers of the Church inspired the urgency to communicate the faith afresh to the modern world. In effect, Vatican II signaled a desire and commitment for a New Evangelization. No less an authority than Pope Paul VI wrote in *Evangelii Nuntiandi*, "The objectives of [the council] are definitively summed up in this single one: to make the Church of the twentieth century ever better suited to proclaim the Gospel to the people of the twentieth century."[1]

Moreover, Paul VI showed his keen awareness of the imperative to continue the conciliar dynamic of *ressourcement/aggiornamento*. He wrote, "[The local churches] have the task of

* This essay was originally published as "Christ Brings All Newness (*EG* 11): The Irenaean Vision of *Evangelii Gaudium*," *PATH, Journal of the Pontifical Academy of Theology* 13, no. 2 (2014): 367–76.

1. Paul VI, *Evangelii Nuntiandi* 2, December 8, 1975, vatican.va. It is noteworthy that in *Evangelii Gaudium,* Pope Francis cites *Evangelii Nuntiandi* a dozen times.

assimilating the essence of the Gospel message and of transposing it, without the slightest betrayal of its essential truth, into the language that these particular people understand, then of proclaiming it in this language."[2] Significantly, Pope Francis displays a like commitment to the creative tension of "appropriation" and "translation." In the section of *Evangelii Gaudium* dedicated to "Preparing to Preach,"[3] the pope creatively applies this basic rhythm to the task of preaching. He writes, simply but profoundly, "A preacher has to contemplate the Word, but he also has to contemplate his people."[4]

This twofold contemplation, this double discernment, structures the preacher's craft, and the homily is its most concrete fruit. But though these contemplative exercises are inseparable, they are not equally primary. The first, the contemplation of the Word, has primacy, as becomes clear in the following section of the apostolic exhortation: "Evangelization and the Deeper Understanding of the Kerygma."[5] Here Pope Francis insists, "[The kerygma] needs to be the center of all evangelizing activity and all efforts at Church renewal."[6] And he states unequivocally, "All Christian formation consists of entering more deeply into the kerygma which is reflected in and constantly illumines the work of catechesis, thereby enabling us to understand more fully the significance of every subject treated."[7]

Though the pope in these sections of *Evangelii Gaudium* speaks explicitly of the tasks of preaching and catechesis, I contend that the principles he invokes apply equally to the task of theology. Like preaching and catechesis, the theological task is to enter more deeply into the apostolic kerygma. For the kerygma,

---

2. *Evangelii Nuntiandi* 63.

3. See Francis, *Evangelii Gaudium* 145–59, apostolic exhortation, November 24, 2013, vatican.va.

4. *Evangelii Gaudium* 154.

5. *Evangelii Gaudium* 160–75.

6. *Evangelii Gaudium* 164.

7. *Evangelii Gaudium* 165.

the primordial and fundamental proclamation of the Gospel, lies at the very heart of the Church's mission. The Church's *raison d'être* is to live and proclaim the joy at the heart of the Gospel: "Jesus Christ loves you; he gave his life to save you; and now he is living at your side every day to enlighten, strengthen, and free you."[8] Thus every ecclesial activity—preaching, catechizing, theological reflection—must have its ongoing point of reference and norm in this apostolic kerygma.

In the face of those who tend to sunder catechesis and theology (seeking thereby, so they suppose, to safeguard the proper role of theological reflection), *Evangelii Gaudium* points to a deeper continuity. For catechesis and theology are rooted in the Trinitarian kerygma of God's love for the world incarnated and revealed through Jesus Christ in the Holy Spirit.

The conciliar rhythm of *ressourcement* and *aggiornamento*, the homiletic rhythm of appropriation and translation, characterizes the theological task as well. But what may have been neglected in the years since the council is that the deepest *ressourcement* is, in reality, a re-Sourcement: a return to the unique Source who is Jesus Christ. Vatican II has been called, with some justification, an "ecclesiological council"—given that two of its constitutions (*Lumen Gentium* and *Gaudium et Spes*) address the nature and mission of the Church, while a third (*Sacrosanctum Concilium*) treats at length the Church's liturgy. But this fact can also conceal how Christologically saturated the documents of the council are. After all, the "Light of the Nations" is not the Church but Jesus Christ to whom the Church bears witness. And the ongoing need for purification and reform in the Church is so that she might be better conformed to Christ her Lord.

In this regard, I maintain that though the four constitutions of the council bear the most authority among its documents, the Dogmatic Constitution on Divine Revelation, *Dei Verbum*,

8. *Evangelii Gaudium* 154.

enjoys the status of a *prima inter pares*. The reason is simple: without the recognition and confession that Jesus Christ is the "mediator and fullness of all revelation,"[9] the Church, the Body of Christ, would have no distinctive identity and her liturgy would lack any sure foundation. All the teaching of the council is governed by this Christological "depth grammar" that confesses the uniqueness and salvific universality of Jesus Christ.

Much has been accomplished since the council in the areas of ecumenical and interreligious dialogue. The council has certainly advanced mutual understanding and respect among Christians and believers in other religious traditions. But this notable gain has sometimes come at the cost of compromising significant distinctions and differences. Thus the uniqueness and originality of Jesus has at times not received due attention. It has even been attenuated. Furthermore, polarization within the Church itself has played a role in neglecting or ignoring the council's robust Christocentricity.

One can sense the anguish with which Benedict XVI composed the foreword to the first volume of his book *Jesus of Nazareth*. The pope wrote about the effect of some historical-critical studies: "Intimate friendship with Jesus, on which everything depends, is in danger of clutching at thin air."[10] While Benedict XVI's immediate concern was the inner life of the Christian community, the late Cardinal Avery Dulles lamented the harmful effect of certain theological approaches and stances upon the Church's evangelizing mission. Dulles spoke of tendencies in contemporary Catholic theology "that inhibit a vigorous program of evangelization" by positing a "soteriological pluralism": different ways of salvation

---

9. Vatican Council II, *Dei Verbum* 2, in *The Word on Fire Vatican II Collection*, ed. Matthew Levering (Park Ridge, IL: Word on Fire Institute, 2021), 17–18.

10. Pope Benedict XVI, *Jesus of Nazareth: From the Baptism in the Jordan to the Transfiguration*, trans. Adrian J. Walker (New York: Doubleday, 2007), xii.

for different peoples and cultures, rather than the unique Way who is Jesus Christ.[11]

In this theological and cultural context the opening words of *Evangelii Gaudium* provide a clarion call to return to the living center of the faith. Pope Francis writes, "The joy of the Gospel fills the hearts and lives of all who encounter Jesus. Those who accept his offer of salvation are set free from sin, sorrow, inner emptiness, and loneliness. With Christ joy is constantly born anew."[12]

Now, beyond this stirring proclamation of the kerygma, Pope Francis also makes a theological claim of surpassing importance. He does so by quoting the evocative declaration of the second-century Father of the Church Saint Irenaeus of Lyons. Irenaeus writes, "By his coming Christ brought with him all newness."[13] So reads the English translation. But the Latin version is even richer and more concentrated: *Omnem novitatem attulit, semetipsum afferens.* Christ brought all newness, in bringing *himself*! It is the person of Jesus Christ, the incarnate Word of God, who is the *novissimus*, the *eschatos*, both "alpha and omega, the first and the last, the beginning and the end" (Rev. 22:13).

Thus a theology apt for the New Evangelization must retrieve and extend this newness which makes Christianity distinctive among the world religions. Or, better, theology for the New Evangelization must become Christocentric in a more daring and comprehensive manner.[14] In this light one may envision the theological task as not only "faith seeking understanding" (in Saint Anselm's classic formulation) but also as "hope seeking understanding." This latter expression derives from the oft-quoted verse of the First Letter of Peter: "Always be prepared to offer an account (*logos*) of the hope that is in you to anyone who inquires of

11. Avery Cardinal Dulles, *Evangelization for the Third Millennium* (New York: Paulist, 2009), 81, 85.

12. *Evangelii Gaudium* 1.

13. Irenaeus of Lyons, *Adversus Haereses*, 4.34.1, quoted in *Evangelii Gaudium* 11.

14. There are helpful essays in Paolo Scarafoni, ed., *Cristocentrismo: Riflessione Teologica* (Rome: Città Nuova, 2002).

you" (1 Pet. 3:15). And it is clear that this hope, which defines the Christian way of life, is founded upon "the resurrection of Jesus Christ from the dead" (1 Pet. 1:3).

Moreover, Christian life is not only the expectation of a future consummation of our hope, but the present experience of the loving encounter with the risen and ascended Jesus. Peter bears witness to the experience of the early Christian community: "Though you have not seen Jesus, you love him. Though you do not now see him, you believe in him and you rejoice with unutterable and exceeding joy; thus you attain the goal [*telos*] of your faith: the salvation of your souls" (1 Pet. 1:8–9). The successor of Peter echoes this when he writes in *Evangelii Gaudium*, "The primary reason for evangelizing is the love of Jesus which we have received, the experience of salvation which urges us to ever greater love of him."[15] Hence, a theology that serves the New Evangelization may rightly be characterized as "love seeking greater understanding." By thus rooting the theological task in the soil of faith, hope, and love, one not only underscores the Christological basis of faith, hope, and love, one also accents the inseparability of theology and spirituality.[16]

Evangelii Gaudium is certainly not a theological treatise. But, as I have been suggesting, it sketches a theology of a markedly Irenaean tenor. In that same Irenaean spirit, Professor Khaled Anatolios, my colleague at Boston College, has spoken of theology as "ordered discourse on the newness of Christ and of the renewal of all things in Christ."[17] It is well known how central to Irenaeus's thought is the Pauline notion of the "recapitulation of all things in Christ" (Eph. 1:10). One of the challenges facing theology

15. *Evangelii Gaudium* 264.

16. See the essays in Piero Coda and Vincenzo Di Pilato, eds., *Teologia "in" Gesù* (Rome: Città Nuova, 2012).

17. Khaled Anatolios, "A Patristic Reflection on the Nature and Method of Theology in the New Evangelization," *Nova et Vetera* 14, no. 4 (Fall 2016): 1070–71. For his study of the "primacy of Christ" as the determinative norm in the development of Nicene Trinitarian doctrine, see Khaled Anatolios, *Retrieving Nicaea: The Development and Meaning of Trinitarian Doctrine* (Grand Rapids, MI: Baker Academic, 2011).

today is to offer a comprehensive vision of reality based upon the primacy of Christ: a "Christological ontology," if you will. Only such a theology can provide the requisite support for *Evangelii Gaudium*'s comprehensive vision of evangelization.

But here another similarity with Irenaeus arises. For we find ourselves in a spiritual and cultural context that, on more than one count, resembles that which confronted Irenaeus in the second century. The proclamation and witness to the faith today transpires in a context of a recrudescent Gnosticism that assumes many guises and disguises. Superficially, there may seem to be little affinity between the overblown metaphysical systems of second-century Gnosticism and the cool skepticism regarding universal claims and grand narratives that characterizes postmodernity. Yet in the "evangelical discernment"[18] that Pope Francis initiates in chapter 2 of the apostolic exhortation, he himself refers to the ongoing "attraction of Gnosticism." He defines this as "a purely subjective faith whose only interest is a certain experience or a set of ideas and bits of information which are meant to console and enlighten but which ultimately keep one imprisoned in his or her own thoughts and feelings."[19]

Like classical Gnosticism, the contemporary manifestation displays an aversion to the material and bodily, preferring "a purely spiritual Christ, without flesh and without the cross,"[20] "a disembodied Jesus who demands nothing of us with regard to others."[21] This Gnostic temptation is further reinforced and skewed by a culture and social order so often marred by "an economy of exclusion and inequality."[22] Indeed, the imperatives of consumer capitalism lead to a "denial of the primacy of the human person"[23]

18. *Evangelii Gaudium* 50.
19. *Evangelii Gaudium* 94.
20. *Evangelii Gaudium* 88.
21. *Evangelii Gaudium* 89.
22. *Evangelii Gaudium* 53.
23. *Evangelii Gaudium* 55.

so that "human beings are themselves considered consumer goods to be used and then discarded."[24]

As in the first century, so today the proclamation of the Gospel must often transpire, especially in the North Atlantic world, in a context that seems "devoid of hope, without God in the world" (Eph. 2:12). And the loss of God is accompanied by the loss of a substantive self. It comes as no surprise, then, that studies have been published over the past few decades, in the English-speaking world, bearing titles like *The Minimal Self* and *The Protean Self*. They depict "selves" uneasy with relationships and wary of binding commitments. Little wonder that so many marriages end in separation and divorce.

The British literary scholar and cultural critic Terry Eagleton has written an intriguing book entitled *Culture and the Death of God*. He speaks of the "spiritual vacuity" of late capitalist society in which men and women are either exploited or reduced to being consumers who are "passive, diffuse, provisional." The sole foundational certitude of "Man the Eternal Consumer" seems to be "I buy therefore I am." In biting words Eagleton writes, "With the advent of postmodern culture, a nostalgia for the numinous is finally banished. It is not so much that there is no redemption as there is nothing to be redeemed. . . . With the emergence of postmodernism, human history arrives for the first time at an authentic atheism."[25] Thus, in his view, "Postmodernism is in many ways a postscript to Nietzsche."[26]

Clearly, there are other cultural contexts (even in the North American world) to which the Church must proclaim the joy of the Gospel. However, through globalization, the consumerist and therapeutic frenzy of late capitalism is spreading apace. As Pope Francis asserts, "In the prevailing culture, priority is given to the

24. *Evangelii Gaudium* 53.

25. Terry Eagleton, *Culture and the Death of God* (New Haven: Yale University Press, 2014), 190.

26. Eagleton, *Culture*, 185.

outward, the immediate, the visible, the quick, the superficial and the provisional."[27] And the consequence is that "the individualism of our postmodern and globalized era favors a lifestyle which weakens the development and stability of personal relationships and distorts family bonds."[28]

In his massive study *A Secular Age*, the Canadian Catholic philosopher Charles Taylor traces the emergence of secularity in modernity. A significant strength of his study lies in his clear appreciation of the real gains that secularization has brought in terms of respect for individual rights and fostering freedom of religion. Therefore, Taylor's recognition of the weaknesses of secularity and its devolution in postmodernity is all the more credible. One of his primary concerns is the attitude he calls "excarnation," an attitude that takes a number of forms. At its most basic, excarnation is the implicit denial of our embodiedness, our constitutive relationality, our vulnerability and mortality. In the face of pervasive excarnational forces in contemporary culture, Taylor contends that Christianity (and Catholicism in particular) must labor "to recover a sense of what the Incarnation can mean."[29]

With this notion of "excarnation," we then rejoin the recognition of the Gnosticizing tendencies latent in so much of our consumerist-driven and privatizing secular culture. These tendencies have been noted and lifted up by figures as diverse as Pope Francis, the cultural critic Terry Eagleton, and the philosopher Charles Taylor. They offer independent and converging discernments regarding the spirits animating so much of contemporary culture. And not all the spirits are beneficent!

Confronted with this situation, Christians turn to the scriptural imperatives as criteria for discernment. Foremost among these is the injunction in the First Letter of John: "Beloved, do not believe every spirit, but test the spirits to see whether they

27. *Evangelii Gaudium* 62.
28. *Evangelii Gaudium* 67.
29. Charles Taylor, *A Secular Age* (Cambridge, MA: Belknap, 2007), 753.

are of God. . . . By this you know the Spirit of God: every spirit which confesses that Jesus Christ has come in the flesh is of God" (1 John 4:1–2). Incarnation, not excarnation, is the first and primary test. But the second extends our understanding of Incarnation to embrace not only the incarnate Son of God but also his Eucharistic Body and his ecclesial Body. Thus, Paul writes, "Let each examine himself or herself, and so eat of the bread and drink of the cup. For anyone who eats and drinks without discerning the body, eats and drinks judgment upon themselves" (1 Cor. 11:28–29). It is clear that Paul's discernment concerns both the Lord's Eucharistic Body and his ecclesial Body that is being sundered between those who suffer physical hunger and those who feast, like Dives, in abundance.

A final New Testament injunction regarding discernment is relevant. Paul exhorts the Romans, "Do not be conformed to this age, but be transformed by the renewal of your mind, that you may discern what is the will of God: what is good and acceptable and perfect" (Rom. 12:2). And the proof of their genuine discernment is that they present their bodies "as a living sacrifice, holy and acceptable to God" (Rom. 12:1).

From these three passages, we can gather three precious criteria of discernment. The principle and foundation is the faith-filled confession that Jesus Christ has come in the flesh. The second is the recognition of the inseparable connection between confession of the lordship of Jesus and realization of his presence in the Eucharist and in the community that worships in his name. Finally, Christians as members of the Body of Christ must both incorporate his once-and-for-all sacrifice in their daily sacrificial living and be a witness to an often hostile world by their transformed existence. Thus, on every count, the Christian way bespeaks incarnation, not excarnation.

The three criteria we have briefly recalled are operative in Pope Francis's "evangelical discernment" throughout *Evangelii*

Gaudium, but they have a particular prominence in chapter 4, which treats "The Social Dimension of Evangelization." He insists that to restrict the salvation wrought in Christ to the private sphere or the purview of the individual is to impoverish Christ's redemptive action. In a striking assertion, the pope writes, "God's word teaches that our brothers and sisters are the prolongation of the incarnation for each of us: 'As you did it for one of these, the least of my brethren, you did it for me' (Matt. 25:40)."[30]

In explicating further, the sense he gives to "the prolongation of the incarnation," Pope Francis draws upon a theme so dear to Saint Irenaeus: that of recapitulation. He insists that salvation concerns the whole person in every aspect of his life, both in this world and in the world to come. The pope writes, "This is the principle of universality intrinsic to the Gospel, for the Father desires the salvation of every man and woman, and his saving plan consists in 'gathering up all things in Christ, things in heaven and things on earth' (Eph. 1:10)."[31]

This "recapitulation" of all things in Christ, putting all under the headship of Christ, is ingredient to the newness that Jesus brings in bringing himself. It bespeaks not merely a moral solidarity but an ontological solidarity in which men and women find their truest identity as members of the Body of Christ and thus members of one another. To recognize this new reality requires a true metanoia, a new consciousness and practice. Indeed, it requires "a new mindset which thinks in terms of community and the priority of the life of all over the appropriation of goods by a few."[32]

Hence all catechetical and theological renewal must be governed by the "epistemic primacy," the absolute *novum* of Jesus

30. *Evangelii Gaudium* 179.
31. *Evangelii Gaudium* 181.
32. *Evangelii Gaudium* 188.

Christ.[33] *Evangelii Gaudium*, from first to last, honors this epistemic primacy of Jesus Christ. Further, it meets Charles Taylor's challenge by setting forth a program of evangelization that offers a comprehensive outline of what the Incarnation means and what its implications are. *Evangelii Gaudium*'s Catholic vision embraces the personal, the social, the economic, and the political. It counters the Gnostic temptation of "excarnation" today, as Irenaeus did in the second century. The Church in this sublime vision serves not only as a "field hospital" but also as a "contrast society."[34]

33. For a careful development of the notion of "epistemic primacy," see Bruce Marshall, *Trinity and Truth* (Cambridge: Cambridge University Press, 2000). For its applicability to the Christian theology of religions, see George R. Sumner, *The First and the Last: The Claim of Jesus Christ and the Claims of Other Religious Traditions* (Grand Rapids, MI: Eerdmans, 2004).

34. I have developed these ideas at greater length in my book *Rekindling the Christic Imagination: Theological Meditations for the New Evangelization* (Collegeville, MN: Liturgical, 2014).

3. "Until Christ Be Formed in You" (Gal. 4:19)

Saint John Henry Newman's Theological-Pastoral Mystagogy

I. INTRODUCTION

I begin with some brief remarks about the title of the essay itself, since it already sums up the thrust of these reflections. By employing the term "mystagogy," literally a leading into the mystery, I raise up Newman's profound sense of God's mystery, God's holiness and otherness from all finite, created reality.

This intense sense of God's holy mystery impressed itself upon Newman from an early age and it evoked from him throughout his life sentiments of awe, reverence, and wonder. His worshipful response finds apt expression in the words of one of his best-loved poem/hymns: "Praise to the Holiest in the height, / And in the depth be praise. / In all his words most wonderful, / Most sure in all his ways."

Newman's foundational sense of God's mystery, like a diamond, is brilliantly reflected in three facets. He (and we) confess and meditate upon the mystery. This is the theological facet. The mystery must be lived and we must conform our lives to its exigencies: the facet of spirituality. And the good news of the mystery must be communicated and shared: the pastoral-ministerial facet.

---

* This essay was originally published as "'Until Christ Be Formed in You': Saint John Henry Newman's Theological-Pastoral Mystagogy," in Kevin O'Reilly, ed., *Heart Speaks to Heart: John Henry Newman and the Call to Holiness* (Leominster, UK: Gracewing, 2021), 103–24.

In Newman's life, these three facets of his encounter with God's holy mystery are inseparable and indispensable. This is one of the prime reasons that he is so exemplary a figure: indeed, a providential saint and teacher for our times. He refuses to countenance any divorce of spirituality, theology, and pastoral ministry, but sees them as constituting a complex and vivifying whole.[1]

A final preliminary point: "mystery" in Catholic theology does not indicate a puzzle or enigma, an absence of light. Rather, it signifies a superabundance of light. And even in the gracious revelation of God's holy mystery, it remains inexhaustible. Indeed, God's supreme revelation in the crucified, risen, and ascended Jesus Christ does not lessen the mystery but only deepens it.

Thus even as we, like Newman, seek to realize something of God's glory revealed in Jesus Christ, even as we confess, meditate, live, and teach this saving mystery, we are constantly drawn back to the foundational doxological imperative of praise. "Praise to the Holiest in the Height, / And in the depth be praise. / In all his words most wonderful, / Most sure in all his ways!"

II. THE MIND OF NEWMAN

One of the distinguishing characteristics of John Henry Newman, making him a particularly apt intellectual and spiritual teacher for our time, is the capaciously catholic breadth of his intellect. He embodies in his person a comprehensiveness of outlook that resists partial views of reality. His is the quintessentially Catholic affirmation of "both/and."

Unlike the narrow rationalists of his own day and ours, Newman's is not a constricted view of reason but one that recognizes legitimate cognitive insights in nonscientific domains, like music

---

1. Louis Bouyer is a sure guide in exploring Newman's holistic vision. See Louis Bouyer, *Newman's Vision of Faith: A Theology for Times of General Apostasy* (San Francisco: Ignatius, 1986).

and poetry. Indeed, he himself was accomplished in both areas.[2] Like the Fathers of the Church whom he so loved, Newman did not divorce mind and heart in the journey to God. His integral vision embraced both and saw that the scientific, the moral, and the aesthetic together comprise an integral anthropology. Ignoring or denying any dimension produces a truncated understanding of the human, harmful not only to the individual but to the community, and ultimately to nature itself.[3]

A key feature of Newman's integral anthropology is the importance he assigns to the imagination. Somewhat surprisingly, "Newman did not set out a definition of the 'imagination.'"[4] Rather he associated this capacity of the mind with the concrete apprehension and appropriation of reality, in particular in the realm of the interpersonal and the affective. In a famous observation, he asserts, "The heart is commonly reached, not through the reason, but through the imagination, by means of direct impressions, by the testimony of facts and events, by history, by description. Persons influence us, voices melt us, looks subdue us, deeds inflame us."[5]

Thus, in speaking of the "mind" of Newman, one must not exclude the "heart" as the seat of affections and imagination. It is both significant and indicative that Newman chose as his cardinalatial motto "Cor ad cor loquitur" ("Heart speaks to heart"). Unlike the great philosophers of modernity, represented by Descartes and Kant, who focus upon the individual, almost in autonomous isolation from others, Newman's whole intellectual disposition is intrinsically interpersonal. In many respects, he anticipated the

2. The indispensable study in this regard is Guy Nicholls, *Unearthly Beauty: The Aesthetic of St John Henry Newman* (Leominster, UK: Gracewing, 2019).

3. Notice the close link Pope Francis draws between an integral anthropology and ecology in his encyclical letter *Laudato Si': On Care for Our Common Home*, chapter 3: "The Human Roots of the Ecological Crisis." For the text of *Laudato Si'*, see vatican.va.

4. Bernard Dive, *John Henry Newman and the Imagination* (London: T&T Clark, 2018), 14.

5. John Henry Newman, *An Essay in Aid of a Grammar of Assent*, ed. I.T. Ker (Oxford: Clarendon, 1985), 65–66.

personalist vision of a Buber or Marcel.[6] Commenting on this aspect of Newman's thought and sensibility, Nicholas Lash writes, "The mode of rationality appropriate to such apprehension is—in its concreteness and irreducible complexity—closer to 'personal knowledge' or to literary and aesthetic cognition, than it is to the 'linear' rationality characteristic of theoretical deduction."[7]

III. A CRUCIAL DISTINCTION: "NOTIONAL" AND "REAL"

In this regard, one of the most characteristic and familiar of Newman's views is the distinction he makes between the "notional" and the "real." He employs it not only in his more technical writings like the *Grammar of Assent*, but it appears prominently in his sermons as he urges his hearers to "realize," to appropriate personally their sacred privileges. In shorthand fashion, one might consider it the distinction between knowledge of the head and knowledge of the heart. One recalls Pascal's famous dictum: "The heart has its reasons which reason does not comprehend."

Yet, as has already been stressed, it is not a question of either/or, as though only the latter were important and the former otiose. Rather, both are required for a comprehensive understanding. However, in matters religious, the ultimate pastoral aim is not merely notional, but real apprehension and appropriation. Nicholas Lash elucidates further, "This latter way of knowing: engaged, experiential, prereflexive, is—and the concept is central to the argument of the *Grammar*—'imaginative.'"[8]

---

6. An important study in this regard is John F. Crosby, *The Personalism of John Henry Newman* (Washington, DC: The Catholic University of America Press, 2014).

7. Nicholas Lash, introduction in John Henry Newman, *An Essay in Aid of a Grammar of Assent* (Notre Dame: University of Notre Dame Press, 1979), 10.

8. Lash, 13.

Newman applies the notional/real distinction (not separation!) to the relation between "religion" and "theology." In a typically balanced and challenging statement, he asserts,

> A dogma is a proposition. . . . To give a real assent to it is an
> act of religion; to give a notional, is a theological act. It is dis-
> cerned, rested in, and appropriated as a reality, by the religious
> imagination; it is held as a truth by the theological intellect.
> Not as if there were in fact, or could be, any line of demarca-
> tion or party-wall between these two modes of assent, the reli-
> gious and the theological. As intellect is common to all men as
> well as imagination, every religious man is to a certain extent
> a theologian, and no theology can start or thrive without the
> initiative and abiding presence of religion. [Still] . . . there is a
> theological habit of mind, and a religious, each distinct from
> each, religion using theology, and theology using religion.[9]

Whether in homilies, catechesis, or theological education, the
context and audience-appropriate union of the two modes of apprehension is imperative, lest the preacher and teacher succumb
either to an arid intellectualism or a flaccid emotionalism.

IV. INCARNATION: THE CENTRAL IDEA AND IMAGE OF REVELATION

In his *Oxford University Sermons,* which explore at length the relation of faith and reason, Newman insists, "It is the Incarnation
of the Son of God rather than any doctrine drawn from a partial

9. Newman, *Assent,* 69.

view of Scripture (however true and momentous it may be) which is the article of a standing or a falling Church."[10]

Once more, his holistic, synoptic vision perceives that the true *novum* of the New Testament is Jesus Christ himself. As he insisted at the end of his *Lectures on Justification* (perhaps his most systematic work), "The true preaching of the Gospel is to preach Christ."[11] Roderick Strange has highlighted this defining dimension of Newman's faith and thought: "From the doctrine of creation to the doctrine of eschatology, the Christ was central for Newman. Any future study of his theology will be obliged to take this fact into account."[12] As will future studies of Newman's preaching.

A helpful beginning is Denis Robinson's study of Newman's sermons. He underscores the inseparability of Newman's theology and his pastoral practice: both are pervasively Christocentric. Robinson writes, "Newman employs all the devices of homiletic rhetoric at his disposal to encourage his listeners to 'realize' the central principle of Christianity, namely, the truth of the Word made Flesh. In Newman's vocabulary, the verb 'to realize' is almost a technical term denoting a personal grasp of the reality of a particular object or truth, a grasp so profound that it can move the believer to action."[13]

Related to the Incarnation as the central principle of Christianity is Newman's famous contention: "From the age of fifteen, dogma has been the fundamental principle of my religion; I know no other religion; I cannot enter into the idea of any other sort

10. John Henry Newman, *Fifteen Sermons Preached before the University of Oxford* [hereafter, *Oxford University Sermons*], 3rd ed. (New York: Scribner, 1872), 35. The quote is from the key second sermon: "The Influence of Natural and Revealed Religion Respectively."

11. John Henry Newman, *Lectures on the Doctrine of Justification* (London: Longmans, 1914), 325.

12. Roderick Strange, *Newman and the Gospel of Christ* (Oxford: Oxford University Press, 1981), 164. Strange has further explored the central place of Christology in *Newman: The Heart of Holiness* (London: Hodder & Stoughton, 2019), 41–49.

13. Denis Robinson, "Preaching," in Ian Ker and Terrence Merrigan, ed., *The Cambridge Companion to John Henry Newman* (Cambridge: Cambridge University Press, 2009), 241–54, at 248.

of religion; religion, as a mere sentiment is to me a dream and a mockery."[14] And, tellingly, he insists, "My battle was with liberalism; by liberalism I mean the anti-dogmatic principle and its developments."[15]

Newman amplified these terse remarks in his well-known "Biglietto Address," delivered in Rome on May 12, 1879, on the occasion of being officially informed of his being raised to the office of cardinal by Pope Leo XIII. Newman spoke these heartfelt words:

> For thirty, forty, fifty years I have resisted to the best of my powers the spirit of liberalism in religion. . . . Liberalism in religion is the doctrine that there is no positive truth in religion, but that one creed is as good as another, and this is the teaching which is gaining substance and force daily. It is inconsistent with any recognition of any religion, as true. It teaches that all are to be tolerated, for all are matters of opinion. Revealed religion is not a truth, but a sentiment and a taste; not an objective fact, not miraculous; and it is the right of each individual to make it say just what strikes his fancy. Devotion is not necessarily founded on faith.[16]

One can only marvel at the acuteness and foresight of these words, anticipating the widespread present-day boast of being "spiritual, but not religious."

The "dogmatic principle" is the claim that there is indeed positive truth in religion and that at the heart of Christianity stands the definitive truth of God's Incarnation in Jesus Christ. But what distinguishes Christianity is the confession that the "dogma" is no abstract principle, but the very person of Jesus Christ.

14. John Henry Newman, *Apologia Pro Vita Sua* (London: Longmans, 1913), 49.
15. Newman, *Apologia*, 48.
16. John Henry Newman, *Spiritual Writings* (Maryknoll, NY: Orbis, 2012), 222.

Thus, commenting on his use of the term "Idea," Keith Beaumont makes this crucial clarification: "When Newman speaks of the living 'idea' of Christianity, he is referring not just to the *thought* of Christ present in men's minds (though it is doubtless on account of this that he uses the term 'idea'), but also, and above all, to the very *Person* of Christ living both in the hearts of individual Christians and in the whole liturgical and sacramental life of the Church—the Church itself being both 'sacrament' and 'mystical body' of Christ, and thereby a vehicle of divine Grace."[17]

The remainder of this essay will bring into prominent relief what Cyril O'Regan calls the "Christological contexting" of the mystery.[18] In so doing, I will seek to show how "Christologically saturated" Newman's spiritual-pastoral theology is. Here again, he appears a much-needed saint and teacher for our time, which is too often marked and marred by "Christological forgetfulness and deficiency."[19]

V. THE PRESENCE OF CHRIST IN THE WORLD

In the Letter to the Romans, Saint Paul teaches that "when Gentiles who do not have the law, do by nature what the law demands, even though they do not have the law, they are a law for themselves. They show that what the law requires is written on their hearts, to which their conscience bears witness" (Rom. 2:14–15a). Here, *in nuce*, I suggest, we find Newman's carefully pondered reflections about "natural religion." He considered the subject at length in his early *Oxford University Sermons* and returned to the theme in the *Grammar of Assent*. In both instances,

17. Keith Beaumont, *Blessed John Henry Newman: Theologian and Spiritual Guide for Our Times* (San Francisco: Ignatius, 2010), 49.

18. Cyril O'Regan, "Newman and von Balthasar: The Christological Contexting of the Numinous," *Eglise et Théologie*, 26 (1995): 165–202.

19. See Robert P. Imbelli, *Rekindling the Christic Imagination: Theological Meditations for the New Evangelization* (Collegeville, MN: Liturgical, 2014), xiii–xxviii, and more recently "No Decapitated Body," *Nova et Vetera*, 18, no. 3 (Summer 2020).

he compared and contrasted "natural religion" with "revealed religion"—as Paul himself had implicitly done.

Newman holds that natural religion is a manifestation of God's providential dispensation for humanity, especially evident in the phenomenon of conscience. In the second of his *Oxford University Sermons,* he writes, "Conscience implies a relation between the soul and a something exterior, and that, moreover, superior to itself; a relation to an excellence which it does not possess, and to a tribunal over which it has no power." He goes further and postulates that "the presentiment of a future life, and of a judgment to be passed upon present conduct, with rewards and punishments annexed, forms an article, more or less distinct, in the creed of Natural Religion."[20]

Conscience intimates the reality of a Lawgiver, even sounding the echo of a Voice. So far "Natural Religion" ventures, yet offers "little or no information respecting what may be called His *Personality.*"[21] In a footnote affixed to this passage in the third edition of the volume, however, Newman avers that this claim is "too strongly said." And in the *Grammar of Assent,* he contends that "if, as is the case, we feel responsibility, are ashamed, are frightened, at transgressing the voice of conscience, this implies that there is One to whom we are responsible, before whom we are ashamed, whose claims upon us we fear."[22]

Nonetheless, he admits that when we consider "the course of human affairs," when we ponder the horrors of human history, "what strikes the mind so forcibly and so painfully is [God's] absence (if I may so speak) from His own world." Thus "my burdened conscience . . . pronounces without any misgiving that God exists:—and it pronounces quite as surely that I am alienated from Him."[23]

20. Newman, *Oxford University Sermons,* 18, 19.
21. Newman, 22.
22. Newman, *Assent,* 76.
23. Newman, 256.

Hence, perhaps the most significant deliverance of natural religion is the recognition of its neediness and incapacity and its anticipation of a remedy for its ills. Newman writes, "Natural Religion is based upon the sense of sin; but it cannot find, it does but look out for the remedy." And he declares, "That remedy, both for guilt and for moral impotence, is found in the central doctrine of Revelation, the Mediation of Christ."[24]

Thus natural religion yearns, however inchoately, for a saving presence that can only be fulfilled in Christ "in whom all the Providences of God centre."[25] And the Gospels, with their inspired depiction of the Image of the Savior, "contain a manifestation of the Divine Nature, so special, as to make it appear from the contrast as if nothing were known of God, when they are unknown."[26]

As Newman hymned in his poem, "Praise to the Holiest,"

> And that a higher gift than grace
> should flesh and blood refine:
> God's Presence and His very self,
> And Essence all-divine.

Moreover, this Incarnation does not serve merely as remedy for sin. It truly recapitulates all those intimations of grace in the lives of individuals and communities. In a passage redolent of his beloved Fathers of the Church, Newman exults, "Christ came for this very purpose, to gather together in one all the elements of good dispersed throughout the world, to make them his own, to illuminate them with Himself, to reform and refashion them into Himself. He came to make a new and better beginning of

24. Newman, 313.
25. Newman, 43.
26. Newman, 81.

all things than Adam had been, and to be a fountain-head from which all good henceforth might flow."[27]

But until Jesus Christ at last appears these elements remain mere prefigurations, at best, but hints and guesses.

VI. THE PRESENCE OF CHRIST IN THE BELIEVER AND IN THE CHURCH

Jesus Christ, the New Adam, in his person is that "fountain-head from which all good might flow." His grace is present and experienced in a surpassing way in the Church in which the idea or image (Newman often uses the two inter-changeably) of Jesus Christ is shared and nourished. As Terrence Merrigan writes,

> Christianity, for Newman, is not the mere perfection of humanity's natural religious instincts, though it does involve the perfection of all the authentic elements of natural religion. It is a revelation of God that would be unthinkable were it not already realized in the person of Jesus and re-presented in the Church by means of certain sacramental extensions of the Incarnation.[28]

The apostolic preaching, the Gospel narratives, the Church's Tradition, and sacraments convey the idea or image to the believer. But it is clear from Newman's sermons and writings that the believer's faith, though mediated by idea and image, does not rest there. Through them believers encounter the living Jesus Christ himself whom their hearts so ardently desire. In a remarkable outpouring, Newman rhapsodizes that "the divinely-enlightened mind sees in Christ the very Object whom it desires to love and worship—the

27. Newman, *Lectures*, 193.

28. Terrence Merrigan, "Revelation," in *The Cambridge Companion to John Henry Newman*, 47–72, at 55.

Object correlative of its own affections; and it trusts Him, or believes, from loving Him."[29] Thus Terrence Merrigan rightly insists, "The dynamism and organizing power of the Christian idea is born of its foundation in the risen Christ, God's living Word in history. . . . He is the ground, the source of coherence, and the continuing dynamic, of Christian life and reflection, in and through which He is now known and apprehended."[30]

Complementary to and in intimate connection with "the dogmatic principle," then, is "the sacramental principle." Newman writes in the *Apologia*, "I was confident in the truth of a certain definite religious teaching, based upon this foundation of dogma; viz. that there was a visible Church, with sacraments and rites which are the channels of invisible grace."[31] As embodied creatures our only access to the spiritual realm is through sacramental embodiment. As Louis Bouyer writes, for Newman, "this sacramental world is dominated by that mysterious presence of God in Christ, here and now already, on earth, which is not only a preparation for heaven but its anticipation."[32] And, though to my knowledge he does not use the term, I think it quite congruent with Newman's Christological vision to say that, by his Incarnation, Jesus Christ is himself the "Ur-Sacrament": the font from whom all spiritual blessings flow.

Through Baptism and Eucharist, the Christian "puts on Christ" and is continually nourished by him. The Christian's "justification" consists in far more than a merely extrinsic imputation of righteousness. Through the sacraments, he or she becomes truly conformed to Christ and embarks on the ongoing journey of transformation in Christ. Such is the burden of Newman's *Lectures on Justification*. In lecture 8, "Righteousness Viewed as a Gift and as a Quality," he writes, "Those who believe that Christ has

29. Newman, *Oxford University Sermons*, 236.
30. Merrigan, "Revelation," 59.
31. Newman, *Apologia*, 49.
32. Bouyer, *Newman's Vision*, 168.

set up a new creation in unity, and that He Himself is the One principle in His Church of all grace and truth, will not be surprised to find that He has superseded the righteousness, as He has abolished the victims, of the ancient time; and that as the grace of the Holy Eucharist is the Presence of Christ Crucified, so the justification of those who approach it is the Indwelling of Christ risen and glorified."[33] One catches distinct resonances of Paul's awe-filled proclamation to the Colossians: "The mystery is this: Christ in you, the hope of Glory" (Col. 1:27).

Jesus Christ justifies us by transforming us, by gracing us with a new relation to God, by incorporating us into his Body.

VII. NEWMAN'S MYSTAGOGY: REALIZING CHRIST

For Newman, as we have seen, the Incarnation is the dogmatic principle par excellence, the Truth of God's Word become flesh in human history, the article of faith which distinguishes the Christian Church, upon which the Church stands or falls. In his *Lectures on Justification*, Newman vindicated this principle against an alternative that prevailed in many quarters of Protestantism. There "justification by faith alone" appeared to be the decisive principle, the criterion of authentic Gospel preaching.

Newman held that this latter view smacked of subjectivism. Its outcome was to place emphasis upon the believer rather than upon the object of belief, thereby usurping the place of Christ. In his final lecture, "On Preaching the Gospel," he expresses his unease and his conviction in words that are as germane today as they were then.

> The fault here spoken of is the giving to our "experiences" a more prominent place in our thoughts than to the nature, attributes, and work of Him from whom they profess to come,

33. Newman, *Lectures*, 201.

—the insisting on them as a special point for the consideration of all who desire to be recognized as converted and elect.
When men are to be exhorted to newness of life, the true Object to be put before them, as I conceive, is "Jesus Christ, the
same yesterday, to-day, and for ever."[34]

Note that Newman is certainly not arguing against exhorting
men and women to "newness of life." Indeed, his sermons brim
with such exhortation. His concern is when the criterion for such
newness becomes one's own "experiences," one's passing "feelings," one's emotional highs, as we might say. In brief, he cautions
against the pitfall of focusing upon one's salvation rather than
upon the person of the Savior.

It may seem paradoxical that one who so stressed the importance of the heart and the affections should seemingly be suspicious of emotion. He himself allows that "no one (it is plain) can
be religious without having his heart in his religion; his affections
must be actively engaged in it; and it is the aim of all Christian
instruction to promote this." But he dreads "lest a perverse use
should be made of the affections." A singular display of this is the
self-deception that "mere transient emotion" can substitute for
true "obedience."[35] And so he concludes, "Let us take warning
from Saint Peter's fall. Let us not promise much; let us not talk
much of ourselves . . . nor encourage ourselves in impetuous bold
language in religion." [36]

A striking corollary of Newman's hermeneutic of suspicion
with regard to emotion bereft of reason is that the great preacher
himself warns against putting excessive emphasis upon preaching—one that places undue burden upon the preacher to effect
conversion, by devices that may even be manipulative, to the

34. Newman, *Lectures*, 325.

35. Quotations are from the sermon "Religious Emotion," in John Henry Newman, *Parochial and Plain Sermons* (San Francisco: Ignatius, 1997), 116. Hereafter *PPS*.

36. Newman, *PPS*, 121.

point of arousing frenzy. For Newman, the proper setting for preaching is within the objectivity of the Church's liturgy. Indeed, the cycle of the liturgical year and the readings designated for the celebrations provide the inspiration and frame for his sermons. Preaching is not an end in itself, but should ever orient toward worship, praise, and thanksgiving—in brief, toward God and not self. For, to stress again, "the true preaching of the Gospel is to preach Christ."[37]

To preach Christ, of course, is not merely to evoke a figure of the past, however much the earthly life, action, and teaching of Jesus are an indispensable point of reference for faith. It is to foster a real encounter with the living Lord, crucified, risen, and ascended, who is truly present in his Church and its sacraments. In an Ascension sermon, "Waiting for Christ," Newman insists that "[Christ] is the only Ruler and Priest in His Church, dispensing gifts, and has appointed none to supersede Him. . . . Christ's priests have no priesthood but His." In line with the Fathers of the Church, he is uncompromising: "When they baptize, He is baptizing; when they bless, He is blessing."[38]

Further, it would be a grievous error to understand Christ's Ascension as though he were no longer present to the Church and the believer. It is true that he is not present physically as he was in first-century Galilee and Judea. But he is present spiritually, which for Newman signifies not a lesser but a truer presence. In an Easter sermon, "The Spiritual Presence of Christ in the Church," he insists,

[The Holy Spirit] has not so come that Christ does not come, but rather He comes that Christ may come in His coming. . . . The Holy Spirit causes, faith welcomes, the indwelling

37. Newman, *Lectures*, 325.
38. Newman, *PPS*, 1337.

44

of Christ in the heart. Thus the Spirit does not take the place of Christ in the soul, but secures that place to Christ.[39]

Newman's own sermons, therefore, are "mystagogic" in that they not only preach Christ, they seek to introduce his hearers into some dimension of the mystery of Christ, to aid their entry into his mystery, to make it their own. He endeavors to midwife their "realization" of the mystery so that they might truly "put on Christ."

Newman uses that last phrase in another Easter sermon, "Difficulty of Realizing Sacred Privileges." In it he shows his keen appreciation of the fact that we require time to come to know the import of our confession of faith, to mature in Christian living. And this not only because of the impediments of human sinfulness but because Christian faith so transcends our human earthbound apprehension. God has raised Christ and has made us heirs of the kingdom in Christ. Hence the need for steadfast perseverance in prayer, meditation, and work; hence the need for fidelity and obedience in daily exercises and practices. These seemingly pedestrian virtues, and not fleeting sentiments or high-sounding words, are the gauge of spiritual seriousness. Thus "Waiting on God day by day, we shall make progress day by day, and approach to the true and clear view of what He has made us to be in Christ."[40]

Ian Ker makes an astute observation regarding the importance of "obedience" in Newman's spirituality and preaching. Ker writes, "Not because obedience is more important than faith and love, but because it is the concrete proof and realization of things more important than itself, things only too easily corrupted or counterfeited."[41] In his piercing Advent homily "Unreal Words,"

39. Newman, 1265–66.
40. Newman, *PPS*, 1249.
41. Ian Ker, introduction to John Henry Newman, *Selected Sermons*, ed. Ian Ker (New York: Paulist, 1994), 49.

Newman broaches forcefully one of his predominant spiritual concerns—namely, employing words and verbal professions that do not reflect the truth of one's lived engagements. He deplores "profession without action, speaking without seeing or feeling."[42] And this, for Newman, is to be "unreal"—the all-too-common condition of a fallen humanity and of a wayward world.

Jesus Christ, who is the very Truth of God Incarnate, first embodied and then spoke an integral Word. He brought to the world a "new language," not merely of words, but of actions, dispositions, and virtues. So Newman, in a splendid peroration, exhorts his hearers,

> It is not an easy thing to learn that new language which Christ has brought us. He has interpreted all things for us in a new way; He has brought us a religion which sheds a new light on all that happens. Try to learn this language. Do not get it by rote, or speak it as a thing of course. Try to understand what you say. Time is short, eternity is long; God is great, man is weak; [man] stands between heaven and hell; Christ is his Saviour; Christ has suffered for him.[43]

"New language, new way, new light!"—Newman clearly is imbued with the New Testament's awe-filled sense of the new beginning that Jesus Christ has brought and is: the New Adam.

Corresponding to this realization of eschatological newness is the persuasion in the New Testament and the Fathers of the radical transformation to which believers are called: not just a better self, a new self. Schooled in Scripture and the Fathers, Newman repeatedly refers to the "new creation" that Jesus Christ has inaugurated. Initiated in the new birth of Baptism, the Christian is destined to grow into the fullness of Christ, toward that

42. Newman, *PPS*, 985.
43. Newman, 986.

"perfection" which Paul in chapter 3 of Philippians holds to be the common goal to which disciples are bent.

In sermon after sermon, Newman takes pains to impress upon his hearers that the journey of faith is no joyride. Or rather, that the surpassing joy is the end, not the starting point. How can it be other if, in the words of one of his most celebrated homilies, "The Cross of Christ" is, for Christian faith, "the Measure of the World?" In our present time, more than in Newman's day, even Christian theology frequently marginalizes the cross, often viewing it as the unhappy consequence of a life disruptive of the "establishment."[44]

Newman's words, then, are even more challenging and imperative. He insists, "In the Cross, and Him who hung upon it, all things meet, all things subserve it, all things need it. It is their centre and their interpretation. For He was lifted upon it that He might draw all men and all things unto Him."[45] And he urges his hearers, "Let us begin with faith; let us begin with Christ; let us begin with His Cross and the humiliation to which it leads."[46]

In concluding this homily, Newman draws the inevitable implications of this doctrine, urging, as always, that believers realize the import of their profession, so that their words not remain "unreal."

> They alone are able to enjoy this world, who begin with the world unseen. They alone enjoy it, who have first abstained from it. They alone can truly feast, who have first fasted; they alone are able to use the world, who have learned not to abuse it; they alone inherit it, who take it as a shadow of the world to come, and who for that world to come relinquish it.[47]

44. See the magisterial study of Fleming Rutledge, *The Crucifixion: Understanding the Death of Jesus Christ* (Grand Rapids, MI: Eerdmans, 2015).

45. Newman, *PPS*, 1241.

46. Newman, 1245.

47. Newman, 1245.

Both in his day and in ours, there are some who object that Newman's vision in these sermons is too severe, too austere. In a Lenten sermon, "The Yoke of Christ," he anticipates the objection. He speaks of those who would soften the scandal and gild the cross. They attempt to attract to religion "by making it appear not difficult and severe." But he dismisses this strategy as "a deceit," just as Jesus himself rebuked Peter for his attempt to repudiate the cross. Indeed, for the one who faithfully follows Jesus on his Way, the burden is "light." "But grace makes it so; in itself it is severe, and any form of doctrine which teaches otherwise forgets that Christ calls us to His yoke, and that yoke is a cross."[48]

Thus, time and again, Newman seeks to impress upon his congregation the cost of discipleship; and, though he readily acknowledges that no one save God can read another's heart, it is clear that he holds that many, even among baptized Christians, ignore the demands of the Gospel and are but lukewarm in their faith. How much more, then, does the "world" hold Christianity at a distance, perceiving it to be a threat to its own earthbound stratagems and devices. The preacher contends that "the world, which chooses the broad way, in consequence hates and spurns the narrow way; and in turn, our Blessed Lord, who has chosen for us the narrow way, hates, scorns, spurns, denounces the broad way."[49] These are words apt to cause serious discomfort for all advocates of (to use Bonhoeffer's indictment) "cheap grace" or, closer to home, a new, supposedly more merciful, "pastoral paradigm."

Newman is unyielding in stressing the newness of the Christian reality and the depth and scope of personal transformation it entails. Taking on Christ's yoke, taking on the mind of Christ, he says, "is the result of a change from a state of nature, a change so great as to be called a death or even a crucifixion of our natural

48. Newman, 1481.
49. Newman, 1486.

state."[50] It is no less than a new creation. Small wonder, then, that, to use the provocative title of another of his sermons, religion is but "a weariness to the natural man."[51]

To characterize the new state and situation of the Christian that is the fruit of Christ's death and Resurrection, Newman often has recourse to a passage from Paul's Epistle to the Colossians. He cites it as the governing text for one of his sermons for the Feast of the Ascension: "Rising with Christ." I transcribe the passage in the translation that Newman himself uses: "If ye then be risen with Christ, seek those things which are above, where Christ sitteth on the right hand of God. Set your affection on things above, not on things on the earth. For ye are dead, and your life is hid with Christ in God" (Col 3:1–3).

Adept mystagogue that he is, Newman often proceeds by way of contrast. Thus, he first sketches the manner of existence of those whose hearts fail to follow Christ in their affections and commitments. In a graphic image, he depicts them as the crowd "thronging and hurrying along the broad way." And he elucidates, "They walk without aim or object . . . [and] follow whatever strikes them and pleases them; they indulge their natural tastes."[52]

In a clear counter position to the "crowd," the disciples of the ascended Lord, "exalted and transfigured with Him," strive "to live in heaven in their thoughts, motives, aims, desires, likings, prayers, praises, intercessions, even while they are in the flesh."[53] Newman recognizes, of course, that such "transfiguration" is never fully realized *in statu viatoris*, thus the importance for the wayfaring Christian of the virtues of patience and perseverance. So, to the tepid or half-hearted, he issues this urgent injunction:

50. Newman, 1485.
51. Newman, 1428–35.
52. Newman, 1316.
53. Newman, 1319.

Start now with this holy season, and rise with Christ. See He offers you His hand; He is rising; rise with Him. Mount up from the grave of the old Adam; from grovelling cares, and jealousies, and fretfulness, and worldly aims; from the thraldom of habit. From the tumult of passion, from the fascinations of the flesh, from a cold, worldly, calculating spirit, from frivolity, from selfishness. . . . I am not calling on you to go out of the world, or to abandon your duties in the world, but to redeem the time . . . in good measure to realize honestly the words of the text, to "set your affections on things above"; and to prove that you are His, in that your heart is risen with Him, and your life hid in Him.[54]

"You are His!" Newman's preaching and teaching far transcend any mere moralism. The obedience to which he exhorts his hearers is, in the root sense of the word, an earnest and attentive "listening to" their and his Lord in whom they will find blessedness and true joy. Yet, in another sermon, he cautions them, "It is not His loss that we love Him not, it is our loss. He is All-blessed, whatever becomes of us. He is not less blessed because we are far from Him. It is we who are not blessed, except as we approach Him, except as we are like Him, except as we love Him."[55]

The obedience of faith is not to a precept but to a person, the person of the Son of God. And its goal is not mere imitation but participation in his own life. In effect, in his theology and spirituality, Newman recovered the ancient Christian tradition of *theosis* or divinization. In a fine essay on the influence of the Fathers of the Church on Newman, Brian Daley writes, "Newman's emphasis on Jesus's divine identity, even in the midst of his human words and activities, leads him to make his own the distinctive Greek Patristic idea of salvation not simply as a change

---

54. Newman, 1323. The phrase "to realize honestly" is Newman's insistent antidote to "unreal words and professions."

55. Newman, 1434–35.

in the believer's relationship with God, thanks to the work of Jesus—as most Protestants had taught since Luther—but as actual transformation, as participation through the Spirit in the divine life and Trinitarian relationships of the Son."[56]

The thrust of the present essay has been not only to underscore Daley's remark but to suggest further that for Newman deification is *Christification*. Just as justification is the indwelling of the risen Christ, so sanctification is progressively to be configured to and transfigured in Jesus Christ. I know of no bolder statement of this on Newman's part than his sermon "Righteousness Not of Us, but in Us." There, he boldly asserts, in a passage I can't forbear from quoting at length,

> What was actually done by Christ in the flesh eighteen hundred years ago, is in type and resemblance really wrought in us one by one even to the end of time. He was born of the Spirit, and we too are born of the Spirit. He was justified by the Spirit, and so are we. He was pronounced the well-beloved Son, when the Holy Ghost descended on Him; and we too cry Abba, Father, through the Spirit sent into our hearts. He was led into the wilderness by the Spirit; He did great works by the Spirit; He offered Himself to death by the Eternal Spirit; He was raised from the dead by the Spirit; He was declared to be the Son of God by the Spirit of holiness on His resurrection: we too are led by the same Spirit into and through this world's temptations; we, too, do our works of obedience by the Spirit; we die from sin, we rise again unto righteousness through the Spirit; and we are declared to be God's sons—declared, pronounced, dealt with as righteous—through our resurrection unto holiness in the Spirit. Or, to express the same great truth in other words; *Christ Himself vouchsafes to repeat in each of*

56. Brian E. Daley, "The Church Fathers," in *The Cambridge Companion to John Henry Newman*, 29–46, at 40.

us in figure and mystery all that He did and suffered in the flesh.
He is formed in us, born in us, suffers in us, rises again in us,
lives in us.[57]

VIII. CHRIST'S REAL PRESENCE

Some years ago, the literary and cultural critic George Steiner
wrote a penetrating book, *Real Presences*. He sets forth his provocative thesis at the very beginning of his study.

> This essay proposes that any coherent understanding of what
> language is and how language performs, that any coherent ac-
> count of the capacity of human speech to communicate mean-
> ing and feeling is, in the final analysis, underwritten by the
> assumption of God's presence. I will put forward the argument
> that the experience of aesthetic meaning in particular, that of
> literature, of the arts, of musical form, infers the necessary pos-
> sibility of this "real presence."[58]

I can only imagine Newman vigorously nodding his assent,
though he would accent what Steiner only hints at: the Real Presence in the world of the Incarnate Word.

I have previously cited Newman's splendid sermon "The
Spiritual Presence of Christ in the Church." Here, he expresses
the very touchstone of his faith:

> Christ has promised He will be with us to the end—be with
> us, not only as He is in the unity of the Father and the Son,
> not in the Omnipresence of the Divine Nature, but personally,
> as the Christ, as God and man; not present with us locally and

---

57. Newman, *PPS*, 1047–48 (emphasis added).
58. George Steiner, *Real Presences* (Chicago: University of Chicago Press, 1989), 3.

sensibly, but still really, in our hearts and to our faith. And it is by the Holy Ghost that this gracious communion is effected.[59]

The presence of the risen and ascended Christ is the very heart of the Church, founding, guiding, nourishing, and sustaining it in the midst of its journey to the fulfillment of God's promise.

Of course, the primordial sacrament of Christ's Real Presence is the Holy Eucharist. In his sermon, "The Eucharistic Presence," Newman meditates upon Jesus's discourse on the Bread of Life in chapter 6 of Saint John's Gospel. He expounds it in this fashion:

> The text speaks of the greatest and highest of all the Sacramental mysteries, which faith has been vouchsafed, that of Holy Communion. Christ, who died and rose again for us, is in it spiritually present, in the fullness of His death and of His resurrection. We call His presence in this Holy Sacrament a spiritual presence, not as if "spiritual" were but a name or mode of speech, and He were really absent, but by way of expressing that He who is present there can neither be seen nor heard; that He cannot be approached or ascertained by any of the senses; that He is not present in place, that He is not present carnally, though He is really present. And how this is, of course, is a mystery. All that we know or need know is that He *is* given to us, and that in the Sacrament of Holy Communion.[60]

It would be well to make two observations apropos this affirmation of faith. First, Newman, as an Anglican, most certainly confessed Christ's Real Presence in the Eucharistic celebration and in the Holy Communion received by the faithful. Second, in his Anglican days, he was chary of the Roman Catholic doctrine of

59. Newman, *PPS*, 1270.
60. Newman, 1272.

"transubstantiation," which he later professed as Catholic and admitted that he had not previously understood its true import.[61] However, it was only as a Catholic that he came to appreciate and draw immense spiritual sustenance from the Real Presence of Christ in the reserved sacrament in Catholic churches throughout the world.[62]

In another sermon, "The Resurrection of the Body," Newman elucidates for his congregation the fruits of the Eucharist: "We eat the sacred bread, and our bodies become sacred; they are not ours; they are Christ's; they are instinct with that flesh which saw not corruption; they are inhabited by His Spirit; they become immortal; they die but to appearance, and for a time; they spring up when their sleep is ended, and reign with Him for ever."[63] And in an Easter sermon, "Christ, a Quickening Spirit," he speaks of "the blessed Sacrament of the Eucharist, in which Christ is 'evidently set forth crucified among us'; that we, feasting upon the Sacrifice, may be 'partakers of the Divine Nature.'"[64] Thus, the Eucharist effects in us what I earlier called *Christification*.

If, in his own day, Newman's theological-pastoral concern issued an urgent challenge to those who "discern not the Lord's Body,"[65] even among the many who attended Church; how much more would his concern be aroused today by the dramatic decline in Church attendance and, apparently, conviction concerning Christ's Real Presence in the Eucharist. We confront a dire situation that, sadly, lends credence to the discernment found in the subtitle of Louis Bouyer's book on Newman: "times of general apostasy." Moreover, if Newman indicted his own culture's growing relativism, what would be his reaction to our contemporary

61. See the careful discussion in Placid Murray, ed., *Newman the Oratorian* (Dublin: Gill & Macmillan, 1969), chapter 3: "The Eucharistic Ministry."

62. See John Tracy Ellis, "The Eucharist in the Life of Cardinal Newman," *Communio* 4, no. 4 (Winter 1977): 320–40.

63. Newman, *PPS*, 176.

64. Newman, 319.

65. Newman, 319.

culture that demonstrates so many tragic signs of being bereft of a sense of real presence and of wandering aimlessly in a wasteland of sheer absence: absence of meaning and of hope?

George Steiner in *Real Presences* speaks of our time as one of the "Epi-logue," the "After-word." The Logos, in which all things cohere and derive meaning, has faded in modern consciousness, and men and women are adrift in a disenchanted world. In his monumental study of modernity, *A Secular Age*, the Catholic philosopher Charles Taylor, while appreciative of many of modernity's gains, forthrightly catalogues its weaknesses, indeed its despairing traits. He analyzes, for example, secularity's "immanent frame" in which all traces of a transcendent realm disappear in the wake of a frenetic consumerism. He also exposes modernity's "buffered self," insulated and isolated from relationships and commitments that might threaten individual autonomy. Finally, he diagnoses the malady of "excarnation," a profound dis-ease with the body, its fragility and ultimate mortality. And he urgently challenges his fellow Christians, "We have to struggle to recover a sense of what the Incarnation can mean."[66]

John Henry Newman, then, appears a providential saint for our time, one who, in the midst of an incipient and spreading secularity, struggled successfully to recover and communicate creatively and imaginatively a profound sense of what the Incarnation means. And he does so, not least, by showing the profound links, in the Christian dispensation, between Incarnation and Eucharist. As he stated in one of his sermons, "No one realizes the Mystery of the Incarnation but must feel disposed towards that of Holy Communion."[67] For Christ's embodiment continues

---

66. Charles Taylor, *A Secular Age* (Cambridge, MA: Belknap, 2007), 753. I confess to finding it odd that, in the book's more than eight hundred pages, there is no mention of John Henry Newman. For another insightful analysis of the spiritual plight of a disenchanted secular world, an age of "de-facement," see the English philosopher Roger Scruton's Gifford Lectures, *The Face of God* (London: Bloomsbury, 2012). He too, however, makes no mention of Newman.

67. Newman, *PPS*, 1281.

in his Eucharistic self-gift for the sake of his Body, the Church, and, through the Church, for the life of the world.

John Henry Newman is not only a saint but also a doctor for our contemporary plight, a guide out of the confinement of a one-dimensional world. He offers us an integral theological-spiritual vision whose center is the Eucharistic Christ, the Christ whose being is to be Eucharist/Gift. Newman can serve as a God-inspired mentor, helping us to rekindle our Eucharistic imagination and to rejoice in Christ's Real Presence in the Eucharist, the paradigmatic expression of heart speaking to heart. He calls us to realize more fully Christ's gift of Real Presence and to join with him in joyful prayer, heart speaking to Heart:

> O most Sacred, most loving Heart of Jesus, you are concealed in the Holy Eucharist, and you beat for us still. Now, as then, you say: "With desire I have desired." I worship you with all my best love and awe, with my fervent affection, with my most subdued, most resolved will.
>
> O my God, when you condescend to suffer me to receive you, to eat and drink you, and for a while you take up your abode within me, make my heart beat with your Heart!
>
> Purify it of all that is earthly, all that is proud and sensual, all that is hard and cruel, of all perversity, of all disorder, of all deadness. So fill it with you, that neither the events of the day, nor the circumstances of the time, may have power to ruffle it, but that in your love and your fear, my heart may have peace. Amen.[68]

68. John Henry Newman, *Prayers, Verses, and Devotions* (San Francisco: Ignatius, 1989), 428. I have taken the liberty of changing Newman's original "thous" to "yous."

I should like to express my gratitude to the Reverend Richard G. Smith for his generous help in suggesting and locating sources for this essay.

4. Joseph Ratzinger's "Spiritual Christology"

INTRODUCTION

This article offers some considerations on the topic: "Joseph Ratzinger's Spiritual Christology." It does so mindful of the frequently alleged disconnect between doctrine and experience manifest in such slogans as "I'm spiritual, but not religious." This slogan has its ecclesiastical counterpart in the increasingly prevalent disjunction between what is "doctrinal" and what is "pastoral." But I also address the topic in light of an ever-growing tendency toward academic specialization that often deems "spirituality" not ingredient to the theological curriculum but "extra-curricular," reserved to the chapel and not the classroom.

I will attempt to show, therefore, how theology and spirituality are intimately and exemplarily related in Ratzinger's thought—just as they were for his theological ancestors and mentors: Augustine and Bonaventure, Newman, Guardini, and de Lubac. For him, as for them, "mystery" and "mysticism" (faith's objective content and its subjective appropriation) are inseparable; and both have a distinctive "Christic form."[1] Ratzinger will come to call this persuasion and approach a "spiritual Christology."

---

* This essay was originally published as "Joseph Ratzinger's 'Spiritual Christology,'" in *Gift to the Church and World: Fifty Years of Joseph Ratzinger's "Introduction to Christianity,"* ed. John C. Cavadini and Donald Wallenfang (Eugene, OR: Pickwick, 2021), 189–212.

1. See de Lubac's important article, "Mysticism and Mystery," in Henri de Lubac, *Theological Fragments*, trans. Rebecca Howell Balinski (San Francisco: Ignatius, 1989), 35–69.

The article will proceed in five parts:

I. Looking Back . . . and Forward to Vatican II
II. Ratzinger on Revelation: The Inextricable Nexus of Theology and Spirituality
III. Introduction to Christianity: Laying the Foundations of a "Spiritual Christology"
IV. Further Delineating "Spiritual Christology"
V. Toward a Eucharistic Mysticism and Spirituality

But let me first dwell briefly upon the two images that accompany this reflection: the risen/ascended Christ bestowing the Holy Spirit upon the Apostles (from the great entrance door of the twelfth-century Basilica of Saint Mary Magdalene in Vézelay, France) and the painting of the Transfiguration by the late thirteenth-century Sienese painter, Duccio di Buoninsegna. (See images on page xxvi and page 228.)

We know the crucial importance of images and of the aesthetic dimension of existence for Joseph Ratzinger/Pope Benedict. In his well-known 2002 address in Rimini, Ratzinger said, "Looking at icons, and in general at the great masterpieces of Christian art, leads us on an interior way, a way of transcendence, and thus brings us, in this purification of sight that is a purification of the heart, face to face with beauty, or at least with a ray of it."[2] A few years later, explaining why he insisted that images of Christian art be included in the *Compendium to the Catechism of the Catholic Church*, then-Cardinal Ratzinger wrote, "In a culture of images, a sacred image can express much more than what can

---

2. "Wounded by the Arrow of Beauty: The Cross and the New 'Aesthetics' of Faith," in Joseph Ratzinger, *On the Way to Jesus Christ*, trans. Michael J. Miller (San Francisco: Ignatius, 2005), 38.

be said in words, and be an extremely effective and dynamic way of communicating the Gospel message."[3]

In this spirit and with this same conviction I offer these two images to recapitulate aesthetically and affectively all that I write here. They depict imaginatively and strikingly *the absolute* novum *of the risen, ascending Jesus Christ and the transformative way of life to which he calls his disciples.* Hopefully, these images will guide our meditations both *ante et post scriptum!* They certainly have continued to inspire my prayer and reflection since I first encountered them during a junior year abroad sixty years ago.

I. LOOKING BACK . . . AND FORWARD TO VATICAN II

Vatican II produced sixteen documents of varied length and importance. But in interpreting the council, in establishing an appropriate "hermeneutic," the four constitutions play a decisive role. They are, of course, *Sacrosanctum Concilium, Lumen Gentium, Dei Verbum,* and *Gaudium et Spes.* However, in many ways it is the Dogmatic Constitution on Divine Revelation, *Dei Verbum,* which holds a primacy among them.[4]

For if God does not take the initiative to reveal himself, there is no foundation for the Church. It becomes only a human association and organization. And if God has not given himself definitively in Christ, there is no basis for liturgy. It becomes a merely human gathering like an American Legion parade or the devoted fans at any sporting event.

A truly distinguishing characteristic of *Dei Verbum*'s presentation of revelation is that it is *explicitly Christocentric.* Though it celebrates God's revelation in the course of the history of the

3. *Compendium to the Catechism of the Catholic Church* (Washington, DC: United States Conference of Catholic Bishops, 2006), xvii.

4. Jared Wicks concurs with this privileging of *Dei Verbum*. See his *Investigating Vatican II: Its Theologians, Ecumenical Turn, and Biblical Commitment* (Washington, DC: The Catholic University of America Press, 2018), 223–24.

people of Israel, it confesses that God's revelation attains its fullness in *the person of Jesus Christ*.[5] It is this Christ-centered understanding of God's revelation and promise that permeates the documents of Vatican II—prominent not only in *Sacrosanctum Concilium* and *Lumen Gentium* but also in *Gaudium et Spes*.

I call attention to *Gaudium et Spes* 10, 22, and 45 as prime instances of Vatican II "rekindling the Church's Christic imagination" and this in its pastoral constitution. These crucial paragraphs of *Gaudium et Spes* give the lie to any facile separation, much less dichotomy, between "dogmatic" and "pastoral" in Church teaching and practice.[6]

Here, for example, is the astonishing claim of *Gaudium et Spes* 45, which concludes part 1 of the pastoral constitution:

> For the Word of God, through whom all things were made, was made flesh so that as perfectly human he would save all human beings and sum up all things. The Lord is the goal of human history, the point on which the desires of history and civilization turn, the center of the human race, the joy of all hearts and the fulfillment of all desires. He it was whom the Father raised from the dead, exalted and placed at his right hand, making him judge of the living and the dead. It is as given life and united in his Spirit that we make our pilgrimage towards the climax of human history which is in full accord with the designs of his love, 'to unite all things in Christ, things in heaven and things on earth' [Eph 1:10]."

Now, one might understandably object: Do you perhaps exaggerate in overstressing the Christocentric nature of Vatican II's understanding of revelation? Did not the Church always confess

---

5. Vatican Council II, *Dei Verbum* 2, in *The Word on Fire Vatican II Collection*, ed. Matthew Levering (Park Ridge, IL: Word on Fire Institute, 2021), 17–18.

6. See the fine article of José Granados, "The Synergy of Doctrine and Life," *Communio* 43, no. 1 (Spring 2016): 104–22, which draws upon Irenaeus, Augustine, and Aquinas.

Christ? Did we not always profess Jesus as Son of God and son of Mary? One divine person in two natures? Certainly, these dogmatic assertions form a lasting part of the Church's deposit of faith.

Yet I contend that Vatican II's re-Sourcement sought to know Christ in a new way: to rediscover the person of Jesus Christ—not only through propositions *about him*, but by inviting and fostering a personal encounter *with him*. An encounter that leads not merely to an assent of the mind but a consent of the heart, and hence to transformation of life. And it sought to bring that renewed sense of Christ's reality and primacy into all facets of the Church's life and its relation to the world. So, all the popes since the council have explicitly advocated a "New Evangelization": a Church in mission to bring the Good News who is Jesus Christ to the world.

Thus, I fully agree with Nicholas Healy, who writes, "Before dogma is something the Church formulates, dogma is something Christ himself is; dogma is first and foremost Christ himself as incarnate Word and enfleshed truth."[7]

The historian of Vatican II, John O'Malley, argues that "the universal call to holiness" weaves through the documents of the council like a golden thread. He suggests that such an emphasis is unique in the history of ecumenical councils. O'Malley writes, "Among the recurring themes of the Council expressive of its spirit, the call to holiness is particularly pervasive and particularly important. . . . It is the theme that to a large extent imbued the Council with its finality."[8]

What I would add, as an essential complement to O'Malley's insight, is that, for the council, the source and enabler of that call is the Holy One himself: Jesus Christ. Indeed, the call to holiness

7. Nicholas J. Healy Jr., "Henri de Lubac on the Development of Doctrine," *Communio* 44, no. 4 (Winter 2017): 667–89, at 679.

8. John W. O'Malley, *What Happened at Vatican II* (Cambridge, MA: Harvard University Press, 2008), 310.

has, in the mind and heart of the council, a distinctive Christological foundation. For the revelation of the uniqueness of Christ is not primarily a propositional truth for our instruction but an existential summons to transformation of life according to the image of Christ: being clothed with Christ, taking on the mind of Christ, living the life of Christ.

Thus, the council notably achieved one of the salient goals of the *Nouvelle Théologie* movement of the 1940s and 1950s. In an excellent article, Paolo Prosperi writes that for *la nouvelle théologie*, "returning to the fathers meant asserting the unity between dogmatic theology and the living experience of Christ in the Church . . . the inseparable bond between mysticism and theology . . . putting back at the center knowledge through *syggeneia* (con-naturality), which for the fathers was the only real way to access the mystery of God."[9]

Vatican II's dialectic of *ressourcement* and *aggiornamento* is founded upon its bold and creative reappropriation of the New Testament confession that "Jesus Christ is the same yesterday, today, and forever" (Heb. 13:8).[10]

If the great achievement of the Second Vatican Council was this evangelical re-Sourcement—a renewed realization of the Christic source of the Church's life and mission—a fair amount of the postconciliar confusion and crisis can be attributed to the misremembering[11] or, worse, willful neglect of this achievement. I have elsewhere sought to elucidate further this loss of the

9. Paolo Prosperi, "The Birth of *Sources Chrétiennes* and the Return to the Fathers," *Communio* 39, no. 4 (Winter 2012): 643–44. For the influence of the series *Sources Chrétiennes* on the labors of Vatican II, see Joseph Ratzinger, "*Sources Chrétiennes* and the One Unique Source," *Communio* 44, no. 2 (Summer 2017): 383–88.

10. Significantly, this verse of the Letter to the Hebrews is quoted in *Gaudium et Spes* 10 at the close of the introduction, thus providing the Christological foundation and orientation for the remainder of the Pastoral Constitution.

11. Cyril O'Regan has insightful and instructive pages on Hegel's "Christological Derailment," which uncannily foreshadows some of Catholicism's postconciliar developments and defections. See Cyril O'Regan, *The Anatomy of Misremembering: Von Balthasar's Response to Philosophical Modernity*, vol. 1, *Hegel* (New York: Crossroad, 2014), 185–204.

Christic center.[12] In doing so, I have been beholden to the analyses of Joseph Ratzinger himself. But before taking up Ratzinger's own assessment of the postconciliar challenges, let us reflect on the theological vision and perspective he brought to the council.

II. RATZINGER ON REVELATION: THE INEXTRICABLE NEXUS BETWEEN THEOLOGY AND SPIRITUALITY

The clearly Christocentric understanding of Revelation in *Dei Verbum* laid the foundation for the Christologically saturated teaching of the council. And a person who helped secure that foundation was the thirty-five-year-old theologian Joseph Ratzinger.

Ratzinger, then a young professor at the University of Bonn, had been chosen by Cardinal Frings of Cologne as his theological advisor. Already in his "Inaugural Lecture" at Münster (to which he had moved in 1963), Ratzinger declared, "Revelation means God's whole speech and action with man; it signifies a *reality* that Scripture makes known but that is itself not simply identical with Scripture. Revelation, therefore, is more than Scripture to the extent that reality exceeds information about it."[13] Thus, revelation exceeds even the divinely inspired images and propositions of Scripture.

And Ratzinger elucidates further the implications of this statement:

> There can be scripture without revelation. For revelation always and only becomes a reality where there is faith. The unbeliever

---

12. Robert P. Imbelli, *Rekindling the Christic Imagination: Theological Meditations for the New Evangelization* (Collegeville, MN: Liturgical, 2014), xv–xviii.

See also Matthew Levering's important book, *An Introduction to Vatican II as an Ongoing Theological Event* (Washington, DC: The Catholic University of America Press, 2017), especially chapter 5: "Vatican II as an Ongoing Theological Event: The Way Forward."

13. Karl Rahner and Joseph Ratzinger, *Revelation and Tradition*, trans. W.J. O'Hara (New York: Herder, 1966), 35.

remains under the veil of which Paul speaks in 2 Corinthians 3. He can read scripture and know what it contains. He can even understand, purely conceptually, what is meant and how its statements cohere, yet he has no share in the revelation. Revelation is in fact fully present only when, in addition to the material statements which testify to it, its own inner reality is operative in the form of faith. Consequently revelation to some degree includes its recipient, without whom it does not exist. Revelation cannot be pocketed like a book one carries around. It is a living reality which calls for the living person as the location of its presence.[14]

I hold that this conviction, inspired to a large degree by his studies of Augustine and Bonaventure, remains as one of the salient motifs of Ratzinger's theological *itinerarium*.[15] Indeed, it clearly anticipates his later thematic "spiritual Christology."

For Ratzinger, as for Augustine and Bonaventure, there is an intimate, inseparable connection between his theology and his spirituality, between the content of faith (*fides quae*) and its experiential appropriation (*fides quā*). Indeed, like them, these are, for him, but two sides of one coin. And, like them, his theological-spiritual vision is *explicitly and pervasively Christocentric*.[16]

14. Rahner and Ratzinger, *Revelation*, 36.

15. Michael Schmaus, one of the two readers of Ratzinger's *Habilitationsschrift* (necessary for teaching at the university level), worried that his position smacked of subjectivism and even modernism. For the "drama" of the dissertation's composition, revision, and defense, see Joseph Ratzinger, *Milestones: Memoirs 1927–77*, trans. Erasmo Leiva-Merikakis (San Francisco: Ignatius, 1998), 106–12.

16. See the insightful reflections of Jordan Haddad, "Kneeling Theology: Believing in Order to See Scripture," *Church Life Journal*, October 17, 2018, churchlifejournal.nd.edu.

III. *INTRODUCTION TO CHRISTIANITY*: LAYING THE FOUNDATIONS OF A "SPIRITUAL CHRISTOLOGY"

In 1983, the now-Cardinal Joseph Ratzinger published a book of essays to which he gave the title *Behold the Pierced One: An Approach to a Spiritual Christology*. In the book's preface, he expressed his intention "to consider Christology more from the aspect of its spiritual appropriation" than he had previously done.[17]

I will return to that book in due course. But the major contention that I would like to argue in this part of the presentation is that the foundation for Ratzinger's "spiritual Christology" was already securely laid in his now-classic *Introduction to Christianity*. The book, of course, originated as lectures delivered at Tübingen in summer 1967, published in German in 1968 and in English in 1969. I maintain that what he later came to call his "spiritual Christology" was already abundantly present in these lectures.

From the very beginning, the book clearly resonated with readers, as it had with its original audience. By 2005, the original German edition had gone through twenty-four reprints, and translations had appeared in twenty-two different languages.

In commenting upon the book, permit me to proceed once more by way of personal reminiscence. I think it evokes some of the turmoil of the postconciliar years in which the book appeared.

My doctoral studies took place at Yale from 1967 to 1970—even before there was a "Yale School"! I was one of the first of a cohort of Catholics to pursue graduate studies in theology at a non-Catholic institution. The years 1967–70 were not happy ones in either the Church or the country. I refer to 1968 in particular as my *annus horribilis*.

I had been ordained barely three years and was living at Saint Thomas More House, the seat of the Catholic chaplaincy at Yale. The talented and well-respected chaplain was on a year's sabbatical.

---

17. Joseph Ratzinger, *Behold the Pierced One: An Approach to a Spiritual Christology*, trans. Graham Harrison (San Francisco: Ignatius, 1986), 9.

In the event, he never returned from the sabbatical and went on to leave priestly ministry—unfortunately, a not-uncommon occurrence in those turbulent years.

Frenzy for change permeated both Church and society. The political crisis of the Vietnam War spilled over into classroom and chapel, provoking tension-filled meetings of newly formed liturgical committees. At times, this seeped into the celebration of the liturgy itself.

One small—though, to my mind, portentous—incident from those days has remained vividly with me. I was at supper with the acting chaplain and we had as a guest the provincial of a small religious congregation. We recited a quite perfunctory grace before meals. Before we had even seated ourselves, the visitor commented, "Oh, I see you still pray: we have gone from formal prayer to informal prayer to no prayer." He said this not as a boast but with a sense of poignant regret. More than fifty years later, the scene seems a paradigm of the disorientation experienced by so many in the wake of the council, as a highly institutionalized Church, with a liturgy unchanged for centuries, sought to find its way in a new religious and cultural landscape where familiar markers were obscured.

In the midst of this turmoil, both institutional and personal, there appeared, literally out of the blue, the English translation of a book by a German scholar, with the not very "jazzy" title *Introduction to Christianity*. It turned out to be an oasis in a parched land. What was it about the book that impressed so deeply?

First was the clear acknowledgment of the theological-spiritual crisis that had erupted in the immediate postconciliar years. In the preface to the first edition, Ratzinger lamented the "confusion about the real content and meaning of Christian faith" and the consequent "watering down of the demands of faith."[18] He

---

18. Joseph Ratzinger, *Introduction to Christianity*, trans. J.R. Foster (San Francisco: Ignatius, 2004), 31.

provocatively employs to this end the parable of "Clever Hans," who successively exchanges the gold that he had inherited for items of lesser value until he is left, at last, with a worthless stone that he then discards.

In a similar vein, in 1992, looking back on the situation in 1972 when the new journal *Communio* was launched, Ratzinger spoke of some in the immediate postconciliar period who made endless appeals to the supposed "spirit" of the council. He wrote, "They sold goods from the old liberal flea-market as if they were new Catholic theology."[19]

Then, in the preface to the new edition of *Introduction to Christianity* in 2000, Ratzinger specifies (what was already clear in the first edition) that the "crisis" in question was—and remains—fundamentally a *Christological crisis*.

He writes,

> If God has truly assumed manhood, and thus is, at the same time, true man and true God in Jesus, then he participates as man in the presence of God, which embraces all ages. Then, and only then, is he, not just something that happened yesterday, but is *present among us, our contemporary in our today*. That is why I am firmly convinced that a renewal of Christology must have the courage to see Christ in all his greatness, as he is presented by the four gospels together, in the many tensions of their unity.[20]

But *Introduction to Christianity* is far from a sustained lament; it presents, rather, a positive vision and proposal. In the original preface, he speaks of "understanding faith afresh as making possible true humanity today."[21] Notice that Ratzinger in no way

---

19. Joseph Ratzinger, "*Communio*: A Program," *Communio* 19, no. 3 (Fall 1992): 436–49, at 437.

20. Ratzinger, *Introduction*, 29 (emphasis added).

21. Ratzinger, 32.

opposes authentic *aggiornamento*: it is intrinsic to his project. What he seeks is theological creativity faithful to the heart of the Church's kerygma and catechesis: the person of Jesus Christ.

Let me select some aspects of *Introduction to Christianity* that advance this constructive vision.

Significantly, Ratzinger sets his entire presentation within the liturgical context of the baptismal profession of faith, articulated in the Apostles' Creed. Clearly for him this is not a polite bow to ritual, a prescribed familiar and familial tradition. Rather, in a phrase that has captivated me since I first read it almost fifty years ago, he declares that faith "is an all-encompassing movement of human existence."[22] It is a radical "turning" marked by existential renunciations and conversions—a personal and person-forming turning to the East, to the risen and ascended Jesus Christ who is ever coming.

He specifies further, "Christian faith is more than the option in favor of a spiritual ground to the world; its central formula is not 'I believe in something,' but '*I believe in you.*' It is the *encounter* with the man Jesus and in this encounter it experiences the meaning of the world as a person."[23] One recognizes here a clear foreshadowing of Benedict XVI's famous assertion in *Deus Caritas Est*: "Being Christian is not the result of an ethical choice or a lofty idea, but the encounter with an event, a person, who gives life a new horizon and a decisive direction."[24]

And Ratzinger sums up his vision and conviction: "Ultimately, all the reflections contained in this book . . . revolve around the basic form of the confession: 'I believe in you, Jesus of Nazareth, as the meaning (logos) of the world and of my life.'"[25]

---

22. Ratzinger, 88. One recalls the "*moto spirituale*" that marks the Pilgrim's descent and ascent in Dante's *Divina Commedia*.

23. Ratzinger, *Introduction*, 79 (emphasis added).

24. Benedict XVI, *Deus Caritas Est* 1 (translation slightly modified), encyclical letter, December 25, 2005, vatican.va.

25. Ratzinger, *Introduction*, 80–81.

Of course, the further question, inseparably both spiritual and theological, is: Who is this man? "Who do you say that I am?"

Ratzinger goes on to devote more than one hundred pages of part 2 of the book to the topic: "Jesus Christ." I offer one quote that is particularly rich and that undergirds his emergent spiritual Christology: "The peculiarity of Jesus' 'I,' of his person . . . lies in the fact that this 'I' is not at all something exclusive and independent, but rather is Being completely derived from the 'Thou' of the Father and lived for the 'You' of men."[26]

Ratzinger's lifelong meditation on the person and unique significance, the *novum*, of Jesus Christ finds expression in his careful exposition of Jesus's relational pattern of existence. For Ratzinger, "relationality" is constitutive of who Jesus is. Jesus the Christ is the one who receives all *from* the Father and shares himself fully, his entire person, *for* the sake of men and women in all their historical concreteness.

Thus, the image that focuses and animates Ratzinger's spiritual Christology is the Johannine image of the crucified/raised Jesus from whose *pierced side* flow blood and water of new life. He makes explicit reference to the image in the important section of *Introduction to Christianity* entitled "Christ, the 'Last Man.'"[27] The "last man" is, of course, Paul's *ho eschatos Adam*, the new man who inaugurates God's new creation. The pierced side reveals Christ as "the completely open man, in whom the dividing walls of existence are torn down, who is entirely *'transitus'* (Passover, 'Pasch')."[28]

This image provides the title of the book that will further thematize his call for a "spiritual Christology," *Behold the Pierced One*, and will be invoked five times in his inaugural encyclical as pope, *Deus Caritas Est*.

---

26. Ratzinger, 208.
27. Ratzinger, 240–41.
28. Ratzinger, 240 (translation slightly modified).

If we truly behold "the Pierced One," if we enter into the movement of existence, the *transitus*, that he realizes and enables, then, of course, we will undergo transformation. Indeed, "Being a Christian means essentially changing over from being for oneself to being for one another."[29] In a real sense it is to "pass over" from being merely an individual to becoming in Christ a person: one defined by his or her relationships.

In one of the most suggestive assertions in the book, Ratzinger writes, "The Christian sees in man, not an individual, but a person. And it seems to me that this passage from individual to person contains the whole span of transition from antiquity to Christianity, from Platonism to faith."[30]

To my mind, the contemporary theologian who shows special kinship with Ratzinger is Rowan Williams. In a profound meditation on the icon of the Transfiguration, Williams writes, "Looking at Jesus seriously changes things. If we do not want to be changed, better not to look too long or too hard."[31] In the writings of both Ratzinger and Williams, one is repeatedly struck by the grammar of "*novum*/transformation" that governs and structures their work. In this, they are manifestly heirs of the Fathers of the Church.[32]

Thus, the issue is far deeper than merely "imitating" Christ by following the path that he indicates. It is rather the *birth of a new self*, on the Way that Jesus has opened through the veil to the Father. Ratzinger's spiritual Christology is mystagogic. It advocates and guides our entering into the mystery of Christ, a "Christification," that goes beyond mere moralism. In a short but rich essay, he writes, "The *sequela Christi* has a much higher goal: to be assimilated to Christ, so as to achieve union with

29. Ratzinger, 252.
30. Ratzinger, 160.
31. Rowan Williams, *The Dwelling of the Light: Praying with Icons of Christ* (Grand Rapids, MI: Eerdmans, 2004), 13.
32. This is abundantly evident in Rowan Williams's new book: *Christ: The Heart of Creation* (London: Bloomsbury, 2018).

God. . . . The *sequela Christi* is not a question of morality. It is a 'mysteric' theme: the conjoining of divine action and our human response."[33]

In *Introduction to Christianity*, he writes, "Christian existence is put with Christ into the category of relationship."[34] Christians, by Baptism, are incorporated into the relational flow of filial existence, *from* the Father, *through* the Son, *in* the communion of the Holy Spirit; and, thus, intrinsic to their identity is to be *for* others. The prepositions are paramount!

Though I will not develop this here at any length, one need not fear that Ratzinger (and the Creed's!) "Christocentrism" risks lapsing into a "Christomonism."[35] Like Augustine and Bonaventure, Ratzinger's Trinitarian vision is foundational to his theological and pastoral reflection. The prime analogue of the "from/for" rhythm of existence is the very life of the Trinity. Relational existence is constitutive of Trinitarian "personhood." It is this dynamic life that the Eternal Word of God incarnates in Jesus Christ.[36]

One must admit that the "spiritual Christology" limned in *Introduction to Christianity* contains scant reference to the

33. Joseph Ratzinger, "The New Evangelization," *Communio* 44, no. 2 (Summer 2017): 389–400, at 398. An important though quite neglected theme of Charles Taylor's monumental *A Secular Age* is that of divinization or *theosis*. I have suggested affinities between the constructive approaches of Ratzinger and Taylor in Robert P. Imbelli, *Rekindling the Christic Imagination: Theological Meditations for the New Evangelization* (Collegeville, MN: Liturgical, 2014), xxi–xxviii.

34. Ratzinger, *Introduction*, 186.

35. In light of my previous remarks concerning a postconciliar loss of the Christic center, one might plausibly argue that the far greater threat today is that of a "Spirit monism." Cyril O'Regan suggests that for Balthasar, "Hegel and his epigones have fundamentally reversed the order of reference and made Christ refer to the Spirit, rather than the Spirit to Christ." The result is that "the community divests itself of the concrete particularity of Christ. . . . Through pneumatic displacement the community's memory of Christ becomes self-referential" (*The Anatomy of Misremembering*, 200). I contend that a similar "misremembering" is by no means absent from the Church today. Indeed, Ratzinger's repeated cautions about a self-referential ecclesial community, especially in its liturgical celebrations, bespeaks just such a concern.

36. In an essay written in 1960, "Christocentrism in Preaching?" the young theologian contends that "Christocentric preaching" is, by its nature, "Trinitarian preaching," "namely the exposition of the way of Christian existence through Christ in the Spirit to the Father." See Joseph Ratzinger, *Dogma and Preaching: Applying Christian Doctrine to Daily Life*, trans. Michael J. Miller and Matthew J. O'Connell (San Francisco: Ignatius, 2011), 46.

Eucharist. The word does not even appear in the index to the English edition (though, not surprisingly, it is listed in the always more exhaustive German). This is understandable in that Ratzinger's chosen perspective in the book is the baptismal profession of the Creed and the movement of existence it initiates. Certainly, in other writings, both as theologian and pope, the Eucharist receives sustained consideration in his development of a spiritual Christology—as it must.

However, there are two places in the volume that merit attention in this regard. In the important and rich "Excursus on Christian Structures," Ratzinger articulates what he calls "The Law of Excess [*Überflusses*]." Here, he makes explicit reference to the change of water into wine at Cana and thus to the Eucharist. He speaks of Jesus Christ as "the infinite self-expenditure (one might even say "wastefulness") of God [*Christus ist die unendliche Selbstverschwendung Gottes*]."[37] That pouring out of Christ finds its supreme sacramental embodiment in the Eucharist.

The other notable reference to the Eucharist occurs in his consideration of "the communion of saints" at the end of the exposition of the Creed. He holds that the "communio sanctorum" refers in first instance to "the holy things" set upon the "Eucharistic table," and derivatively, but inseparably, to the "Eucharistic community" they effect.[38] But it is crucial to affirm the proper order: while the Church, indeed, "confects" the Eucharist, it is the Eucharistic Christ who constitutes the Church in the Spirit. Because Ratzinger's spiritual Christology is at its heart Eucharistic, I will return to the Eucharist in the final section of the article.

There is one final theme to lift up from *Introduction to Christianity*. This, too, comes from the section "Excursus on Christian Structures," or as Ratzinger calls it in another place: "Principles of Christian Existence."[39] Principle five concerns "Finality and

37. Ratzinger, *Introduction*, 261.
38. Ratzinger, 234.
39. Ratzinger, 269.

Hope." Here, he addresses again the uniqueness and eschatological reality of God's definitive revelation in Jesus Christ. There is thus no "Third Age" of the Spirit, if that is understood as a surpassing of the fullness realized in Christ Jesus. Thus, in company with both Bonaventure and Aquinas, his insistence upon "finality." The end time has truly been initiated in the Death, Resurrection, and Ascension of Jesus Christ.

And yet . . . there remains a "not yet"; and, hence, a hope. "The union that has taken place at the one point 'Jesus of Nazareth,' must attain the whole of mankind, the whole one 'Adam,' and transform it into the body of Christ. So long as this totality is not achieved, so long as it remains confined to one point, what has happened in Christ remains simultaneously both end and beginning."[40] We recognize here the Pauline vision of the eschatological achievement of the one "perfected person" (Eph. 4:13—*eis andra teleion*), lovingly exegeted by Augustine as the *totus Christus.*

I call attention to one implication of this affirmation of both "finality and hope" that entails serious responsibilities for preaching and teaching. In this very section of his book, Ratzinger maintains that "faith can have final [definitive] statements in which its intrinsic finality is articulated." Dogmatic statements are of crucial import. Still, he continues, "This does not mean that these formulas cannot open further in the course of history and thus be understood in fresh ways, just as the individual must continually learn to understand the faith afresh as a result of his or her own experiences of life."[41] Was this not John XXIII's intention for the council: not new truths but new understanding and expression?[42]

---

40. Ratzinger, 263–64.

41. Ratzinger, 265.

42. For a nuanced understanding of Pope John's famous opening address to the council, with its distinction between the content of the faith and its mode of expression, see Thomas Guarino, *The Disputed Teachings of Vatican II: Continuity and Reversal in Catholic Doctrine* (Grand Rapids, MI: Eerdmans, 2018), 34–37.

Indeed, in the essay on "Christocentrism in Preaching" (to which I referred earlier), Ratzinger laments that "perhaps nothing in recent decades has done more harm to preaching [and I would add "teaching"] than the loss of credibility that it incurred by merely handing on formulas that were no longer the living intellectual property of those who were proclaiming them."[43] John Henry Newman castigates these merely rote repetitions as "unreal words!"[44]

IV. FURTHER DELINEATING "SPIRITUAL CHRISTOLOGY"

In this section I will supplement these reflections on *Introduction to Christianity* by turning to *Behold the Pierced One*, the book of essays in which Ratzinger formally announced his intention "to consider Christology more from the aspect of its spiritual appropriation than I had hitherto done."[45]

In the first essay, "Taking Bearings in Christology," he sought to spell out how such spiritual appropriation is "realized." Advisedly, I use that word, so dear to John Henry Newman, and will return to it again. Ratzinger proceeds by articulating several theses—the third and fourth of which are particularly relevant to my purpose.

Thesis 3 states, "Since the center of the person of Jesus is prayer, it is essential to participate in his prayer if we are to know and understand him."[46] One hears echoes here of Evagrius's well-known dictum: "The theologian is one who prays and one who prays is a theologian."

43. Ratzinger, *Dogma*, 57.
44. John Henry Newman, "Unreal Words," in *Parochial and Plain Sermons* (San Francisco: Ignatius, 1997), 977–87.
45. Ratzinger, *Behold*, 9.
46. Ratzinger, 25.

But one also recalls Newman's famous distinction between "notional" and "real" apprehension. I contend that Ratzinger's "spiritual Christology" is a pastoral-theological call, ever more urgent in this era of the "Nones," to move from a merely notional apprehension, a purely academic Christology if you will, to a *lived, personally appropriated Christology*. To know spiritually is participatory knowing, not distance education. Spiritual exercises are incumbent upon the seeker.

Thus, toward the end of his elaboration of the thesis, he writes, "Real advances in Christology can never come merely as the result of the theology of the schools . . . as important as schools are. It must be complemented by the theology of the saints, which is theology from experience. All real progress in theological understanding has its origin in the eye of love and in its faculty of beholding."[47]

One catches resonances of the famous conclusion to Saint Bonaventure's *Itinerarium*, where he exclaims, "If you wish to know how such things come about, consult grace, not doctrine; desire, not understanding; prayerful groaning, not studious reading; the Spouse, not the teacher; God, not man; darkness, not clarity."[48] Neither Bonaventure nor Ratzinger would endorse a dichotomy here. But each, I think, would assign a primacy.

Thesis 4 then adds a further important dimension to Ratzinger's understanding of a "spiritual Christology."

> Sharing in Jesus' praying involves *communion* with all his brethren. Fellowship with the person of Jesus, which proceeds from participation in his prayer, thus constitutes that all-embracing fellowship that Paul calls the 'Body of Christ.'

47. Ratzinger, 27.
48. Bonaventure, *The Journey of the Mind to God*, trans. José de Vinck, in *The Works of Bonaventure* (Patterson, NJ: St. Anthony Guild, 1960), 1:58.

So the Church—the 'Body of Christ'—is the true subject of our knowledge of Jesus.[49]

And Ratzinger professes the conviction that permeates all his pastoral-theological endeavors: "In the Church's memory [*anamnesis*] the past is present because *Christ is present and lives* in her."[50] In his Body, the Church, the Christian *encounters Christ*, not merely as the object of exegetical study but most crucially as the living Lord of the Church, its beloved spouse. We recognize here the persuasion that inspires Benedict XVI's *Jesus* books.

Clearly related to this theme of Christ's ongoing presence and greatly deserving of further study is the critical significance of Christ's Ascension for Ratzinger's spiritual Christology. In general, the Lord's Ascension often languishes as a rather neglected topic in contemporary theology. How often, even among liturgists, is the "Paschal Mystery" truncated to the Lord's Death and Resurrection without reference to its completion in the Ascension.[51]

Ratzinger, both as theologian and preacher, does not slight the mystery of the Ascension. In the splendid epilogue to *Jesus of Nazareth: Holy Week*, he writes, "The departing Jesus does not make his way to some distant star. He enters into communion of power and life with the living God, into God's dominion over space. Hence he has not 'gone away,' but now and forever, by God's own power, he is present with us and for us." Therefore, Ratzinger insists, "[Jesus'] going away is in this sense a coming, a new form of closeness, of continuing presence."[52]

---

49. Ratzinger, *Behold*, 27 (emphasis added).

50. Ratzinger, 27 (emphasis added).

51. I have considered the topic more fully in Robert P. Imbelli, "*Sursum Corda*: Ascension Theology and Spirituality," in *Sufficit Gratia Mea*, ed. Manlio Sodi (Vatican City: Libreria Editrice Vaticana, 2019), 359–68. See also the fine study by Anthony Kelly, *Upward: Faith, Church, and the Ascension of Christ* (Collegeville, MN: Liturgical, 2014).

52. Pope Benedict XVI, *Jesus of Nazareth: Holy Week: From the Entrance into Jerusalem to the Resurrection*, trans. Philip J. Whitmore (San Francisco: Ignatius, 2011), 283.

I think it consonant with Ratzinger's theological vision to say that Christ's Ascension establishes a new, redeemed order of existence, a reconfiguration of space and time, centered around the person of Jesus Christ, which is the present visible order brought to transfigured fulfillment. Indeed, Ratzinger maintains that the Christian understanding of heaven is constitutively Christological. Thus, in *Introduction to Christianity*, he writes, "Heaven and the Ascension of Christ are indivisibly connected; it is only this connection that makes clear the Christological, personal, history-centered meaning of the Christian tidings of heaven."[53]

This new order of existence, the Pauline "new creation," inseparably comprises three interrelated dimensions. Ratzinger develops this insight in another essay of *Behold the Pierced One*, entitled "Eucharist, Christology, Ecclesiology: The Christological Core." Here, he shows how these three are dimensions of *the one mystery of Christ* "in whom the whole fullness [*plērōma*] of deity dwells bodily [*sōmatikōs*]" (Col. 2:9). Somatic relationality intimately binds the ascended Lord with his Eucharistic and ecclesial body.

A salient consequence of the absolute uniqueness of Jesus Christ, the New Adam—*ho eschatos Adam* (1 Cor. 15:45)—is the depth of the transformation to which disciples are called. A remarkable passage of this essay declares, "The goal of Eucharistic communion is a total recasting of a person's life, breaking up a man's whole 'I' and creating a new 'We.' Communion with Christ is, of necessity, a communion with all those who are his: it means that I myself become part of this new 'bread' which Christ creates by transubstantiating all earthly reality."[54] In the next section, we will further consider the scope of the transformation which the Eucharist sacramentalizes and empowers.

53. Ratzinger, *Introduction*, 313.
54. Ratzinger, *Behold*, 89.

Joseph Ratzinger's spiritual Christology thus exhibits a profoundly challenging theological-pastoral dialectic. To realize concretely the newness of Jesus Christ is to realize that we are summoned by Jesus to a radically transformed way of life. And, as we
enter more deeply into that new life (Dante's *Vita Nuova*), we are
led to a deeper realization of the identity and mission of Jesus, the
firstborn of creation and firstborn of the dead.

Jesus's prayerful attentiveness to the will of the Father and his
total dedication to the true good of others—his "pro-existence"—
are to be replicated in his disciples who are called to become *filii
in Filio*. But this stupendous vocation can only be realized *in
Spiritu Sancto*, in the communion of the Spirit that is the Body
of Christ.[55]

The classics of spirituality, from Augustine and Bonaventure
through Teresa of Avila and John of the Cross to Thérèse of Lisieux and Teresa Benedicta of the Cross "flesh out" the concrete
shape of transformation, of what configuration to Christ entails.
Hence, they are not extracurricular activities; they are integral to
the theological curriculum itself. They are integral to and indispensable for a truly spiritual Christology.

V. TOWARD A EUCHARISTIC MYSTICISM AND SPIRITUALITY

In this final section, I want to relate more explicitly Ratzinger's
insistence upon encounter with the living Jesus Christ, and the
transformed life to which it calls Christians, to the reality of the

---

55. See the striking remarks of Yves Congar: "If I were to draw but one conclusion from
the whole of my work on the Holy Spirit, I would express it in these words: no Christology
without pneumatology and no pneumatology without Christology." Indeed, he insists, "The
vigor of a lived pneumatology is to be found in Christology. There is only one body which the
Spirit builds up and quickens and that is the body of Christ." See Yves Congar, *The Word and the
Spirit*, trans. David Smith (San Francisco: Harper and Row, 1986), 1, 6.

Eucharist. Here, mystery and mysticism are concentrated and receive paradigmatic expression.

I think Peter John McGregor is exactly right when he says that "the goal of Ratzinger's spiritual Christology is Eucharistic."[56] Some of his fine homilies and meditations from the later 1970s have been published in English under the title *God Is Near Us: The Eucharist, the Heart of Life*.[57] Here, Ratzinger's Eucharistic vision and spirituality are set forth in a succinct and accessible way. They manifest once more the inseparable nexus of the doctrinal and pastoral.

But I will concentrate in particular upon Benedict XVI's *Sacramentum Caritatis*, the apostolic exhortation he wrote following the Synod on the Eucharist (2005). There, he evokes once again the figure of the pierced crucified One and explicitly relates it to the Eucharist. He writes,

> A contemplative gaze upon him whom they have pierced (Jn. 19:37) leads us to reflect on the causal connection between Christ's sacrifice, the Eucharist, and the Church. . . . The Eucharist is Christ who gives himself to us and continually builds us up as his Body. . . . The Church is able to celebrate and adore the mystery of Christ present in the Eucharist precisely because Christ first gave himself to her in the sacrifice of the cross. . . . The Church's ability to 'make' the Eucharist is completely rooted in Christ's self-gift to her. . . . We too, at every celebration of the Eucharist, confess the primacy of Christ's gift . . . it was Christ who loved us first (1 Jn. 4:19).[58]

---

56. Peter John McGregor, *Heart to Heart: The Spiritual Christology of Joseph Ratzinger* (Eugene, OR: Pickwick, 2016), 197.

57. Joseph Ratzinger, *God Is Near Us: The Eucharist, the Heart of Life*, trans. Henry Taylor (San Francisco: Ignatius, 2003).

58. Benedict XVI, *Sacramentum Caritatis* 14, apostolic exhortation, February 22, 2007, vatican.va.

Here, we see once more the warning against a community's liturgical celebration that becomes self-referential—a theme so prominent in Ratzinger's *The Spirit of the Liturgy*.[59] It is a warning against what I have called the "decapitated Body," a community that in its liturgical practice is effectively and affectively sundered from its Head. Ratzinger insists that Jesus Christ, the Head of the Body, does not exercise an absent lordship but is present, nourishing and building up his Body, the Church, through the gift of his Body, his Eucharistic self. Jesus's Ascension does not remove him but establishes a new and lasting presence.[60]

But if it is truly united with its Head, the community, whose very identity, whose "subsistence" (whose very "personhood"[61]) is founded in the Eucharist, will cultivate a "Eucharistic Form of Life." Thus part 3 of *Sacramentum Caritatis* is entitled "The Eucharist, A Mystery to Be Lived" and the first section is "The Eucharistic Form of the Christian Life." Such a Eucharistic form of life entails taking on the heart and mind of Jesus Christ so that Eucharistic spirituality becomes the measure of our thoughts and actions and the criterion by which we discern the values and disvalues of a given culture.[62] For the theologian pope, Romans 12:1–2 serves as ongoing inspiration and imperative: "I appeal to you brethren, by the mercies of God, to present your bodies as a living sacrifice, holy and acceptable to God, your spiritual worship [*logikē latreia*]. Do not be conformed to this world, but be

59. Joseph Ratzinger, *The Spirit of the Liturgy*, trans. John Saward (San Francisco: Ignatius, 2000).

60. Paul Griffiths writes, "The principal condition of the possibility of the Eucharist is exactly that Jesus has ascended. . . . After the Ascension, his flesh, veiled as bread, and his blood, veiled as wine, can be touched and tasted everywhere and at once, without constraint by the metronome of time or the map grid of space." Paul J. Griffiths, *Christian Flesh* (Stanford, CA: Stanford University Press, 2018), 51.

61. Heribert Mühlen's pioneering work remains a salutary spur to systematic theology: *Una Mystica Persona* (München: Schöning, 1964).

62. For challenging reflections, see the concluding section, "Eucharistic Passages," in Jan-Heiner Tück, *A Gift of Presence: The Theology and Poetry of the Eucharist in Thomas Aquinas*, trans. Scott G. Hefelfinger (Washington, DC: The Catholic University of America Press, 2018), 301–39.

transformed by the renewal of your mind, that you might discern what is the will of God, what is good and acceptable and perfect."

A Eucharistic form of life is not, for Benedict, one of withdrawal into some supposedly uncontaminated spiritual realm.[63] Like the Eucharist itself, it is radically material, fruit of the earth and work of human hands, transformed by the power of the Word and the Spirit. Indeed, I would not hesitate to speak of Ratzinger/Benedict's "Eucharistic mysticism."[64] But it is a mysticism rooted in the Eucharist and is, thus, corporeal, communal, and cosmic: in a word, "somatic."[65]

Benedict contends that "every great reform in the Church has in some way been linked to the rediscovery of belief in the Lord's Eucharistic presence among his people."[66] Karl Rahner once famously claimed that "the Christian of the future will be a mystic—one who has experienced something—or will not be."[67] Joseph Ratzinger is, perhaps, more diffident in employing the term "mystic." Yet I maintain that his "spiritual Christology" in effect proposes that "the Christian of the future will be a Eucharistic mystic—one who has experienced Someone, the living Lord—or will not be."

Throughout his long service to Christ's Church, Joseph Ratzinger/Benedict XVI had an overriding theological-pastoral concern to foster real friendship with Jesus. Exploring his spiritual Christology leads, mystagogically, to the realization that *Jesus Christ's very being is to be Eucharist.* The sacrament of the

63. The considerations of Timothy O'Malley are apposite: "Joseph Ratzinger Is Not a Platonist," *Church Life Journal,* October 16, 2018, churchlifejournal.nd.edu.

64. See my audio presentations *Christic Imagination: How Christ Transforms Us,* especially Lecture Nine: "Dwelling in Christ's Transfigured Presence: the Mystic Dimension of Christian Faith," Learn25, https://www.learn25.com/product/christic-imagination-how-christ-transforms-us/.

65. In *On the Way to Jesus Christ,* 124–28, under the heading "The Eucharist as the Sacrament of Transformations," Ratzinger delineates a fivefold transformation that Christ effects.

66. *Sacramentum Caritatis* 6.

67. Karl Rahner, "Christian Living Formerly and Today," in *Theological Investigations,* vol. 7, trans. David Bourke (New York: Herder, 1971), 15.

Eucharist is the privileged locus where friendship with Jesus is nourished and cultivated. To the extent that we become present to his Real Presence, our very self becomes Eucharistic: a living out of gratitude to the Father and generosity toward our brothers and sisters.[68]

In Eucharistic celebration and adoration, as nowhere else, the believer can echo Saint Paul's daring and joyful exclamation: "It is no longer I who live, but Christ lives in me. And the life I live now in the flesh, I live by faith in the Son of God who loves me and gives himself for me" (Gal. 2:20). And can join Joseph Ratzinger in quoting his beloved *Rule of Saint Benedict*: "Christo nihil omnino praeponere"—cherish Christ above all![69]

CONCLUSION

In 1970, when I first began to teach at the New York Archdiocesan Seminary, I chose, as major text, the newly translated work of Professor Doctor Joseph Ratzinger. I used it in each of my eight years there.

It provided for me and, I hope, for my students what Henri de Lubac's *Catholicism* had provided the young seminarian Joseph Ratzinger in 1949. Speaking, years later, of de Lubac's classic work, Cardinal Ratzinger called it "an essential milestone on my theological journey." It opened for him, he says, a vivid sense of the "*Catholica*," the "all-embracing": "the inner unity of I and Thou and We," rooted in the Triune God.[70]

And de Lubac achieves this by returning theology to its Christic center, drawing upon its own deepest resources, its life-giving source. Yet, Ratzinger insists, de Lubac is not engaged

---

68. For further considerations on this theme, see Essay 10: "A Eucharistic Form of Life."

69. Benedict of Nursia, *Rule* 62.11 (my translation).

70. Joseph Ratzinger, foreword to Henri de Lubac, *Catholicism: Christ and the Common Destiny of Man*, trans. Lancelot C. Sheppard and Sister Elizabeth Englund (San Francisco: Ignatius, 1988), 11.

upon an antiquarian exercise. De Lubac is in constant dialogue with his contemporaries and brings their most intimate questions to his task, and thus can offer real, not fabricated, answers.

Can one find a more apt characterization of Joseph Ratzinger's own achievement in *Introduction to Christianity*?

5. The Eucharistic Vision of Pope Benedict XVI

I. INTRODUCTION

Riven between consolation and desolation, the young Gerard Manley Hopkins, SJ, "Fled with a fling of the heart to the heart of the Host" ("The Wreck of the Deutschland").[1] In less poetic but no less intense terms, Joseph Ratzinger, a cardinal at the time, understood the Eucharist to be "the mystical heart of Christianity, in which God mysteriously comes forth, time and again, from within himself and draws us into his embrace." "The Eucharist," he wrote in *Pilgrim Fellowship of Faith*, is "the fulfillment of the promise" made by Jesus: "I, when I am lifted up from the earth, will draw all to myself" (John 12:32).[2]

Throughout his long ecclesial and academic ministry, there was never, for Joseph Ratzinger, a divorce between theology and spirituality, between Christian thought and devotion. In this he was manifestly a keen and grateful student of Saint Augustine: pastor, doctor, spiritual guide. Pope Benedict's homilies, like Augustine's, are theologically rich and his theological works spiritually nourishing. Whether homilies, catechesis, or treatises, they all testify to a profound spiritual and theological sensibility. They will continue to be read and appropriated for generations.

---

* This essay was originally published as "Pope Benedict XVI's Eucharistic Vision: A Key to Understanding His Life and Theology," *America: The Jesuit Review*, December 31, 2022, https://www.americamagazine.org/.

1. Gerard Manley Hopkins, "The Wreck of the Deutschland," Poetry Foundation, poetryfoundation.org.

2. Joseph Ratzinger, *Pilgrim Fellowship of Faith: The Church as Communion*, trans. Henry Taylor (San Francisco: Ignatius, 2005), 121.

In the quotation from Hopkins above, the Jesuit poet no doubt had first in mind the consecrated Host present in the tabernacle. But one also senses intimations of the Host who is Jesus himself: "the heart of the Host." Heart speaks to heart, as the mentor of Hopkins, John Henry Newman, exclaimed. Newman also deeply influenced Pope Benedict, who had the joy of beatifying him during his apostolic visit to England in 2010. Like Newman, Benedict placed the Real Presence of Jesus Christ in the Eucharist at the very center of Catholic faith and devotion.

Perhaps nowhere is Pope Benedict's Eucharistic vision set forth so fully as in his apostolic exhortation "The Sacrament of Charity." It was written to sum up and disseminate more widely the fruit of the meeting of the Synod of Bishops on the Eucharist. The very first sentence reads, "The sacrament of charity, the Holy Eucharist is the gift that Jesus Christ makes of himself, thus revealing to us God's infinite love for every man and woman."[3] Of course, it is the Gospels' narrative of the life, death, and new life of Jesus that vividly displays the height and breadth and length and depth of the love of Jesus. Meditation upon the Gospels' story preceded for Ratzinger, as it did for Saint Ignatius Loyola, the contemplation on God's love that is the climax of the *Spiritual Exercises*. The meditative Liturgy of the Word prepares the table for the more contemplative Liturgy of the Eucharist. Scripture and sacrament, story and supper, mutually illumine each other.

II. ACCESS TO JESUS

However, one confronts, in our contemporary context, a challenge unknown to Saint Ignatius Loyola and the many guides to the Christian life of previous centuries. Some present-day biblical studies seem to block rather than foster access to the Jesus of

---

3. Benedict XVI, *Sacramentum Caritatis* 1, apostolic exhortation, February 22, 2007, vatican.va.

Christian faith. Pope Benedict expresses his concern in the fore-word to the first volume of his trilogy, *Jesus of Nazareth*. Reliance on historical-critical approaches alone has led to the spread of unwarranted skepticism concerning our knowledge of Jesus. The unhappy result is that the figure of Jesus becomes "increasingly obscured and blurred." And Benedict voices a heartfelt lament: "Intimate friendship with Jesus, on which everything depends, is in danger of clutching at thin air."[4]

What accounts for the fact that Benedict devoted such com-mitment and labor to bring his volumes on Jesus to term, save for his conviction that friendship with Jesus, and through Jesus with the Father, stands at risk? Benedict's proposed Christolog-ical reading of Scripture does not entail rejection of the legiti-mate exercise of historical-critical analysis. He sought, rather, to broaden and deepen it through a faith-filled apprehension that did not leave Jesus as a strange figure from the past, but as one with whom personal relationship is possible today.

It may be suggestive, then, to consider Benedict's *Jesus* vol-umes as contemporary spiritual exercises designed to render accessible once again the Jesus of the Gospels who, as Benedict insisted, is the real Jesus. The crucified and risen Jesus is as con-temporary to us as he was to the first disciples. The exercise of critical reason needs to be complemented by the insights of the reasons of the heart. For, as Joseph Ratzinger wrote, "Love seeks understanding. It wishes to know even better the one whom it loves. It 'seeks his face,' as Augustine never tires of repeating."[5]

4. Pope Benedict XVI, foreword to *Jesus of Nazareth: From the Baptism in the Jordan to the Transfiguration*, trans. Adrian J. Walker (New York: Doubleday, 2007), xii.

5. Joseph Ratzinger, *The Nature and Mission of Theology: Essays to Orient Theology in Today's Debates*, trans. Adrian Walker (San Francisco: Ignatius, 1995), 27.

III. BEHOLD THE PIERCED ONE

In both his homilies and his other writings, Benedict showed great sensitivity to the spiritual importance of images. Perhaps no image from the Gospels so captivated him as that of the pierced side of Jesus, described in the Gospel of John (19:31–37). He titled one of his books *Behold the Pierced One*, and the image recurs five times in his encyclical "God Is Charity" (2005). In consonance with many Fathers of the Church, Benedict saw the blood and water pouring from the pierced heart of Jesus as symbols of sacramental life in the Church: Baptism and Eucharist. He taught in the encyclical that "one must constantly drink anew from the original source, who is Jesus Christ, from whose pierced heart flows the love of God."[6] And he ceaselessly affirmed the enduring presence of Christ's love in the Eucharistic mystery.

But the Eucharistic mysticism Benedict propounded is not merely a contemplative gazing upon the Lord, crucified and risen. It is entering, in communion with Christ, into his Paschal Mystery: his Death, Resurrection, and Ascension. There is an actualism to his understanding of the Eucharist, a *participatio actuosa* in Christ's Eucharistic action. Benedict writes in "God Is Charity," "The Eucharist draws us into Jesus' act of self-oblation. . . . We enter into the very dynamic of his self-giving."[7]

So intimate is the communion the Eucharist effects between Christ and the Christian that Joseph Ratzinger did not hesitate to speak of our becoming Eucharist in Christ. In a rich essay, "Eucharist and Mission," he comments upon the First Eucharistic Prayer:

> We ask that Christ's sacrifice might become present not just
> in an exterior sense, standing over against us and appearing,
> so to speak, like a material sacrifice, that we might gaze upon

6. Benedict XVI, *Deus Caritas Est* 7, encyclical letter, December 25, 2005, vatican.va.
7. *Deus Caritas Est* 13.

(as people once gazed upon the physical sacrifices of old). We would not in that case have entered into the New Covenant at all. We are asking rather that we ourselves might become a Eucharist with Christ, and thus become acceptable and pleasing to God.[8]

IV. *TOTUS CHRISTUS*

The intimacy of the relation of the individual to Jesus could lead to the suspicion that Benedict's Eucharistic mysticism, though intense, is purely individualistic. That would be a complete misreading of Benedict's theological-spiritual vision. Though the Christian's relation to Jesus, Savior and Lord, is supremely personal, it is never private. The reception of the Eucharistic Body of Christ incorporates the recipient into the risen Lord's ecclesial Body. Benedict built upon (indeed, he probably played a major role in composing) John Paul II's last encyclical, *Ecclesia de Eucharistia* (2003). The Church arises from the Eucharist, as blood streams forth from the pierced heart of Christ, sanctifying the disciples standing at the foot of the cross.

Augustine provided Joseph Ratzinger with a core insight that the theologian pope explored throughout his ministry: that of the *totus Christus*. In the section of *Sacramentum Caritatis* where he develops the concept, he teaches that the Eucharistic celebration is the work of the whole Christ, Head and members.[9] Christ, of course, is the prime agent. He is the Bridegroom who continues to give himself to nourish his beloved. Benedict often repeated Augustine's insistence that unlike ordinary food, the Eucharist transforms those who feast upon it into Christ. They do not transform Christ into themselves; they are incorporated into the Body whose sole Head is Jesus Christ. Yet Christ's grace is such

8. Ratzinger, *Pilgrim Fellowship*, 116.
9. See *Sacramentum Caritatis* 36 and 37.

that he always associates his Church with his Eucharistic sacrifice offered "for you and for many."

Thus it would be a serious error to understand Benedict's Eucharistic mysticism as countenancing any Gnostic removal of the earthly and the bodily. Rather, in reading him, one is repeatedly struck by how *corporeal* and *corporate* this "mysticism" is. It can serve as a salutary antidote to a widespread New Age Gnosticism. Thus, he writes in *Behold the Pierced One*: "The most intimate mystery of communion between God and man is accessible in the sacrament of the Body of the Risen Lord; conversely, then, the mystery lays claim to our bodies and is realized in a Body. The Church, which is built upon the sacrament of the Body of Christ, must herself be a body. And she must be a single body, corresponding to Jesus Christ's uniqueness."[10]

Central to Benedict's teaching about the triform Body of Christ—the risen body of the Lord, his Eucharistic Body, and his ecclesial Body—is its constitutive *relationality*. Through his risen body, Christ is totally communicable. His Eucharistic Body is the sacramental realization and sharing of his new life. His ecclesial Body is the incorporation of the many into loving communication with their redeemer. There is a mutual indwelling (what Charles Williams and Bishop Robert Barron, learning from Dante, have called "co-inherence") among the participants—an enhancement, not a diminishment, of personhood. For the outcome of Eucharistic relationality is not fusion but communion in the Spirit. *Indeed, through Christ and in Christ we become fully relational, truly persons.*

10. Joseph Ratzinger, *Behold the Pierced One: An Approach to a Spiritual Christology*, trans. Graham Harrison (San Francisco: Ignatius, 1986), 94.

V. *NOVUM* AND TRANSFORMATION

The supple structure that undergirds Pope Benedict's reflections might be called the grammar of newness and transformation. The *novum*, the newness, is Christ himself, fully revealed in his Paschal Mystery: his Passion, Death, Resurrection, and Ascension. The New Testament, Benedict insisted, does not give witness to new ideas but to the new person, the New [*eschatos*] Adam. By his death and Resurrection, Jesus has accomplished the true Exodus, transforming death itself into newness of life. He has inaugurated the new creation.

The Eucharist, celebrated on the Lord's Day of Resurrection, the eighth day of the new creation, immerses all who celebrate it into this mystery of faith. It offers a love beyond our capacity, one that we can only gratefully receive. Truly to receive it does not entail a passive undergoing, but an active transforming, a radical shift in our center of gravity.

In a now-famous commencement address at Kenyon College in 2005, the late David Foster Wallace spoke of "the default setting" into which we seem naturally "hard-wired": namely, our self as "the absolute center of the universe."[11] Though Wallace did not use the word, the condition he described seems strikingly similar to what the tradition terms "original sin."

If Baptism orients us away from this primordial self-referential condition toward the renewal of creation in Christ, the Eucharist plunges us ever more deeply, if we allow it, into paradise regained. In his most systematic work, *Eschatology: Death and Eternal Life*, Ratzinger speaks of the fundamental assent of faith made at Baptism. But he goes on to say of our assent, "Only with difficulty can it peer out from behind the latticework of an egoism we are powerless to pull down with our own hands."[12] We

11. See David Foster Wallace's 2005 commencement speech at Kenyon College, "This is Water," available at https://web.ics.purdue.edu/~drkelly/DFWKenyonAddress2005.pdf.

12. Joseph Ratzinger, *Eschatology: Death and Eternal Life*, trans. Michael Waldstein (Washington, DC: The Catholic University of America Press, 1988), 231.

are, indeed, the recipients of God's mercy, Ratzinger writes, yet this does not relieve us of the need to be transformed. The privileged encounter with the Lord in the Eucharist fosters this ongoing transformation. For Jesus's very being is to be Eucharist: loving thanksgiving to the Father, loving sacrifice for the sake of the many.

In numerous places Benedict sketched the contours of this Eucharistic transformation of the recipients. In one of his most striking passages, he writes,

> The Eucharist is never an event involving just two, a dialogue between Christ and me. Eucharistic Communion is aimed at a complete reshaping of my own life. It breaks up man's entire self and creates a new "we." Communion with Christ is necessarily also communication with all who belong to him: therein I myself become a part of the new bread he is creating by the transubstantiation of the whole of earthly reality.[13]

VI. EUCHARISTIC FORM OF LIFE

Sacramentum Caritatis unfolds in three major sections: the Eucharist is a mystery to be believed, celebrated, and lived. The third section, "A Mystery to Be Lived," speaks of the Eucharistic form of the Christian life. Benedict writes, "A Eucharist which does not pass over into the concrete practice of love is intrinsically fragmented." It is no longer the breaking of the host to be shared among many, but the breaking of the unity of the Body of Christ. Hence, Eucharistic mysticism is intrinsically social and calls forth a new way of being, thinking, and acting, for "the union with Christ brought about by the Eucharist also brings

---

13. Ratzinger, *Pilgrim Fellowship*, 78.

a newness to our social relations: this sacramental mysticism is social in character."[14]

Each pope brings to the Petrine ministry a distinct set of gifts, a particular style unique to himself. Many have commented upon the distinctive styles of Pope Benedict and Pope Francis. Yet, these words of *Sacramentum Caritatis* could well have been penned by either of these successors of Saint Peter: "The mystery of the Eucharist inspires and impels us to work courageously in our world to bring about that renewal of relationships which has its inexhaustible source in God's gift. . . . In a particular way, the Christian laity, formed at the school of the Eucharist, are called to assume their specific social and political responsibilities."[15] The Eucharist is the sacrament of the kingdom, inspiring and impelling the faithful toward its eschatological consummation.

VII. REORIENTATION AND RECAPITULATION

When one thinks of Joseph Ratzinger in connection with the Church's liturgical practice, the first association for many is his advocacy of celebrating the Eucharist *ad orientem*, "facing east." Clearly, he expressed his preference for this and gave theological and pastoral reasons for this option. But he never made it the only valid position. Indeed, throughout his pontificate he celebrated Mass in St. Peter's Basilica *versus populum*, facing toward the people. Of course, because of St. Peter's geographical placement, the celebrant both faces east and faces the congregation.

As always for Benedict, the fundamental issue and principle is Christological. Facing east is facing toward the rising sun, the cosmic symbol of the Christ who comes. He writes in *The Spirit of the Liturgy*, "The fact that we find Christ in the symbol of

14. *Sacramentum Caritatis* 89.
15. *Sacramentum Caritatis* 91.

the rising sun is the indication of a Christology defined eschatologically."[16]

Many have lamented the loss of an acute sense of the eschatological in contemporary Catholicism. Benedict's Eucharistic mysticism gives form to the conviction that Jesus Christ, the New [eschatos] Adam, by his death and Resurrection has inaugurated the "last days." But he is equally clear that the final consummation of all things in Christ has not yet been fully realized; thus his reorientation of Christian faith, hope, and love toward the Christ who is present and yet is to come. At the very beginning of his book *Eschatology*, he writes, "The Eucharist is at once the joyful proclamation of the Lord's presence and a supplication to the already present Lord that he may come, since, paradoxically, even as the One who is present, he remains the One who is to come."[17]

It is in this light that Benedict's *ad orientem* proposal takes its correct bearing. Far from being a "turning of the priest's back to the people," as it is too facilely criticized, it is the symbolic embodiment of both priest and people on pilgrimage toward their coming Lord. From this perspective, the geographic East is less important than the spiritual East—the reorientation of our bodies and our being toward Christ that he may "easter in us" (as Hopkins prays).[18] Indeed, "Every Eucharist is Parousia, the Lord's coming," Benedict writes, "and yet the Eucharist is even more truly the tensed yearning that he would reveal his hidden Glory."[19] The universal call to holiness issued anew by the Second Vatican Council can be enabled and sustained only by the risen Lord, who alone is the Holy One, the true revelation of God's glory.

When, then, Jesus Christ comes again "to judge the living and the dead," his coming will recapitulate all in himself, put

16. Joseph Ratzinger, *The Spirit of the Liturgy*, trans. John Saward (San Francisco: Ignatius, 2000), 69.

17. Ratzinger, *Eschatology*, 6.

18. Gerard Manley Hopkins, "The Wreck of the Deutschland," Poetry Foundation, poetryfoundation.org.

19. Ratzinger, *Eschatology*, 203.

under his headship, both human history and the whole of creation. Significantly, the final section of *The Spirit of the Liturgy* is devoted to "matter."[20] Unlike much of ancient thought influenced by Plato, the authentic Christian tradition does not counsel flight from the body and matter but their transformation. It comes as no surprise that Benedict, both as theologian and pope, voiced appreciation for the vision of Pierre Teilhard de Chardin, SJ. Like Teilhard's, Benedict's Eucharistic mysticism descends to the depths of matter so that rising it may converge on Jesus Christ who is alpha and omega, Lord of history and cosmos. To him the whole Eucharistic assembly raises the cry, "Amen. Come, Lord Jesus" (Rev. 22:20).

I suggest that Benedict XVI's lasting challenge and legacy to the Church he loved and served so wholeheartedly may be summed up in these words from "The Sacrament of Charity":

> The Sacrament of the Altar is always at the heart of the Church's life: thanks to the Eucharist, the Church is reborn ever anew! The more lively the Eucharistic faith of the people of God, the deeper is its sharing in ecclesial life in steadfast commitment to the mission entrusted by Christ to his disciples. . . . Every great reform has in some way been linked to the rediscovery of belief in the Lord's Eucharistic presence among his people.[21]

May Benedict's witness and teaching help enkindle anew the Church's Eucharistic faith.

---

20. Ratzinger, *Spirit of the Liturgy*, 220–24.
21. *Sacramentum Caritatis* 6.

6. The Heart Has Its Reasons

Giving an Account of the Hope that Is in Us

I. INTRODUCTION

October 2, 2012, was a true "kairos" moment. For it saw the conjunction of three significant ecclesial events: the fiftieth anniversary of the opening of the Second Vatican Council, the beginning of the Year of Faith, and the meeting of the Synod of Bishops on the New Evangelization. Thus, the 2013 Convention of the College Theology Society occurred in the light of an auspicious constellation of events. It thereby provides an opportunity to respond afresh to the challenge they represent.

Allow me a personal reminiscence. October 2, 2012, was, for me, a particularly "graced moment." I was present in Rome for the Mass celebrating the fiftieth anniversary of the council and the inauguration of the Year of Faith. It was a sun-drenched October morning, and present at the Mass, along with the participants at the synod, were the patriarch of Constantinople and the archbishop of Canterbury. In his homily Pope Benedict extolled the documents of Vatican II as the indispensable basis upon which to build as we confront the challenges of the present and the future.

I had also been present in Saint Peter's Square fifty years before for the council's opening. I had just arrived in Rome as a first-year Seminarian to begin theological studies at the Gregorian

* This essay was originally published as "The Heart Has Its Reasons: Giving an Account of the Hope That Is in Us," *Origins* 43, no. 7 (June 20, 2013): 103–11. It also appeared in *Handing on the Faith*, College Theology Society Volume 59 (2013) (Maryknoll, NY: Orbis, 2014), 21–42.

University. The four years I spent in Rome were remarkable by any account. Though I had fine professors in the classroom (people like Bernard Lonergan, Francis Sullivan, and René Latourelle—to name but three), there is no doubt that the events outside the classroom had even more of an impact. Ordained to the priesthood in Rome in 1965, my almost fifty years of priestly ministry and teaching have been indelibly marked by the council.

Hence, being in Rome in October 2012 filled me with a deep sense of gratitude, a sense of personally having come full circle.

Fifty years are certainly a long period in the life of an individual—as I can fully attest! But it is a relatively short time in the life of the Church and in the reception of a council, especially one as "revolutionary" as Vatican II.

II. SIGNS OF THE TIMES

One of the phrases used by the council has come into theological and even popular currency: "reading the signs of the times." The theme of the 2013 Convention of the College Theology Society, "Teaching Theology and Handing on the Faith: Challenges and Convergences," and the accompanying questions fleshing out the theme indicate that a number of those signs have evolved since the council. I make no claim to originality in enumerating issues such as the following:

1. the decline if not the disappearance of the Catholic subcultures that formed and nourished folk like me (and perhaps a few of you);

2. the precipitous decline in Catholic schools on the elementary and secondary level, with the consequent effect on both religious formation and practice;

3. the widespread biblical and theological illiteracy we

encounter among our college students—acknowledged from all points on the Catholic compass;

4. polarization among members of the Catholic community (of which some blog sites serve as a house-of-horrors mirror);

5. as a subspecies of that polarization: tension among theologians and bishops with particular instances too well-known to require further specification;

6. and drawing closer to the 2013 convention theme: the issue of the identity and mission of Catholic colleges and universities.

III. CURRENT CONCERNS

Of course, we all inevitably read these signs of the times from a particular vantage point. Let me briefly sketch something of the perspective I bring.

I have spent twenty-seven years at Boston College—six as director of the Institute of Religious Education and Pastoral Ministry and over twenty as teacher in the theology department—teaching both undergraduate core courses (in my case "Exploring Catholicism: Tradition and Transformation") and graduate seminars. For the past ten years, I have been active in Boston College's "Church in the 21st Century" initiative. In connection with the initiative, I edited the volume *Handing on the Faith: The Church's Mission and Challenge* and the Spring issue of "C21 Resources" on "The Catholic Intellectual Tradition."

In these years, I have often voiced two concerns that bear on the topic of the convention. First, the tendency in college and university mission statements to camouflage "Catholic" and to substitute phrases like "in the Jesuit tradition" or its equivalent. Moreover, in parsing the tradition invoked, often the content has been reduced to some colorless generality like "educating men and women for others."

The second tendency I have decried is the ritualistic distancing of theology from catechesis, as in the oft-repeated refrain: "We're doing theology not catechesis." Often, this eventuated not in a distinction but a divorce between the two.

These two tendencies may have been understandable in light of the signs of the times of the immediate post–Vatican II era. The council rightly stressed the indispensable role of lay men and women in the total life of the church. It showed the deep bonds uniting Catholics with their fellow Christians and, indeed, with all people of good will. It spoke of the need for a revival and reform of theological studies.

The aftermath of the council saw the loosening of the tight juridical and clerical bonds of our institutions of higher education. It also witnessed the growing conviction of the need for theology in the United States to establish its academic integrity and credentials. Paradoxically, this has led in some instances to a move from theology to a more neutral espousal of "religious studies."

But in light of new signs of the times, some of which I alluded to above, a new discernment seems called for. Indeed, I sense a course change over the past fifteen years. I perceive a greater willingness to affirm the Catholic identity of colleges and universities, animated perhaps by Pope John Paul II's apostolic constitution *Ex Corde Ecclesiae*. This is sometimes done via an exploration of "The Catholic Intellectual Tradition" and its bearing upon curriculum decisions and design.

I also think there is a growing sense that kerygma, catechesis, and theology form a differentiated continuum, rather than completely discrete ecclesial tasks. Since this latter point bears upon the theme of the 2013 convention, let me elaborate further to stimulate and contribute to the discussions of these days.

IV. CATECHESIS AND/OR THEOLOGY

In an article in *Commonweal*, Michael Peppard of Fordham University wrote,

> Just about every day, theological educators must channel Paul at the Areopagus, tailoring our methods to an audience that has no idea what we are talking about (Acts 17). Following Paul's lead, we meet our students where they are, in order, God willing, to bring some of them forward on a path (*educere*). In that process of theological education—not catechetical instruction (*instruere*)—we learn and change together.[1]

I agree with much in Peppard's thoughtful piece, but the passage I just quoted struck me, because it seemed to suggest a dichotomy between "theological education" and "catechetical instruction" that I find problematic. I posted the quote on the *Commonweal* blog under the heading: "Theology and/or Catechetics." A lively conversation ensued.[2]

Enriched by that conversation, let me offer a few clarifications. First, Peppard's disjunction between the tasks of *educere* and *instruere* does not do justice to either the college classroom or the catechetical setting. *Educere* and *instruere*, I contend, are operative in both.

Second, however, there is a clear difference in audience and goal. In catechesis, the goal of the education is to form members of the community by "handing on the faith." In theological education, as it currently takes place in many of our institutions, the goal is to convey notional knowledge of a particular religious tradition to students who may or may not be participants in that tradition. Put in other terms: catechesis aims at personal transformation in light of the faith tradition handed on; theological

1. Michael Peppard, "Testing the Boundaries," *Commonweal*, April 12, 2013, 16.
2. Robert P. Imbelli, "Theology and/or Catechesis," *Commonweal*, April 8, 2013, https://www.commonwealmagazine.org/theology-andor-catechetics.

education aims at intellectual appropriation of the matter conveyed—in the case I am considering: the Catholic theological
tradition. Thus, by insisting on the nexus between catechesis and
theology, I am not advocating the collapse of the two ecclesial
undertakings in an undifferentiated fusion.

However, and this is central to my presentation this evening,
I maintain that the theological educator must respect not only the
tradition which the student may espouse, but he or she must also
respect the uniqueness of the tradition that is being presented.
In the case I am reflecting upon: the genius of Catholicism, its
distinctive form or *gestalt*.[3]

Hence, I do not deny differentiations. But I hold that both
theological education and catechesis "hand on," communicate,
the faith's content. Thus, my insistence on "differentiated continuity." In terms of the convention's theme: I do not deny the
"challenges" but stress the "convergences."[4]

I will try, in the main part of this essay, to illustrate the convergences by reflecting upon the theological task as I understand
it. What are we teaching when we teach theology in the Catholic
Christian tradition? Here is where the continuum catechesis/the-
ology needs to be extended to embrace the kerygma, the proclamation of God's salvation in Jesus Christ. Or, perhaps more to
the point, the kerygma needs to be acknowledged as the matrix
and ongoing reference of both catechesis and theology. I believe
myself to be in the good company of Karl Rahner in making
this claim. Rahner writes, "Since theology reflects and serves the
giving of a critical answer for the faith, it is essentially oriented
to testimony and preaching. Hence all theology is 'kerygmatic.'"[5]

3. The notion of "form" is key to the theological vision of Hans Urs von Balthasar. See
Aidan Nichols, *A Key to Balthasar* (Grand Rapids, MI: Baker Academic, 2011), 12–48.

4. In the exchange on the *Commonweal* blog, I raised the question: Is Joseph Ratzinger's
Introduction to Christianity a work of catechetics or theology? In my view, it is inseparably both.

5. Karl Rahner, "Theology," in *Sacramentum Mundi: Encyclopedia of Theology*, vol. 6 (New
York: Herder, 1970), 234.

V. AN UNDERSTANDING OF CATHOLIC THEOLOGY

A 2013 article in *America* by the Jesuit theologian James Hanvey, "*Quo Vadis?* Reflections on the Shape of the Church to Come," contains this challenging observation (which I fully make my own):

> Too often, in its migration to the university, theology has lost its sense of service, not just to the academy but to the church and its mission. It needs to claim its own freedom and legitimacy within the campus, without sacrificing its subject to the gods of secular reason. Theology must not allow itself to forget that only in service of the mystery of Christ and his church is it preserved from vacuity.[6]

I take my point of departure from the theme sounded in Hanvey's last phrase—"only in service of the mystery of Christ and his church is [theology] preserved from vacuity." I propose, then, three variations on the theme of the mystery of Christ and his Church as giving specific form to Christian theology. The variations take the theological virtues, faith, hope, and love, as ways of structuring an approach to Christian theology.

1. Many here will recognize and accept an approach to theology that takes its point of departure from Anselm's assertion that theology is faith seeking understanding (*fides quaerens intellectum*) or, even more succinctly, theology is the understanding of the faith (*intellectus fidei*).

I want to draw out two implications of this understanding that are not always to the fore as they should be. One implication is that there is a *prior given* not always sufficiently acknowledged. The faith upon which theology reflects is responsive to a

6. James Hanvey, "*Quo Vadis*: Reflections on the Shape of the Church to Come," *America*, March 18, 2013, 15.

revelation that it has not itself generated. There is an *objectivity* of the Christian fact that precedes any subjective appropriation, including that of the theologian.

Let me illustrate this point with reference to the Second Vatican Council. Though the council's four constitutions represent the key documents that must have pride of place in the ongoing interpretation and reception of Vatican II, *Dei Verbum*, the Dogmatic Constitution on Divine Revelation, should be considered *prima inter pares*, "first among equals." For without the revelatory given, neither liturgy nor Church nor mission and service to the world has any theological reason for being. To be even more specific, without *Dei Verbum*'s confession that "the deepest truth about God and the salvation of man shines out for our sake in Christ, who is both the mediator and the fullness of all revelation,"[7] there is no foundation upon which Christian theology may wisely build.[8]

As Pope Francis said in his homily to the cardinals the day after his election, without Christ and his cross at the center, the Church would only be "a charitable NGO (Non-Governmental Organization), but not the Church, the Bride of the Lord."[9]

The second implication of seeing theology as faith seeking understanding is that the faith is transmitted, handed on to the theologian by the Church. Theologians reflect upon that which they have received. We hand on to you what we also have received. And the bearer of that tradition is, of course, the Church in its kerygma, its liturgy, and its catechesis.

The *credo* of the believer is always derivative from the *credimus*: the faith of the Church into which he or she is baptized.

7. Vatican Council II, *Dei Verbum* 2, in *The Word on Fire Vatican II Collection*, ed. Matthew Levering (Park Ridge, IL: Word on Fire Institute, 2021), 17–18.

8. Ormond Rush makes a similar point in his article, "Toward a Comprehensive Interpretation of the Council and its Documents," *Theological Studies* 73, No. 3 (September 2012): 550: "the theological focus of *Dei Verbum* can function as a lens for interpreting the more ecclesiologically focused constitutions *Sacrosanctum concilium*, *Lumen gentium*, and *Gaudium et spes*."

9. Pope Francis, "'Missa Pro Ecclesia' with the Cardinal Electors," March 14, 2013, vatican.va.

Thus, if we take faith seeking understanding as a helpful approach to the task of theology, it highlights theology's ecclesial nature and responsibility. The faith the theologian seeks better to understand is the faith received from the Church; and the further understanding it seeks is to serve the Church and its mission.[10]

2. As a second "riff" upon the theme that Hanvey sounded, let me pass the lead to the Apostle Peter and, in particular, his first letter. 1 Peter 3:15 is often cited as justification for the theological task: "Reverence in your hearts Christ as Lord. Always be ready to make a defense to anyone who asks you for an account of the hope that is in you." The word translated here as "account" is *logos*: thus, always be ready to speak a word, to give a reason for the hope that is in you. I have often been struck that the author does not say, "Give an account, speak a word about your faith," but about your hope. One could thus play a variation of Anselm and say that theology is hope seeking understanding.

Now what is the hope that the First Letter of Peter evokes? The response is clear from the letter's opening "benediction": "Blessed be the God and Father of the Lord Jesus Christ! By his great mercy we have been born anew to a living hope through the resurrection of Jesus Christ from the dead" (1:3). The ground of Christian hope, therefore, is the Resurrection of Jesus from the dead. Indeed, this living hope extends the horizon of believers to a transcendent realm, "to an inheritance which is imperishable, undefiled, and unfading kept in heaven" (1:4).

In his fine book *The Spirit of Early Christian Thought*, the patristics scholar Robert Wilken does not hesitate to say, "The Resurrection of Jesus is the central fact of Christian devotion and the

---

10. I find myself, therefore, in substantial agreement with Avery Dulles's articulation of an "ecclesial/transformative" understanding of the theological enterprise. See his *The Craft of Theology: From Symbol to System* (New York: Crossroad, 1995), 18–21.

ground of all Christian thinking."[11] He is only drawing out the implications of Paul's famous declaration in the First Letter to the Corinthians: "If Christ has not been raised, then our preaching is in vain and your faith is in vain" (1 Cor. 15:14). And Peter would insist, "Your hope is in vain." It would have no objective basis; it would be mere illusion and delusion. Indeed, Paul himself continues, "If for this life only we have hoped in Christ, we are of all men and women most to be pitied" (1 Cor. 15:19).

This hope is not founded in the expectation of a general resurrection of the dead on the "last day." Its assurance is based upon the concrete and singular occurrence of the Resurrection of the one who had been crucified. As Peter proclaimed in his Pentecostal kerygma reported in Acts, "This Jesus God raised up, and of that we are all witnesses . . . God has made him both Lord and Christ, this Jesus whom you crucified" (Acts 2:32,36).

David Bentley Hart draws out the implications of the narrative. He writes, "The crucifixion and resurrection of Jesus tell us nothing in the abstract about human dereliction or human hope. . . . [They] concern first what happened to Jesus of Nazareth, to whose particular truth and radiance all the general 'truths' of human experience must defer."[12] The scandal of particularity indeed!

If, then, we approach the theological task as reflection upon Christian hope seeking understanding, the *novum* of the risen Christ will stand at the very center of our theological vision. Theology will ponder Jesus Christ, "the concrete universal" who fulfills all human yearning. In *Gaudium et Spes*, Vatican II strikingly proclaims that

---

11. Robert Louis Wilken, *The Spirit of Early Christian Thought: Seeking the Face of God* (New Haven: Yale University Press, 2003), xv.

12. David Bentley Hart, *The Beauty of the Infinite: The Aesthetics of Christian Truth* (Grand Rapids, MI: Eerdmans, 2003), 27.

God's Word, by whom all things were made, was Himself made flesh so that as perfect man He might save all men and sum up all things in Himself. The Lord is the goal of human history, the focal point of the longings of history and of civilization, the center of the human race, the joy of every heart, and the answer to all its yearnings.[13]

3. I can now add a third voice to the chorus: the beloved disciple. In the wonderful "epilogue" to the fourth Gospel, John narrates the encounter of the risen Jesus with Peter. The famous three-fold question, "Simon, son of John, do you love me?" evokes the heartfelt confession: "Yes, Lord, you know that I love you" (John 21:15).

We catch an echo of this scene at the very beginning of the First Letter of Peter. Peter tells the community, "Without having seen [Jesus], you love him; though you do not now see him, you believe in him and rejoice with unutterable and exalted joy" (1 Pet. 1:8).

Robert Wilken says forthrightly,

The church gave men and women a new love, Jesus Christ, a person who inspired their actions and held their affections. This was a love unlike others. For it was not only that Jesus was a wise teacher, or a compassionate human being who reached out to the sick and needy, or even that he patiently suffered abuse and calumny, and died a cruel death, but that after his death God had raised him from the dead to new life. He who once was dead now lives.[14]

Consequently, Christian existence is lived in intimate relation with the risen Lord. The risen Jesus is not primarily a figure of the

13. Vatican Council II, *Gaudium et Spes* 45, in *The Word on Fire Vatican II Collection*, 267.

14. Wilken, *Early Christian Thought*, xv.

past, for "he always lives to make intercession for us" (Heb. 7:25). Pope Benedict, in his three-volume *Jesus of Nazareth*, acknowledges the important contribution of the historical-critical method to biblical study. But he discerns that, left to itself, it relegates Jesus to the distant past. Therefore, it must be complemented by a theological hermeneutic that mediates an encounter with the living Lord of the Church and nourishes a personal relationship with him.[15]

This love relationship to the living Jesus is at the heart of Christian discipleship. Christian theology, in service to the mystery of Christ and his Church, is that love seeking understanding. We ever desire to know better the one whom we love.[16]

VI. A CHRISTOCENTRIC TURN

My purpose in this probing of the theological virtues as points of departure for Christian theology is to underscore that theological education and handing on the faith are configured around the person of Jesus Christ. Christ is the fulfillment of the revelation that faith recognizes and affirms, his Resurrection is the unique ground of Christian hope, and loving relationship with him is the distinctive mark of Christian discipleship. In the absence of this Christic center, things fall apart.[17]

Thus, though it is understandable that, for the sake of inter-religious dialogue, one often hears that there are three "religions of the book"—Judaism, Christianity, and Islam—it is truer to

15. Pope Benedict XVI, *Jesus of Nazareth: Holy Week: From the Entrance into Jerusalem to the Resurrection* (San Francisco: Ignatius, 2011), xiv–xvii.

16. See the perhaps insufficiently appreciated essay by Karl Rahner, "What Does It Mean to Love Jesus?", in *The Love of Jesus and the Love of Neighbor*, trans. Robert Barr (New York: Crossroad, 1983), 9–61.

17. For a scathing indictment of "Christological collapse" in the contemporary Catholic context, see Luke Timothy Johnson, "On Taking the Creed Seriously," in Robert P. Imbelli, ed., *Handing on the Faith: The Church's Mission and Challenge* (New York: Crossroad, 2006), 63–76. For an irenic but incisive analysis of the "de-centering of Christ" in some contemporary theology, see Harold Wells, *The Christic Center* (Maryknoll, NY: Orbis, 2004), chapters 4 and 6.

the distinctiveness of Christianity to call it the "religion of the person," because of the uniqueness of its identity-defining relation to the person of Jesus Christ. In its 2011 document, "Theology Today," the International Theological Commission writes, "The Church greatly venerates the Scriptures, but it is important to recognize that 'the Christian faith is not a "religion of the book"; Christianity is the "religion of the word of God," not of "a written and mute word, but of the incarnate and living Word."'"[18]

Hence, both for the sake of a fuller appropriation of its distinct identity and to elucidate better the connection between "teaching theology and handing on the faith," theology needs to recover and renew its Christocentric focus. Doing so will promote a deeper reception of the Second Vatican Council and will support and strengthen efforts toward the New Evangelization.[19]

A "Christocentric turn" in theology will by no means negate the valid insights of the "anthropological turn" that Karl Rahner cogently thematized and that has characterized much of postconciliar Catholic theology. But it will root the Christian vision of the human in the New Adam, who both reveals and enables humanity's true dignity and transcendent destiny.[20]

I am convinced that Vatican II's singular, though neglected, accomplishment was its recovery of a robust and renewed

18. International Theological Commission, "Theology Today: Perspectives, Principles, and Criteria," 2011, chapter 1, no. 7, available at www.vatican.va. (The inner quotation in the passage cited is from Benedict XVI's post-synodal apostolic exhortation *Verbum Domini*.)

19. In his essay "The New Evangelization and Theological Renewal," Avery Dulles argues that a Christ-centered theology is essential for promoting the new evangelization. See Avery Cardinal Dulles, *Evangelization for the Third Millennium* (New York: Paulist, 2009), 78–89.

20. One of Rahner's interpreters, Francis Schüssler Fiorenza, makes this insightful observation: "Rahner's method is such that he does not take a secular modern version of humanity and project it back to Christology, but rather makes the concrete existence of Jesus the norm for understanding Christian existence." See "Method in Theology" in *The Cambridge Companion to Karl Rahner*, ed. Declan Marmion and Mary Hines (Cambridge: Cambridge University Press, 2005), 70. In the article "Theology," Rahner says that "theology is and remains perpetually linked to the historical event of salvation which took place once and for all" (see n. 5 of this essay).

Christocentricity.[21] The finest fruit of its program of *ressourcement* and *aggiornamento* was its "re-Sourcement": its faithful and creative return to the Source who is Jesus Christ himself.[22]

Taking up and developing Vatican II's teaching on the primacy of Jesus Christ also entails heeding the council's call for a renewal of theological education in this light. Here, the council only provides general orientations, but they are suggestive. Thus, *Dei Verbum* declares that "the study of the Sacred Page is, as it were, the soul of sacred theology" and that theology should proceed "by investigating, in the light of faith, all the truth that is stored up [*conditam*] in the mystery of Christ."[23] Further, the "Decree on Priestly Formation," *Optatam Totius*, asserts the need to renew theological disciplines through a "more living contact with the mystery of Christ *ex vividiore cum Mysterio Christi . . . contactu*.[24]

These desiderata of the council are still a work in progress.[25] Let me sketch two lines of thought worth pondering as we consider the meaning and implications of theology in the Catholic tradition. I characterize one as "epistemological" and the other as "ontological." The point of departure for these further reflections is the famous affirmation of Vatican II's Pastoral Constitution on the Church in the Modern World, *Gaudium et Spes*:

21. See Robert P. Imbelli, "Do This in Memory of Me: Vatican II Calls Us to a Renewed Realization of the Primacy of Christ," *America*, April 22, 2013, 18–20.

22. Ormond Rush writes, "One of the most significant teachings of the Council is its retrieval of the nature of divine revelation as first and foremost God's loving, personal self-communication to humanity in Christ through the Spirit . . . God's continuous revelatory and salvific presence and activity in human history in Jesus Christ through the Holy Spirit." Rush, "Towards a Comprehensive Interpretation," 564.

23. *Dei Verbum* 24.

24. Vatican Council II, *Optatam Totius* 16, in *The Word on Fire Vatican II Collection: Declarations and Decrees*, ed. Matthew Levering (Park Ridge, IL: Word on Fire Institute, 2023), 264.

25. Gerald O'Collins laments the scarce treatment of the Resurrection of Christ in sacramental and moral theology. See *Believing in the Resurrection: The Meaning and Promise of the Risen Jesus* (New York: Paulist, 2012), chapter 8: "The Resurrection's Impact on Sacramental and Moral Theology."

In fact, it is only in the mystery of the incarnate Word that light is shed on the mystery of humankind. For Adam, the first human being, was a figure of Him who was to come, namely Christ the Lord. It is Christ, the final Adam [*novissimus Adam*], who fully discloses humankind to itself and manifests its sublime calling, by the revelation of the mystery of the Father and His love. It is not surprising, then, that in Christ all the truths stated here find their source and attain their fulfillment.[26]

VII. EPISTEMOLOGICAL IMPLICATIONS

If the living Lord Jesus Christ stands at the center of Christianity's theological vision, then theology will engage a mode of knowing beyond the historical and empirical. It will also appeal to a more experiential, participative, and personalist mode of thought. It is this that Pascal alludes to when he speaks of "the reasons of the heart"—a more integral, incarnational form of human knowing.

Recall how Bernard Lonergan exegetes Pascal. Lonergan writes, "Besides the factual knowledge reached by experiencing, understanding, and verifying, there is another kind of knowledge reached through the discernment of value and the judgments of value of a person in love." And he goes on to speak of faith as "such further knowledge when the love is God's love flooding our hearts."[27]

For the Christian, this experiential, affective knowledge of God's love is always mediated through Jesus Christ. As Saint Paul exults at the climax of the magnificent chapter 8 of Romans, "For I am sure that neither death, nor life, nor angels, nor principalities, nor things present, nor things to come, nor powers, nor height, nor depth, nor anything else in all creation, will be able to separate us from the love of God in Christ Jesus our Lord" (Rom.

26. *Gaudium et Spes* 22.
27. Bernard Lonergan, *Method in Theology* (New York: Herder, 1972), 115.

8:38–39). Paul's assurance of things hoped for is firmly rooted in his personal experience and knowledge of "the Lord Jesus, who loved me and gave himself for me" (Gal. 2:20).

Such affective cognition also permeates the Johannine tradition. Here are two salient examples from the First Letter of John: "The one who does not love does not know God, for God is Love" (1 John 4:8); and "By this we know that we abide in him and he in us, because he has given us of his own Spirit" (1 John 4:13). Again, the Johannine tradition is clear that such knowing is always mediated through the Son, as Jesus himself states in his "High Priestly Prayer" in the Gospel: "that they may know you, the only true God, and Jesus Christ whom you have sent" (John 17:3).

I suggest, therefore, that participatory "knowledge of the heart" introduces us to the mystical depth of theology. Gregory the Great recapitulated this persuasion in his well-known and oft-cited dictum: "Amor ipse notitia est"—"Love is itself knowledge."[28] If Christianity is, as affirmed above, preeminently the "religion of the person," then personal knowledge, the knowledge of persons in relation, must have a crucial place in theological reflection upon Christian faith.[29]

Let me draw out further consequences of this claim. The privileged locus for theology is the celebration of the liturgy, where knowledge born of love is both expressed and nurtured. In the liturgy, the Bible becomes Scripture, *Sacra Pagina*.[30] Scripture

28. Gregory's phrase regarding affective cognition is developed in the fine book of the English philosopher John Cottingham: *The Spiritual Dimension: Religion, Philosophy, and Human Value* (Cambridge: Cambridge University Press, 2005). It will come as no surprise that Cottingham, in this book, draws appreciatively on Pascal.

29. Students of Lonergan, like Robert Doran and Patrick Byrne, have creatively extended Lonergan's "intentionality analysis" to posit a "fifth level of intentional consciousness": the interpersonal dimension.

30. In setting forth his understanding of an "ecclesial-transformative" approach to theology, Avery Dulles writes: "A privileged locus . . . is the worship of the Church, in which the biblical and traditional symbols are proclaimed and 're-presented' in ways that call for active participation (at least in mind and heart) on the part of the congregation." Dulles, *Craft of Theology*, 19. It is noteworthy that in the expanded edition of *Craft of Theology* (1995), Dulles added a new chapter on "Theology and Worship."

studies, in the Catholic tradition, cannot prescind from this li-turgical setting if they hope to avoid a reductionistic approach that leads to an ever-more-fragmented text. Gerhard Lohfink has reminded us that "the gospels, after all, are the church's texts and their true 'life situation' is the liturgy. There they are celebrated as the word of God. There they are proclaimed as Gospel and authentically interpreted."[31]

Tellingly, Lohfink goes on to assert that "faith is true knowl-edge, true recognition, but a recognition of a different kind from that which analyzes, that is, literally, dissolves." He goes on to speak of personal knowledge and its consequences: "Whoever wants to truly recognize another as a person must expect to en-counter the unexpected and be led into a new world of which previously one had no idea—a world whose strangeness fascinates but also frightens."[32] If this is true of everyday human encounters, how much more is it true of the encounter with the person of Jesus Christ!

A further consequence is that the classics of spirituality, such as Augustine's *Confessions*, Dame Julian's *Revelations*, Teresa of Avila's *Interior Castle*, Merton's *New Seeds of Contemplation*, be-come crucial theological sources—not merely "extracurricular reading" but intrinsic to the curriculum.[33] Sarah Coakley draws boldly upon these sources, especially the Greek fathers, to retrieve the notion of "the spiritual senses." She writes, "This tradition charts in some detail the proposed capacity of our gross physical senses to undergo profound transformative change, or sharpen-ing in the Spirit." This entails "a very particular, and normally

---

31. Gerhard Lohfink, *Jesus of Nazareth: What He Wanted, Who He Was*, trans. Linda M. Maloney (Collegeville, MN: Liturgical, 2012), 8.

32. Lohfink, *Jesus of Nazareth*, 21.

33. One of the achievements of Frans Jozef van Beeck is his masterful integration of the classics of spirituality into the fabric of systematic theology. See *God Encountered: A Contempo-rary Catholic Systematic Theology*, vol. 1 (Collegeville, MN: Liturgical, 1989).

CHRIST BRINGS ALL NEWNESS

undiscussed, form of epistemic receptivity" that requires a dispos-session of self, an "undoing of epistemic blockage."[34]

To lift up the classics of spirituality as important theological resources is to underscore that theology reflects upon revelation not as, in the first instance, providing information but as issu-ing a summons to transformation. By placing "conversion" as the subject of the functional specialty, "Foundations," Lonergan ar-gues that "one's interpretation of others is affected by one's under-standing of oneself"; and he goes on to insist that "the converted have a self to understand that is quite different from the self that the unconverted have to understand."[35] The theologian enjoys no exemption from the Gospel's summons to ongoing conversion.

Thus, what makes the classics of spirituality so important for theological education is their mapping of the logic of transforma-tion from the truncated, in-turned self to the self liberated and renewed in Christ, the New Adam. This theme of the new "self" features prominently in the paraenetic portions of the letters to the Colossians and Ephesians. So, in Colossians, "You have put off the old self [*ton palaion anthrōpon*] with its practices and have put on the new self [*ton neon*], which is being renewed in knowl-edge, according to the image of the one who is creating" (Col. 3:9–10). And in Ephesians, "Put off your old nature [*ton palaion anthrōpon*] which belongs to your former manner of life and is corrupt through deceitful lusts, and be renewed [*ananeousthai*] in the spirit of your minds; and put on the new self [*ton kainon anthrōpon*] created according to God in true righteousness and holiness" (Eph. 4:22–24).[36]

34. Sarah Coakley, "The Identity of the Risen Jesus," in Beverly Roberts Gaventa and Richard Hays, eds., *Seeking the Identity of Jesus* (Grand Rapids, MI: Eerdmans, 2008), 312n21, 313.

35. Bernard Lonergan, *op. cit*, 271.

36. A quite personal reflection on the shape of the old self and the new self in Christ is Miroslav Volf, *Free of Charge: Giving and Forgiving in a Culture Stripped of Grace* (Grand Rapids, MI: Zondervan, 2005).

In this vein, Sarah Coakley insists upon the importance of spiritual practices, a formation for transformation, if you will. She sees the need for "a cumulative tangle of practices—meditative, sacramental, but also moral—in order to sustain this paradoxical form of unknowing/knowing."[37]

I am not necessarily advocating that the theological classroom incorporate practices that may be more proper to the catechumenate—though certain practices may indeed by conducive to foster a more meditative climate even in the classroom. But in keeping with my stress on continuity rather than discontinuity between the two ecclesial undertakings, the teaching of theology ought at least to be sensitive to more affective modes of presentation of the Catholic theological vision, theological forms that speak to the heart as well as the head.

A final consequence, therefore, is the recognition that the study of theology bears special affinity to poetry, art, and music. I say this not to deprecate more conceptual modes of knowing but to complement them for the sake of a more integral and integrated understanding of the human. Thereby, we seek to do some measure of justice not only to claims about truth and goodness but about beauty as well. I confess to resonating deeply with David Bentley Hart's claim that "Bach is the greatest of Christian theologians, the most inspired witness to the *ordo amoris* in the fabric of being. . . . No one as compellingly demonstrates that the infinite is beauty and that beauty is infinite."[38] Reference to "the fabric of being" leads, then, to a reflection on some ontological implications of a theology centered on Christ.

---

37. Coakley, "Identity of the Risen Jesus," 316.
38. Hart, *Beauty of the Infinite*, 282, 283.

VIII. ONTOLOGICAL IMPLICATIONS

What vision of reality emerges from reflection upon Christian existence that flows from conversion to Christ? It is the vision of a personal universe whose alpha and omega is the tripersonal God.

The great Tradition of the Church has pondered over the centuries the mystery of the threefold Name that is at the heart of its liturgical celebrations. From Baptism "in the Name of the Father, and the Son, and the Holy Spirit," to the Eucharist offered to the Father through the Son in the Spirit, the reflection of the Church has elucidated and explored the Trinitarian grammar of its confession.[39]

The dogmatic formulae of Nicaea and First Constantinople sought to provide an authentic reading of Christian experience, as it is constituted and nourished by word and sacrament, to affirm and guide that experience, not to replace it. In the course of the centuries, theological giants like the Cappadocians and Augustine, Richard of Saint Victor and Thomas Aquinas, Karl Rahner and Joseph Ratzinger have sought to provide some *intellectus fidei*, some understanding of the Church's faith (and, of course, I would add the Church's hope and love).

With regard to the mystery of the most Holy Trinity, a fertile approach has been to think in two registers: substantive and relational. So, the "persons" of the Trinity are understood in terms of the reciprocal subsistent relations among Father, Son, and Spirit. It is not my intention to investigate in any detail the sense and significance of the Church's Trinitarian doctrine.[40] What I want to highlight is that, in the theological tradition, "person" is exegeted in a richly relational key.

39. A splendid account is found in Khaled Anatolios, *Retrieving Nicaea: The Development and Meaning of Trinitarian Doctrine* (Grand Rapids: MI: Baker Academic, 2011).

40. A brief but substantial treatment is Joseph Ratzinger, *Introduction to Christianity*, trans. J.R. Foster (San Francisco: Ignatius, 2000), 162–90. A fuller presentation is Luis Ladaria, *The Living and True God: The Mystery of the Trinity*, trans. Maria Isabel Reyna and Liam Kelly (Miami, FL: Convivium, 2010).

If this offers some analogical access to a consideration of the mystery of the Trinity, it also entails consequences for theological anthropology, for a theological understanding of the human mystery. Man and woman themselves are called to relationality, to enter into personal relationship with one another and, inseparably, with the three-personed God. Indeed, such relationality is ingredient to their becoming persons.

Hans Urs von Balthasar has suggestively distinguished the "individual" and the "person." The latter is preeminently a theological category rooting personal identity in the assumption of a dramatic role within a network of relations. He thus situates the emergence and enrichment of personhood within a relational context. We become more fully persons as we enter more deeply and richly into the field of life-giving relations that replicate the eternal rhythms, the relational fecundity and generosity, that is the life of Father, Son, and Spirit.

The *telos* of these relations is *koinonia*/communion.[41] Not the resolution of individuals into an undifferentiated unity but the abiding of persons in peaceful and mutually enriching relational interaction. The vision of a personal universe, founded in belief in a three-personed God, supports the realization of a communion of persons in which "if one member of the body suffers, all suffer; if one is honored, all rejoice together" (1 Cor. 12:26). It is the vision poetically painted at the end of Dante's *Paradiso*: the image of the White Rose, the communion of holy ones in the Triune God. Lest we take this vision for granted, it is well to ponder the striking contrast that Nicholas Lash draws with another ontological vision—one all too prevalent in our culture. Lash writes,

---

41. Following the hint in Second Corinthians regarding the "*koinonia* of the Spirit" (2 Cor. 13:13), one can consider communion to be the distinctive *proprium* of the Spirit both in the economy of salvation and in the Godhead. See Robert P. Imbelli, "The New Adam and Life-Giving Spirit: The Paschal Pattern of Spirit Christology," *Communio* 25, no. 2 (Summer 1998): 233–52. In the same issue, note the important article of Joseph Ratzinger, "The Holy Spirit as *Communio*: Concerning the Relationship of Pneumatology and Spirituality in Augustine."

"In the beginning, according to Nietzsche, there is violence, the struggle for mastery, the will to power. Christianity announces and enacts another tale, according to which in the beginning, and in the end, is peace, pure donated peacefulness which, in the times between, makes its appearance in the endless uphill labor of transfigurative harmony."[42]

Lash's fine phrase, "the endless uphill labor of transfigurative harmony," well captures the situation of the Christian in the world. But it also points to what sustains the journey and the end to which it is directed. Christ's Resurrection and Ascension have brought to full realization humanity's vocation to transfiguration. Not in some disembodied state but precisely in his Body transformed in the Spirit, what Paul calls the *"sōma pneumatikon"* (1 Cor. 15:44).

Thus, we can take a further step in reflecting upon the ontological implications of Christian theology's Christological concentration. I speak of it as the vision of a "Christological ontology" wherein the glorified and transfigured humanity of Jesus Christ reveals the depths of reality itself. Salvation, in the Christian understanding, is participation in the very Body of Christ. Jesus Christ does far more than show the way to salvation. He creates the way in his own Body into which all believers become incorporate.

Indeed, the Tradition speaks of the triform body of Christ. There is the glorified body of the risen Jesus Christ, which still bears the signs of his Passion; there is the ecclesial Body of the Lord, encompassing both Head and members; there is the Eucharistic Body, which mediates new life from Head to members. Hence, the Christian vision is radically and pervasively personal, corporeal, and communal. It counters all Gnostic temptations to

---

42. Nicholas Lash, *The Beginning and the End of "Religion"* (Cambridge: Cambridge University Press, 1996), 232.

"excarnation." The new creation will bring embodied relationality to transfigured fulfillment.[43]

Robert Barron articulates something of what I have been suggesting in these pages. He writes,

> If, as the Prologue to the Gospel of John insists, Jesus Christ is the visible icon of the Logos through which God has made all things, and if, as the Letter to the Colossians makes clear, Jesus is the one in whom and for whom all things exist and through whom they are maintained, then Jesus is the interpretive lens through which reality is properly read. Jesus Christ is for Christians epistemically basic. . . . We Christians claim to know in a distinctive way, but this does not exclude us from the general human conversation, quite the contrary. It allows us to enter it more honestly, effectively, and creatively.[44]

And, I would add, to bring to that conversation Good News that is genuinely new. In the words of the Letter to the Colossians, "To make known the riches of the glory of the mystery, which is Christ in you, the hope of glory" (Col. 1:27).

IX. THE NOTIONAL AND THE REAL

I have sought in this essay to indicate the intimate nexus between "Teaching Theology and Handing on the Faith." My strategy has been to make a case for an understanding of Catholic theology that is radically Christocentric. The teaching of theology in the Catholic tradition, whatever the audience to which it is directed, must honor this Christocentric originality. Doing so entails

---

43. A very stimulating article that probes this triform body of the risen and ascended Christ is Anthony Kelly, "'The Body of Christ: Amen!' The Expanding Incarnation," *Theological Studies* 71, no. 4 (2010): 792–816.

44. Robert Barron, "The Metaphysics of Co-Inherence: A Meditation on the Essence of the Christian Message," in *Handing on the Faith*, 83–84.

"handing on the faith" by communicating what is most proper to it. I insist, however, that this does not mean engaging in the effort to "convert" the students taking the course, proselytizing in the invidious sense it has acquired.

Here, Cardinal Newman's distinction between the "notional" and the "real" may be of help. What I ask of students is that they exhibit a notional understanding of the distinctive claims and implications of the Catholic theological tradition, in whatever aspect or area it is presented them. Whether this "notional apprehension" becomes a "real assent" is the work of their own discernment and conscience—and the Holy Spirit.

Some may wonder whether, in so focusing upon a Christocentric approach to theology, I have ventured perilously close to that dread disease labeled "Christomonism." It is too late in the essay to offer more than a brief assurance that I do indeed affirm the Trinity and the third person. I would stress, however, that we have no reason for confessing a Triune God save for the Incarnation of the Son in Jesus Christ. As Khaled Anatolios writes, "A Christological reconception of divine transcendence was foundational for the deep structure of the developing trinitarian grammar of what came to be associated with 'Nicene' faith."[45] Indeed, the Holy Spirit is ever sent from the Father through the Son.

Pentecost is the fruit and gift of Christ's Paschal Mystery. As *Gaudium et Spes* professes, "The Holy Spirit . . . offers to everyone the possibility of being associated with [Christ's] paschal mystery."[46] I can hardly do better, in this matter, than make my own the conviction of Yves Congar: "The vigor of a lived pneumatology is to be found in Christology. There is only one body which the Spirit builds up and quickens and that is the body of Christ."[47]

45. Anatolios, *Retrieving Nicaea*, 9.

46. *Gaudium et Spes* 22.

47. Yves Congar, *The Word and the Spirit*, trans. David Smith (San Francisco: Harper and Row, 1986), 6. See also Robert P. Imbelli, "The Holy Spirit," in Joseph Komonchak, Mary Collins, Dermot Lane, eds., *The New Dictionary of Theology* (Wilmington, DE: Michael Glazier, 1987), 474–89.

Since I have extolled the indispensable place of poetry, music, and the arts in the Catholic theological tradition, I close by invoking a contemporary poet who has written of the need for a "poetics of belief"—that is, the need for "a language capacious enough to include a mystery that, ultimately, defeats it, and sufficiently intimate and inclusive to serve not only as individual expression but as communal need."[48]

In that same reflection, Christian Wiman pens these words, which may serve us as both recapitulation and challenge:

> Modern spiritual consciousness is predicated upon the fact that God is gone, and spiritual experience, for many of us, amounts mostly to an essential, deeply felt and necessary, but ultimately inchoate and transitory feeling of oneness or unity with existence. It is mystical and valuable, but distant. Christ, though, is a shard of glass in your gut. Christ is God crying *I am here*, and here not only in what exalts and completes and uplifts you, but here in what appalls, offends, and degrades you, here in what activates and exacerbates all that you would call not-God. To walk through the fog of God toward the clarity of Christ is difficult because of how unlovely, how "ungodly" that clarity often turns out to be.[49]

---

48. Christian Wiman, *My Bright Abyss: Meditation of a Modern Believer* (New York: Farrar, 2014), 124.

49. Wiman, 121.

7. Three Tantalizing Enigmas in Dante's Heaven of the Sun

In canto 10 of the *Paradiso*, Dante and Beatrice arrive in the Heaven of the Sun, the heaven of the theologians. They will abide here through canto 14. The sun is the first of the heavenly spheres that escapes the shadow cast by earth. Thus, it is fittingly the place where the wise manifest themselves to Dante in undimmed splendor.

Significantly, canto 10 begins with an invocation of the Trinity. "Gazing on his Son with the Love / the one and the other eternally breathe forth."[1] Though the Trinitarian character of the poem is clearly evident in its *terza rima* versification and in the numerological division of its presentation (three cantica, each of thirty-three cantos, plus an introductory canto), in these cantos, where Wisdom is celebrated, Trinitarian doxology plays a perspicuous role. It is as though we were hearing an anticipatory echo of Dante's glorious vision of the Triune God that is the culmination of the poem in canto 33.

Twin dancing circles of resplendent flames, each circle composed of twelve saints, inspire and inform the revelatory movement of these cantos. Each of the luminous circles has a spokesman who opens some portion of Wisdom's book to Dante. The two are Thomas Aquinas and Bonaventure, both deceased a bare

---

* This essay was originally published as "Three Tantalizing Enigmas in Dante's Heaven of the Sun," *Church Life Journal*, September 22, 2020, https://www.churchlifejournal.nd.edu.

1. Dante Alighieri, *Paradiso* 10.1–3, in Dante, *Paradiso*, trans. Robert Hollander and Jean Hollander (New York: Anchor, 2008).

quarter century before the *Divine Comedy's* symbolic occurrence in the Holy Year 1300.

One of the wonders of Dante's poetic imagination receives striking expression in this heavenly sphere. Transcending earthly rivalries, Aquinas the Dominican sings the praise of Francis, while the Franciscan Bonaventure extols Dominic. Conversely, each levels harsh criticism at the failure of the members of their own order to follow their Founder faithfully. Thomas laments that faithful Dominicans have become so few that only a little cloth would suffice to stitch their cowls—a sentiment Bonaventure picturesquely echoes in his own diatribe against his feuding brethren.

The energetic praise and lament that constitute the substance of cantos 11 and 12 give way to canto 13, which, by contrast, reads like a rather dry scholastic disquisition by Thomas on God's direct and indirect creative action. Thomas argues that Solomon was not the wisest of creatures (that distinction is accorded to the humanity of Adam and of Christ, directly created by God), but, rather, the wisest of rulers. The canto even concludes with some pedantic (if salutary) cautions by Thomas concerning the failure to make distinctions and the consequent hasty judgments indulged in by both intellectuals and ordinary folk.

Robert Hollander, the fine Dante scholar and translator, acknowledges the "unpoetic quality" of this canto.[2] And others agree. However, I fail to find in the commentators I have read any suggestion that Dante, who leaves little to chance, may have intended precisely this effect—and affect. In other words, canto 13 is a "set up" for canto 14 to follow, which is one of the most "poetic" and affective of the entire *Divine Comedy*.

It may be telling therefore that at the beginning of canto 14 the poet remarks of the loquacious Aquinas (in my reading, a bit wryly): "Si tacque la gloriosa vita di Tommaso"—"the

---

2. Dante, *Paradiso*, p. 356, note to lines 49–51 of canto 13.

glorious living soul of Thomas fell silent."[3] I am reminded (no doubt mischievously) of the beginning of the fourth movement of Beethoven's Ninth Symphony. Just before launching into the exuberant choral finale of the symphony, the bass intones, "O friends, no more these sounds! Let us sing more cheerful songs, more full of joy!"

The song of joy that bursts forth in the fourteenth canto celebrates both the ever-living Trinity and the resurrection of the glorified body. As we shall see further, for Dante there seems a surprisingly intimate nexus between the two themes, the two realities of Trinity and bodily resurrection.

In this sequence of cantos, Dante the Pilgrim, for the only time in the *Divine Comedy*, does not speak. It is Beatrice who articulates the pilgrim's unspoken concern: whether the risen body will be so overwhelmed by the glorious splendor of the soul as to be blinded, its senses annihilated. And the respondent to his *dubium* is neither Thomas nor Bonaventure, as we might have been led to expect, but, rather, one of the "flames," whose name is never given, save by indirection. Earlier, as a member of the first circle of souls, he was introduced by Thomas as "tra noi più bella"—"the most beautiful among us . . . whose wisdom had no rival."[4] Now, still unnamed, he steps forward from among the dancing circles as "la luce più dia"—"the most brilliant light."[5]

The great majority of commentators concur in identifying this figure with King Solomon, the wisest of Israel's kings and the canonical author of the Old Testament's "Song of Songs." Pointedly, the poet prefaces Solomon's response by remarking upon his "modest voice" that resembled that of the angel's to Mary.[6] So the reader must ready herself to be privy to a new annunciation.

3. *Paradiso* 14.6.
4. *Paradiso* 10.113–14.
5. *Paradiso* 14.34.
6. *Paradiso* 14.35–36.

The first of the enigmas that these cantos present, then, is why is Solomon thus privileged among the twin circles of the wise, surpassing his soulmates?

Consensus among the commentators is to dwell upon two aspects of Solomon's fame that have a particular appeal for Dante. First, of course, is his fame as ruler, who prayed the Lord for wisdom to govern his people and, in doing so, found favor with God (1 Kings 3:3–14). Dante, the great promoter of the emperor as guarantor of unity and universal peace, promotes Solomon as precursor to a restored empire.

The second aspect of Solomon's figure, perhaps even more salient, is his authorship of the "Song of Songs." In this regard, Solomon appears not only as precursor to the ardently desired emperor. He is precursor to the ever-so-present poet: Dante.

In the Church's tradition, the Song of Songs represents the mystical love of Christ and his spouse, the Church. For Dante, it testifies to the possibility of the transfiguration, not renunciation, of earthly love, of eros. Indeed, this is the very leitmotif of the *Divine Comedy*: earthly loves—for nature, native place, human accomplishments, concrete others—not denied but purified and transformed on the way to deification: the *trasumanar* of *Paradiso* 1.70. And Dante, who scorns false modesty, clearly asserts the originality of his poetic enterprise—and of himself as its pioneer.

At the very beginning of canto 10, he had put his readers on notice: "Now all my force is focused on that matter of which I have been made the scribe."[7] "Scribe," like Solomon! Presumptuous? Here is how, later in *Paradiso*, he speaks passionately of his undertaking: "'1 poema sacro/al quale ha posto mano e cielo e terra"—"The sacred poem upon which both heaven and earth have set their hand."[8] Dante is the evangelist, not of a new dispensation, but of a new realization of the order of grace.

7. *Paradiso* 10.26–27.
8. *Paradiso* 25.1–2.

In his penetrating study of Dante in the third volume of *The Glory of the Lord*, Hans Urs von Balthasar (no tyro in his knowledge of the whole of the theological tradition) daringly declares of Dante's undertaking,

> The love, which began on earth, between two human beings, is not denied, is not bypassed on the journey to God; it is not, as was always, naturally enough, hitherto the case, sacrificed on the altar of the *via negativa*; no, it is carried right up to the throne of God, however transformed and purified. This is utterly unprecedented in the history of theology.[9]

So it is scarcely by chance that Dante entrusts the celebration of the resurrected body to the author of the Song of Songs, that paean to love human and divine.

However, there may be a further reason that the chosen celebrant is Solomon, not Thomas. Thomas most certainly taught the doctrine of bodily resurrection. Moreover, he steadfastly maintained that disembodied souls lack a fundamental constituent of their very nature as the form of the body. Yet Thomas also taught that the resurrected body will be resplendent, not of itself, but due to the overwhelming brightness of the soul that animates it. He writes in his *Summa contra Gentiles* that "the soul enjoying the beatific vision is filled with a spiritual luminosity, so that, by a certain overflow from the soul to the body, the body itself, in its own manner, is clothed with a glorious brightness" (*Sicut igitur anima divina visione fruens, quadam spirituali claritate replebitur, ita, per quamdam redundantiam ex anima in corpus, ipsum corpus suo modo claritatis gloriae induetur*).[10]

Solomon exults, "When we will be clothed again in our flesh, made glorious and holy, our person will be more pleasing for

---

9. Hans Urs von Balthasar, *The Glory of the Lord*, ed. John Riches, trans. Andrew Louth et al. (San Francisco: Ignatius, 1986), 3:32.

10. Thomas Aquinas, *Summa contra Gentiles* 4.86 (translation mine).

being all complete"—"più grata fia per esser tutta quanta."[11] And Thomas Aquinas, of course, would assent.

But then Solomon goes further and rhapsodizes, "This radiance which already encircles us [referring to the disembodied soul] will be surpassed in its visibility by the flesh which earth still covers"—"fia vinto in apparenza da la carne."[12] Thus, not only will the body have a radiance proper to it, it will even surpass that of the soul.

Robert Durling, in the notes to his translation of *Paradiso*, opines, apropos these verses, "Dante somewhat complicates the matter by imagining a glory proper to the body."[13] But I contend that the "complication" is the point! Dante here strides beyond Aquinas and, perhaps, the entire Scholastic tradition. No wonder Solomon serves as his chosen spokesperson.

So then the second enigma arises. If indeed we witness here a provocative advance beyond the theology of the schools, in what does it consist? What is the import of the view attributed to no less an authority than the scripturally sanctioned Solomon?

I think we discover significant clues in the remarks that the poet annexes to Solomon's astonishing attestation. First, he records the joyful response that issues from the double ring of the wise. Both choirs intoned an "Amen!" thus showing "their ardent desire for their dead bodies"—"che ben mostrar disio d'i corpi morti."[14] Tellingly, however, Dante uses the Tuscan dialect form for Amen: "Amme!" The great proponent of the use of the vernacular, here introduces even its colloquial expression into the heavenly realm.

Rather than a provincialism on the part of the proud Florentine, there is a deeply human impulse that becomes clarified in

11. *Paradiso* 14.43–45.

12. *Paradiso* 14.55–57.

13. Dante, *The Divine Comedy of Dante Alighieri*, vol. 3, *Paradiso*, trans. and ed. Robert M. Durling (Oxford: Oxford University Press, 2011), 295.

14. *Paradiso* 14.63.

his remarkable commentary upon the ardent desire he has just described. He says that the desire is "not for themselves alone perhaps, but for their mothers, for their fathers, and for the others who were dear to them before they became everlasting flames"— "forse non pur per lor, ma per le mamme, / per li padri e per li altri che fuor cari / anzi che fosser sempiterne fiamme."[15]

The use of the familial "mamme" (rather than "madri") arises not merely from the exigencies of rime but from a sensibility to the intimacy of relations that bind: from mother tongue to mother's milk, embracing all those who have shaped the persons we have finally become.

What drives these crucial verses of canto 14, then, is not sentimental nostalgia but affective wisdom. It is the wisdom that recognizes and celebrates the constitutive nature of the relationships inscribed in our very bodies—what I call "somatic relationality." It is this realization that accounts for the surpassing brilliance of the glorified body, for it extends beyond the individual to the person defined by his or her relationships.

In this light, the striking presence of Trinitarian invocations and doxologies in these cantos takes on new meaning. For the Trinitarian relations that constitute the persons of the Godhead are the *arche* and *telos* of every person's journey, coming forth from the Father through the Word in the Spirit and returning in the Spirit through the Word to the Father. This is the very journey that Dante's theological-poetic masterpiece depicts. It celebrates the profoundly corporeal nature of salvation, incorporating in Christ *cari, comunità, cosmo*: dear ones, community, the cosmos itself.

No sooner does the poet cease his comment on the ardent desire expressed by the double circles that the third enigma bursts upon us. It takes form as the sudden epiphany of a bedazzling third circle.

15. *Paradiso* 14.64–66.

"Behold," marvels the poet, "like a brightening horizon, there arose a splendor surpassing the former"—"un lustro sopra quel che v'era."[16] He continues, "I seemed to see new figures forming a ring beyond the other two"—"un giro di fuor da l'altre due circunferenze."[17] A new, third circle of numerous souls appear, underscoring the Trinitarian imagery that pervades these cantos.

The sight elicits this exclamation from the wondering poet: "O true shining forth of the Holy Spirit! / How sudden and splendorous it appears / That my eyes, overwhelmed, could not bear it." "Oh vero sfavillar del Santo Spiro / come si fece sùbito e candente / a li occhi miei che, vinti, nol soffriro!"[18]

Robert Hollander rightly characterizes these verses as "this supercharged passage," so vatic and enigmatic do they appear. He and others speculate that Dante, following in the wake of Joachim of Flora, here foresees the coming of a "Third Age" of the Holy Spirit, perhaps even distancing from the previous ages of the Father and the Son. The third circle of countless, still nameless, personages would be, then, those "spirituals" liberated from the constrictions of the previous eras.

However, I think this hypothesis implausible. First, because Bonaventure in his criticism of his Franciscan brethren in canto 12 had specifically inveighed against Umberto da Casale, leader of the so-called "Spiritual Franciscans." It is unlikely that Dante would here repudiate what he had Bonaventure pronounce. Second, and more crucially, the reality and symbolism of the Trinity is so central to Dante's vision that any implication of Trinitarian supercessionism would undermine his entire endeavor.

Yet clearly in "this supercharged passage" a *novum* is being proclaimed. In what does it consist? How resolve this third, clearly prophetic, enigma? If not a new age, then what? Hans Urs von Balthasar provides a promising orientation when he speaks of

16. *Paradiso* 14.68.
17. *Paradiso* 14.74.
18. *Paradiso* 14.76–78.

Dante as the "originator" of a "new third theology." Perhaps one might say a new "integration": of sacred and secular, Christianity and antiquity, Church and empire, theology and poetry, reason and affectivity, whose focus is always the concrete particularity of human persons, forged by their affective interpersonal relations in history. And the privileged vehicle to express this integration is the vernacular, the mother tongue in which these relations transpire.

Hence the appropriateness of the *Santo Spiro*, the Holy Spirit, as matrix of this new poetic theology. The Holy Spirit, not as the inaugurator of "Third Age," but as the communion of persons both in the Godhead and among the Trinity's created images. Thus, the "Third Age" dawning is not Joachite but Dantean. Dante the Pilgrim, who has never once spoken in the Heaven of the Sun, had no need to speak. He himself has become the inspired scribe of this new mystical-political theology whose inauguration is the "Sacred Poem" itself.

In my reading, the commentators seem to have paid insufficient attention to the link that closely binds what I have been calling the "three enigmas": the choice of Solomon as the final speaker, the extraordinary celebration of the risen body with its myriad defining relationships, and the mysterious epiphany of a third circle of theologians enfolding the other circles. Each enigma builds upon the former and, together, they mutually illumine one other. But they also significantly anticipate the climax of the *Comedy* in the last cantos of *Paradiso*.

Readers of Dante know that the pilgrim's journey culminates in his great beatifying vision of the Trinity in the thirty-third canto of *Paradiso*—the hundredth of the entire *Commedia* (both numbers replete with Trinitarian significance). Even more than before, the poet struggles to give voice to the finally ineffable reality he experiences. The "apophatic" strain of the poem has been widely commented upon and appreciated. Dante does not presume to circumscribe the vision, but to be circumscribed, encircled by it.

Here are the verses in the Hollander translation:

> In the deep, transparent essence of the lofty Light there appeared to me three circles having three colors but the same extent, and each one seemed reflected by the other as rainbow is by rainbow, while the third seemed fire equally breathed forth by one and by the other.[19]

And yet the ultimate reality is not a beckoning void or inscrutable nothingness but manifests Trinitarian—personal and relational—contours. Even more, the "cataphatic" element is boldly confessed, as it must be in a work of Christic inspiration. For the vision reveals a further depth. Addressing the very Godhead the poet exclaims,

> That circling which, thus conceived, appeared in you as light's reflection, once my eyes had gazed on it a while, seemed within itself and in its very color, to be painted with our likeness, so that my sight was all absorbed in it.[20]

What Dante perceives, enfolded in the very mystery of the Triune God, is the glorified humanity of the Son. Christ's Incarnation finds fulfillment, achieves its *telos*, in his Ascension whereby humanity is deified. Indeed, the glorified humanity of Jesus is the very condition for the possibility of every spiritual journey whose true destiny is a humanity transfigured.

The close association of Trinity and humanity's bodily resurrection that we glimpsed in the Heaven of the Sun, we now contemplate fully realized in this last canto. The God who lovingly

19. *Paradiso* 33.115–20.
20. *Paradiso* 33.127–32.

formed humankind from the dust, Adam from earth, brings his beloved creation home—*tutta quanta* ("whole and entire").

Those familiar with Charles Taylor's monumental study *A Secular Age* recall that the last chapter is entitled "Conversions."[21] In it, Taylor introduces the reader to a number of figures who, in his view, have "converted," ventured beyond the limitations and negativities of modernity, to embrace a more fully human mode of existence and to articulate a more ample vision of reality. Among secularity's constrictions that he identifies are the reduction of reality to an "immanent frame" that allows no scope for transcendence and the cultivation of a "buffered self," supposedly liberated from entanglements and commitments.

Taylor suggestively sums up the deleterious undertow of secularity with the word "excarnation." Excarnation is radical discomfort with bodily existence: with relationships and their demands, with community and its commitments, with history and its challenges.

Among those he celebrates for their conversion to a deeper vision and a fuller reality are Gerard Manley Hopkins and Charles Péguy. Hopkins's vivid sacramental sense, expressed in incomparable poetry, breaks out of the stifling one-dimensionality of the immanent frame. Péguy's passionate advocacy of community and communion lays bare the impoverished state of the buffered self. Both hymn a world "charged with the grandeur of God."[22] They thereby echo the opening verse of *Paradiso*: "The Glory of Him who moves all things / Permeates the universe"—"La Gloria di Colui che tutto move / per l'universo penetra."[23]

I would happily count both Hopkins and Péguy in the company of that third circle of living flames whom Dante prophetically foresaw. But since the number of participants is both

---

21. See Charles Taylor, *A Secular Age* (Cambridge, MA: Belknap, 2007).

22. Gerard Manley Hopkins, "God's Grandeur," Poetry Foundation, poetryfoundation. org.

23. Dante, *Paradiso* 1.1–2.

manifold and incomplete, the circle is open for new membership. With Hopkins and Péguy, I would personally enroll figures like Pascal and Newman. Others may enlist other bards of this incarnational poetic, celebrants of embodied particularity. God knows the need is great and excarnation ever threatens. But in that third circle, however many join the dance, Dante will remain the coryphaeus—even after seven hundred years.

8. "He Is the Head of the Body, the Church" (Col. 1:18)

Salvation as Incorporation into Christ

"The mysteries of the Ascension and Transfiguration breach the ultimately dehumanizing boundaries of the immanent frame and the buffered self and inaugurate the new creation."

The following essay explores a crucial yet neglected dimension of the mystery of salvation in Christ. Because the issue of the salvation that Jesus Christ proclaims and enacts lies at the very heart of the Church's evangelical and pastoral mission and ministry, it must be a central and ongoing concern of theology as an ecclesial discipline in service to that mission.

In a fine article, Father Khaled Anatolios offers an approach to theology with which I am fully in accord. He writes, "Theology, from the perspective of the new evangelization, [is] ordered discourse on the newness of Christ and of the renewal of all things in Christ."[1] This perspective will govern my presentation. One might call it a reading of the *Summa* from the vantage of the *Tertia Pars*.

The essay will proceed in five steps: (1) some indication of the *status quaestionis* regarding the theme of salvation; (2) some

---

* This essay was originally published as "'He Is the Head of the Body, the Church' (Col 1:18): Salvation as Incorporation into Christ," *Communio* 46, no. 2 (Summer 2019): 288–309.

1. Khaled Anatolios, "A Patristic Reflection on the Nature and Method of Theology in the New Evangelization," *Nova et Vetera* 14, no. 4 (2016): 1067–81, at 1070.

concerns about the state of Catholic life and theology today; (3) the Christo-logic of the Letter to the Colossians; (4) the crucial importance of Christ's Ascension and headship for realizing salvation in Christ; and (5) the conclusion: toward a Eucharistic mysticism.

I. STATUS QUAESTIONIS

On February 22, 2018, the Congregation for the Doctrine of the Faith released a brief but important document, *Placuit Deo*, "On Certain Aspects of Christian Salvation." It was signed by the prefect of the congregation, then-Archbishop, now-Cardinal Luis Ladaria, SJ, and expressly approved by Pope Francis. Significantly, its opening sentence, from which its title *Placuit Deo* derives, is a direct citation of a crucial paragraph from *Dei Verbum*, the Second Vatican Council's Dogmatic Constitution on Divine Revelation:

> In his goodness and wisdom God chose to reveal Himself and to make known to us the hidden purpose of his will (see Eph. 1:9) by which through Christ, the Word made flesh, man might in the Holy Spirit have access to the Father and come to share in the divine nature (see Eph. 2:18; 2 Peter 1:4). . . . The deepest truth . . . about God and the salvation of man shines out for our sake in Christ, who is both the mediator and the fullness of all revelation.[2]

---

2. Vatican Council II, *Dei Verbum* 2, in *The Word on Fire Vatican II Collection*, ed. Matthew Levering (Park Ridge, IL: Word on Fire Institute, 2021), 17–18.

That the salvation of humanity is revealed and accomplished in Christ is the central conviction that the CDF document seeks to elucidate more fully.

Placuit Deo begins with the forthright admission that the Church's "teaching on salvation in Christ must always be deepened."[3] I suggest that two realities impel this assertion. First, of course, is that the mystery of our salvation in and through Jesus Christ is inexhaustible and thus is open to an ever-deepening contemplative and speculative appropriation.

But the other reality that drives the need for ongoing and renewed reflection is the evolving social context that poses new questions and challenges to the received wisdom. Indeed, the CDF document admits that "the contemporary world perceives not without difficulty the confession of the Christian faith, which proclaims Jesus as the only Savior of the whole human person and of all humanity."[4]

Placuit Deo identifies the difficulties in question in terms of two perennial temptations that, following the writings of Pope Francis, it designates as "Pelagianism" and "Gnosticism."[5] These deformations of the human spirit take on a particular coloration in our consumerist and therapeutic culture. On the one hand, the stress on the radical autonomy of the individual leaves little place for the in-breaking of God's grace. On the other hand, alienation from the material world and even one's own body propels a retreat into the inner *sanctum* of some untainted "spiritual" self. Both tendencies conspire to produce that condition (and here I move beyond the CDF document) so poignantly depicted by Walker Percy in his book, *Lost in the Cosmos*.[6]

---

3. Congregation for the Doctrine of the Faith, *Placuit Deo* 1, February 22, 2018, vatican. va.

4. *Placuit Deo* 2.

5. See, for example, Francis, *Evangelii Gaudium* 93–94, November 24, 2013, vatican.va.

6. Walker Percy, *Lost in the Cosmos: The Last Self-Help Book* (New York: Farrar, 1983).

Let me probe this plight further, calling upon the thought of the Canadian Catholic philosopher Charles Taylor in his monumental study *A Secular Age*.[7] Taylor, who certainly acknowledges the gains of modernity and secularity in areas like religious freedom and tolerance, nonetheless recognizes what might be called "the dark side of secularity." There is the reduction of the social imaginary to "the immanent frame" where a sense of transcendence cedes to this-worldly concerns and imperatives. This experiential narrowing tends to produce the "buffered self": a self closed off from influences emanating from a transcendent realm and, increasingly, even from vital interactions with human others—a problem that has grown even more acute since the book's appearance twelve years ago.[8]

But to my mind, most interesting (and I think rather neglected by commentators on Taylor's work) is his introduction of the category of "excarnation" to describe our modern plight. Ancient Gnosticism was, of course, wary of the flesh, with its messiness and fragility. Its existential "grammar" was deeply "excarnational," as its proponents sought refuge in some spiritual realm beyond the vicissitudes and afflictions of the flesh.

But secularity for all its touted sexual liberation is often deeply "excarnational." Many men and women today are suspicious of history and tradition, hesitant to form binding relations, prone to use others as objects to satisfy fleeting emotions, as they practice death avoidance and denial.[9] These are manifest symptoms of excarnation—a profound unease with and alienation from our bodily reality.

Charles Taylor sums up the contemporary predicament and, astonishingly, in a work of historical and philosophical analysis,

7. Charles Taylor, *A Secular Age* (Cambridge, MA: Belknap, 2007).

8. See the pointed reflection by the political and social commentator, Andrew Sullivan, on internet addiction: "I Used to Be a Human Being," *New York Magazine*, September 19, 2016, http://nymag.com/intelligencer/2016/09/andrew-sullivan-my-distraction-sickness-and-yours.html.

9. A classic analysis is Ernest Becker, *The Denial of Death* (New York: Free Press, 1973).

points to a remedy. He writes, "Christians today . . . live in a world where objectification and excarnation reign, where death undermines meaning. We have to struggle to *recover a sense of what the Incarnation can mean*."[10]

2. CONCERNS ABOUT THE STATE OF CATHOLIC LIFE AND THEOLOGY

"To recover a sense of what the Incarnation can mean." Clearly, Taylor is not suggesting that a mere repetition of doctrinal formulas and propositions will be a sufficient remedy—however important such propositions remain. What is required is a new "realization" (in Newman's strong sense) that is at once spiritual, intellectual, and affective. If I may be permitted to use the phrase, we need a "rekindling of the Christic imagination!"[11]

But I fear that we may be ill-equipped to respond creatively to our contemporary predicament, because there are disturbing indications that not a few areas of Catholic life and theology have succumbed (whether innocently or wittingly) to secularity's "immanent frame." We risk "misremembering" the Tradition's insistence (beginning with the New Testament and continuing through the Second Vatican Council) of the absolute *novum* of Jesus Christ and the profound *transformation* to which he summons us. To call attention to this anomalous condition, I have used the intentionally provocative phrase "the *decapitated body* of contemporary Catholicism."

There are a number of "symptoms" of this loss of the "headship" of Christ in the contemporary Church. Let me briefly suggest three (and ask whether they are recognizable in the readers' own experience).

10. Taylor, *Secular Age*, 753 (emphasis mine).

11. Robert P. Imbelli, *Rekindling the Christic Imagination: Theological Meditations for the New Evangelization* (Collegeville, MN: Liturgical, 2014).

The first is a "horizontalism" in the liturgy that the theologian Joseph Ratzinger / Benedict XVI so often deprecated, for it obscures the absolute primacy of Jesus Christ. As Benedict wrote in his apostolic exhortation *Sacramentum Caritatis,*

> The Eucharist is Christ who gives himself to us and continually builds us up as his body. . . . The Church is able to celebrate and adore the mystery of Christ present in the Eucharist precisely because Christ first gave himself to her in the sacrifice of the Cross. . . . We too, at every celebration of the Eucharist, confess the primacy of Christ's gift. The causal influence of the Eucharist at the Church's origins definitively discloses both the chronological and ontological priority of the fact that it was Christ who loved us "first." For all eternity he remains the one who loves us first.[12]

Such horizontalism has perhaps been abetted by the celebration of the Eucharist *versus populum.* But certainly, that is but one element in a pervasive ideological stance that, in its most blatant expression, argues, "What is important is not what is on the altar, but who is around the altar"—namely, the congregation. The second "decapitated body symptom" is the "Christological derailment" that has been a mark of Protestant liberalism since Kant and Hegel and that has clearly taken root in some quarters of postconciliar Catholic theology. It is characterized by the reduction of Jesus Christ to a sublime exemplar of moral living, a sort of "superstar."

Cyril O'Regan provides, I think, a perceptive delineation of one characteristic thrust of this reductionism. He writes of Hegel and those who followed him that they offered a "rinsed rendition of Christ." They "reversed the order of reference, and made Christ

12. Benedict XVI, *Sacramentum Caritatis* 14, apostolic exhortation, February 22, 2007, vatican.va.

refer to the Spirit rather than the Spirit to Christ." The result is one that has haunted Protestant liberalism for two hundred years. "The community divests itself of the concrete particularity of Christ, and in its reference to Spirit concludes in abolishing transcendence altogether. Through pneumatic displacement the community's memory of Christ becomes self-referential."[13] Such a reductive Christology inevitably capitulates to secularity's immanent frame.

A prime manifestation of such Christological reductionism, as Fleming Rutledge's *The Crucifixion* magisterially highlights, is the marginalization of the cross. A fair amount of contemporary theological reflection upon the crucifixion of Jesus sees it solely as the punishment inflicted by an oppressive political-religious establishment upon a provocative threat to its power. When asked whether anything salvific transpired *on* the cross, many today would demur.

For liberal Christian theology, the salvific ministry of Jesus unfolded in his life of teaching and healing and social advocacy. But his death itself was only the consequence of his radical challenging of the "powers that be." The more extreme advocates of liberation and feminist approaches to theology go so far as to savage theories of the atonement as evidence of heavenly parental "child abuse." In so doing, they render incomprehensible the Gospel narrative, both in the synoptics and John, where the cross is the culmination of Jesus's mission, summed up in the centurion's cry, "Truly this man was the Son of God" (Mark 15:39), or the Johannine Jesus's own testimony, "It is consummated" (John 19:30).

Thus, Rutledge writes, "The cross, incomparably vindicated by the resurrection, is the *novum*, the new factor in human experience, the definitive and world-changing act of God that makes

---

13. Cyril O'Regan, *The Anatomy of Misremembering: Von Balthasar's Response to Philosophical Modernity*, vol. 1, *Hegel* (New York: Crossroad, 2014), 200.

the New Testament proclamation unique in all the world." And she insists, "The crucifixion is the touchstone of Christian authenticity, the unique feature by which everything else, including the resurrection, is given its true significance."[14]

The Christological deficit of liberalism leaves a Christian congregation bereft of its Lord, a headless body of believers that echoes Magdalene's lament: "They have taken the Lord and we do not know where they have laid him" (John 20:2). Absent Christ, who is the Way, the Truth, and the Life, Christian self-understanding inevitably succumbs to what Joseph Ratzinger has decried as "the dictatorship of relativism."[15] And no salvation is to be found there.

The late Cardinal Avery Dulles identified a third sign of Christological derailment. In the very last book he published, Dulles (prophetic in this as in much else) warned of a growing "soteriological pluralism" in theology, by which he meant the view that Jesus is one of a number of bringers of salvation, normative, perhaps, for Christians, but not to be imposed in imperialistic fashion upon others.[16]

Flowing inevitably from this soteriological ambiguity is the "benevolent" neglect accorded Dei Verbum. What is arguably the Second Vatican Council's primary document, from which all the others receive their theological foundation and justification, tends often to be ignored in theological journals and conferences.[17] The Christic soteriological universalism of Dei Verbum—"the deepest truth . . . about God and the salvation of man shines out for

---

14. Fleming Rutledge, *The Crucifixion: Understanding the Death of Jesus* (Grand Rapids: Eerdmans, 2015), 61, 71. See also the stimulating article by Gil Bailie, "Making Peace through the Blood of His Cross," *Communio* 45, no. 3–4 (Fall–Winter 2018): 471–93.

15. See Ratzinger's memorable "Homily at the Mass 'Pro Eligendo Romano Pontifice'" April 18, 2005, available at www.vatican.va.

16. Avery Dulles, *Evangelization for the Third Millennium* (New York: Paulist, 2009), 81, 85.

17. For the particular significance of *Dei Verbum*, see Imbelli, *Rekindling*, xv; see also Jared Wicks, *Investigating Vatican II: Its Theologians, Ecumenical Turn, and Biblical Commitment* (Washington, DC: The Catholic University of America Press, 2018), 223.

our sake in Christ, who is both the mediator and the fullness of all revelation"—(which, as we saw, gives *Placuit Deo* its point of departure and orientation) is thus not only lost to view, it is in practice denied.

Accordingly, there is an urgent need to recover, both theologically and spiritually, the extraordinary claims of the New Testament regarding the salvation realized by the crucified and risen Jesus of Nazareth in his uniqueness and universality. Those unique claims are proclaimed in striking fashion in the Letter to the Colossians.

3. THE CHRISTO-LOGIC OF THE LETTER TO THE COLOSSIANS

Every Wednesday at Vespers, the Church prays and confesses an extraordinary hymn: the Christological hymn of the Letter to the Colossians.

We know it so well that we can take it for granted, failing to wonder at its radical, even revolutionary, assertions. It can remain merely notional, not impacting and reorienting one's whole stance toward reality itself.

Recall the context in which the hymn appears. Paul is recounting to the Colossians the reason for their common thanksgiving. God the Father has delivered them from the domain of darkness and brought them into the kingdom of his beloved Son "in whom we have redemption, the forgiveness of sins" (Col. 1:14). Then begins the great profession of Christological faith:

> He is the image of the invisible God, the first-born of all creation. For in him all things were created, in heaven and on earth, visible and invisible, whether thrones or dominions or principalities or authorities. All things were created through him and for him. He is before all things and in him all things

hold together. He is the head of the body, the Church. He is the beginning, the first-born of the dead, that in everything he might be preeminent. For in him all the fullness of God was pleased to dwell, and through him to reconcile to himself all things, whether on earth or in heaven, making peace by the blood of his cross. (Col. 1:15–20)

A little later in the letter, the Apostle draws out implications of the hymn in further remarkable affirmations: "In Christ are hid all the treasures of wisdom and of knowledge" (2:3); "for in Christ the whole fullness of deity dwells bodily" (2:9).

Yet this intense Christological concentration of Colossians does not induce a "Christomonism," because believers themselves are intimately caught up in—indeed, defined by—the mystery of Christ. For Colossians proclaims the mystery to be this: "Christ in you, hope of glory" (1:27).

This glory, furthermore, must become manifest in newness of life that can only be truly lived if believers cohere in Christ, allowing themselves to be transformed through dependent union upon him who is their Head. They must live, therefore, as those who form one body with Christ the Head. As their new condition is to be in Christ, so must they live in and through Christ. Hence, any separation of "doctrinal" and "pastoral" is insidious. New identity and new mode of living are inextricably related.

As Douglas Moo writes in his fine commentary on Colossians,

Few texts in the New Testament make the case so clearly that Christian living must be rooted in Christ. He is the "head" who supplies power to the whole body (2:19). It is by our existence "in him," the "new self," or "new man," that renewal in the image of God takes place (3:10). . . . Our very mind-set must be governed by "the things above" where Christ is and with whom we have been raised to new life (3:1–2).[18]

Among the challenges Colossians confronted seems to have been an ambivalence, on the part of some believers, as to whether Christ is the unique Savior, the one who alone can be relied upon. The letter aims to counter a Gnostic lust for salvific assurance elsewhere than in Christ—a sort of hedging of one's salvific bets—which Colossians decries as "not holding fast to the Head" (2:19). Moo writes, "Against those arguing that ultimate spiritual experience had to be sought in places in addition to Christ, Paul holds up Christ as the one who is the true and only source of life for the body. Just as Christ is preeminent in the universe, so he is preeminent within the new creation, the assembly of new covenant believers."[19] True salvation is ever in and through Jesus Christ.

Thus, Colossians insists that it is from Christ the Head that the whole Body is "nourished and knit together" and grows "with a growth that is from God" (2:19).

A further development of Paul's argument is important to note. (It will play an important role in the thought of both Augustine and Aquinas.) He begins chapter 3 of Colossians with almost a recapitulation of what he has written thus far:

> Since you have been raised with Christ, seek the things that are above, where Christ is seated at the right hand of God. Be mindful of the things that are above, not the things of earth. For you have died, and your life is hid with Christ in God. When Christ, who is our life, appears, then you also will appear with him in glory. (3:1–4)

18. Douglas Moo, *The Letters to the Colossians and to Philemon* (Grand Rapids, MI: Eerdmans, 2008), 69–70.

19. Moo, *Letters*, 128.

Here again we see the "grammar" of *novum*/transformation that governs the New Testament: the absolute newness of Jesus Christ ("Christ seated at the right hand of God") and the radical personal transformation to which we are called in Christ ("You have died, and your life is hid with Christ in God"). Colossians is a privileged summation of the Gospel of salvation through and in Christ. The letter highlights in a singular way that salvation (redemption, forgiveness of sin, fulfillment of God's eternal plan, friendship, and communion with God) is realized through incorporation into Christ. And Christians remain somatically dependent upon the ongoing salvific action of the Lord who has been exalted to God's right hand, in whom "all the fulness of deity dwells bodily" (Col 2:9).

In this, Colossians provides a powerful counter-testimony to those negative trends in secularity that Charles Taylor identified: its constricted, immanent frame; its excarnational thrust; its sundering of communal bonds; its failure to satisfy the inchoate human aspiration for a fullness of human flourishing.

4. THE CRUCIAL IMPORTANCE OF CHRIST'S ASCENSION AND HEADSHIP FOR REALIZING SALVATION IN CHRIST

In this fourth section, I argue that an imperative of contemporary Catholic spirituality and theology is to explore existentially and systematically the closely connected doctrines of Christ's Ascension and headship. Though I do not presume to specialized knowledge of either Augustine or Aquinas, I think it important to begin by offering some brief indications of the resources that each might lend this crucial theological-spiritual recovery and exploration.

4.1 Augustine on the Ascension and Headship of Christ
In one of his many homilies on the Lord's Ascension, Augustine
exhorts his congregation,

> Today our Lord Jesus Christ ascended into heaven; let our
> hearts ascend with him. Listen to the words of the Apostle: "If
> you have risen with Christ, set your hearts on the things that
> are above where Christ is, seated at the right hand of God; seek
> the things that are above, not the things that are on earth" [Col.
> 3:1–2]. For just as he remained with us even after his ascension,
> so we too are already in heaven with him, even though what is
> promised us has not yet been fulfilled in our bodies.
>
> Christ is now exalted above the heavens, but he still suffers on
> earth all the pain that we, the members of his body, have to
> bear. He showed this when he cried out from above: "Saul,
> Saul, why do you persecute me?" and when he said: "I was
> hungry and you gave me food." . . .
>
> These words are explained by our oneness with Christ, for he is
> our head and we are his body. . . .
>
> Out of compassion for us he descended from heaven, and al-
> though he ascended alone, we also ascend, because we are in
> him by grace. Thus, no one but Christ descended and no one
> but Christ ascended; not because there is no distinction be-
> tween the head and the body, but because the body as a unity
> cannot be separated from the head.[20]

Emmanuel Durand comments,

> If the Incarnation constitutes Christ as the Head of humanity
> by his sharing of our condition, the salvific efficacy of such a

---

20. Taken from the Office of Readings for the Solemnity of the Ascension in *The Liturgy of the Hours*, vol. 2, *Lenten Season – Easter Season* (New York: Catholic Book Publishing, 1976), 920–922.

claim is revealed and accomplished by his Ascension, which exerts a supernatural effect upon the members of his body, bearing them toward God [*un effet surnaturel d'entraînement vers Dieu*]. Augustine here recovers the Pauline emphasis upon the Ascension perceived as the decisive stage in fully unfolding the role of Christ the Head on behalf of his members who are still *in via*.[21]

Here, we find richly present Augustine's singular understanding of the *totus Christus*—the whole Christ composed by Head and members in most intimate union. This teaching lies at the heart of Augustine's ecclesiology. The uniqueness of the Head is not compromised since he is the ever-active source and stay of the Body's life. However, the members of his Body truly participate in the dignity and supernatural life of their Head. His Ascension anticipates and enables their final destiny.[22]

Augustine's extraordinary sensitivity to and insight into the corporate/ecclesial nature of salvation in Christ perhaps receives consummate lyrical expression in this splendid passage from his *Sermons on the First Letter of Saint John*:

> The sons of God are the Body of the unique Son of God. And since he is the Head and we the members, the Son of God is one. Thus, he who loves the sons of God loves the Son of God. Who are the sons of God? The members of the Son of God. And, by loving, he becomes himself a member, and through love is joined to the Body of Christ. And there will be one Christ loving himself.[23]

21. Emmanuel Durand, *L'Offre universelle du salut en Christ* (Paris: Cerf, 2007), 255 (translation mine).

22. For a good discussion of the importance of *totus Christus* in Augustine's theology and spirituality, see David Vincent Meconi, *The One Christ: St. Augustine's Theology of Deification* (Washington, DC: The Catholic University of America Press, 2013), 195–216.

23. Augustine, *Tractatus in epistolam Ioannis ad Parthos* 10.3 (translation mine): "Filii Dei corpus sunt unici Filii Dei. Et cum ille caput, nos membra, unus est Filius Dei. Ergo qui diligit

One can scarcely imagine a more radical sense of the intimate union binding Redeemer and redeemed, Savior and saved, than Augustine's teaching of the *totus Christus*. Its recovery is sorely needed for the life of the Church and world today.

4.2 Thomas Aquinas on the Ascension and Headship of Christ

The noted Thomist scholar Jean-Pierre Torrell comments upon Thomas's path-breaking discussion of the salvific effects of the Ascension. Speaking of *Summa theologiae* 3.57.6, "Utrum ascensio Christi sit causa nostrae salutis" (Whether Christ's Ascension is the cause of our salvation?), Torrell extols "the sheer originality of this article." And he adds, "If one wishes to gauge this originality, one can say that the salvific efficacy of the Ascension, in contemporary teaching, was even less prominent than that of the Resurrection."[24] One might well wonder whether the salvific significance of the Ascension is any more to the fore today?[25]

In the body of this article, in his usual succinct fashion, Thomas notes a number of salvific effects of the Ascension. The Ascension fixes our minds on Christ and evokes the saving virtues of faith, hope, and charity. Indeed, as our Head, he prepares for us the way to fullness of life. In very Augustinian fashion, Thomas says, "Opportet illuc sequi membra quo caput praecessit"—the members must follow where the Head has gone.

Further, the ascended Christ enters heaven itself *ad interpellandum pro nobis*. And his intercession is that "God, who has thus exalted human nature in Christ, will have mercy on us for whom the Son of God assumed that nature."

filios Dei, Filium Dei diligit. Quos filios Dei? Membra Filii Dei. Et diligendo fit et ipsum membrum, et fit per dilectionem in compage corporis Christi. Et erit unus Christus amans seipsum."

24. Jean-Pierre Torrell, *Le Christ en ses mystères: la vie et l'oeuvre de Jésus selon saint Thomas d'Aquin*, vol. 2 (Paris: Desclée, 1999), 664 (translation mine).

25. There are two studies of the theology of the Ascension that I have found especially insightful: Douglas Farrow, *Ascension Theology* (London: Bloomsbury, 2011), and Anthony Kelly, *Upward: Faith, Church, and the Ascension of Christ* (Collegeville, MN: Liturgical, 2014).

Another key assertion Thomas makes (though, unfortunately, it is not developed here at length) is that the ascended Christ will send *divina dona hominibus* (appealing to Eph. 4:10).

In his response to the second objection, Thomas gives almost a summary of the salvific efficacy of the Ascension: "Ascensio autem Christi est directe causa ascensionis nostrae, quasi inchoando ipsam in capite nostro, cui oportet membra coniungi." Torrell translates, "The Ascension of Christ is the direct cause of ours, because our ascension might be said to begin in that of our Head, to whom, as his members, we are necessarily united."[26] For Torrell, this brings decisively forward "l'identité mystique entre la Tête et les membres" (the mystical identity of Head and members).

Let me add two further references that may draw out a little more the radical implications of these observations of Aquinas. In question 8, article 6 of the *Tertia Pars*, Thomas raises the issue: "Utrum esse caput Ecclesiae sit proprium Christo"—Whether it is proper to Christ to be head of the Church? I find it noteworthy that in the *sed contra* that launches him into his positive response, he cites the dense sentence of Col. 2:19: "The Head, from whom the whole body, nourished and knit together through its joints and ligaments, grows with a growth that is from God." And Thomas remarks simply, "Sed hoc soli Christo convenit. Ergo solus Christus est caput Ecclesiae"—now this belongs only to Christ; therefore, only Christ is the Head of the Church.

Finally, let me mention the striking phrase that appears in question 48, article 2. The issue he poses is "Utrum passio Christi causaverit nostram salutem per modum satisfactionis"—Whether Christ's Passion brought about our salvation by way of satisfaction? In his reply to the first objection, Thomas says, "Caput et membra sunt quasi una persona mystica. Et ideo satisfactio Christi ad omnes fideles pertinet sicut ad sua membra"—Head

---

26. Torrell, *Le Christ en ses mystères*, 668 (translation mine).

and members are as one mystical person; and therefore, Christ's satisfaction belongs to all the faithful as being his members.

In another rich study, Torrell cites this very text of Aquinas and does not hesitate to speak of "une solidarité mystique" that transcends the purely natural order and opens upon the order of grace.[27] Christ is the Head from whom life flows to the Body, but the members of the Body truly participate in this new life of grace that conforms us to Christ and incorporates us into his Body.

Further, in his study *Spiritual Master*, Torrell writes, "The historical Christ, today glorified, touches us by each of the acts of his earthly life, which is thus the bearer of a divinizing life and energy." And again, "Our grace is the grace of adoptive sons, but also a grace of suffering, death, Resurrection, and Ascension through Christ, with him, and in him. We are here at the heart of the ontological exemplarism and of the mystery of Christ-conforming grace."[28] And, in an intriguing comment about Thomas's teaching on the headship of Christ, Torrell writes, "The Master from Aquino soon felt the limits of the analogy of the instrument and, without rejecting it—since it allowed for some definite advance—he moved toward a deepening of the Pauline contribution about the Body of Christ."[29]

Torrell appears to suggest here that however important Thomas's systematic advance in considering Christ's humanity as the "instrument" of his divinity, he was moving toward a yet deeper appreciation of the uniquely intimate union of the Head and members of the Body: forming, indeed, *una persona mystica*.

In sum, I am arguing that one of the key tasks before us is to deepen further our realization and appreciation of the ascended Jesus Christ as the Head whose self-giving continues to nourish his Body and of the intimate ties and the consequent

27. Jean-Pierre Torrell, *Pour nous les hommes et pour notre salut* (Paris: Cerf, 2014), 265.

28. Jean-Pierre Torrell, *Saint Thomas Aquinas*, vol. 2, *Spiritual Master*, trans. Robert Royal (Washington, DC: The Catholic University of America Press, 2003), 139, 141.

29. Torrell, *Spiritual Master*, 145.

responsibilities binding the members of the Body into the new transcendent reality that is *una persona mystica*.

Placuit Deo intimates as much when it declares, "Salvation, then, consists in our incorporation into [Christ's] life, receiving his Spirit (cf. 1 John 4:13). He became, 'in a particular way, the origin of all grace according to his humanity.' He is at the same time Savior and Salvation."[30] Christian salvation is, of its nature, corporate and somatic. And Catholicism, from this vantage, does not so much have a theology of the body, as it is a theology of the Body of Christ. Thus, voluntaristic individualism and Gnostic excarnation are deceptive counterfeits. They may strut and prance on the stage of Facebook and Twitter, but they cannot save.

4.3. Toward a Mystagogy of Christ's Ascension and Headship

As we have seen, even Charles Taylor admits to the poverty and dark side of secularity's "social imaginary." It constricts human experience and apprehension to the immanent sphere; it foments a spurious, often alienated individualism, a condition that recalls the terrible discernment of the Letter to the Ephesians: "Separated from Christ, alienated from the commonwealth of Israel, strangers to the covenants of promise, having no hope and without God in the world" (Eph. 2:12). The urgent theological-pastoral task of the Church is to bring the light of salvation in Christ to those "who dwell in darkness and the shadow of death" (Luke 1:79).

The task is most decidedly a mystagogic one, and, in particular, one that requires theological-pastoral soundings of the mystery of Christ's Ascension and headship. And it will have inseparable speculative and liturgical dimensions. Its point of departure might well be the short yet telling question 8, article 3 of the *Tertia Pars*: "Utrum Christus sit caput omnium hominum"— Whether Christ is the Head of all men? It, therefore, requires of all of us a new kindling of our Christic imagination.

---

30. *Placuit Deo* 11. The interior quote is from Thomas Aquinas, *De veritate* 29.5.

Let me, therefore, mention briefly three contemporary authors whose work, I believe, provides resources for our task. To cite them is also to acknowledge gratefully my debt to them. The first is the indefatigable and incisive Australian Jesuit Gerald O'Collins, who taught for many years at Rome's Gregorian University. His recent book is entitled *A Christology of Religions*.[31] In some ways, it is an initial exploration, though one that is rich and suggestive. What impresses is that in a day of soteriological relativism, it contains a robust assertion of the unique and universal salvific efficacy of Jesus Christ. It could well be read as a commentary upon the verses of Colossians: "In Christ all the fullness of God was pleased to dwell, and through Christ to reconcile to himself all things, whether on earth or in heaven, making peace by the blood of his cross" (Col. 1:19–20).

Clearly, O'Collins refuses to marginalize the cross, but sees it inscribed upon all history and the cosmos itself. Indeed, a distinctive feature of the book is O'Collins's focus upon the high priestly intercession of the ascended Christ, not only for the Church, but for the world. The Lamb, once slain, stands in eternal intercession before the throne of God, continuing his salvific mission and exercising present agency.

And by uniting itself to the ascended Jesus's eternal sacrifice for all, the Church, the Body of the Savior, furthers the transformation of the world. As the Third Eucharistic Prayer pleads, "May this sacrifice of our reconciliation, we pray, O Lord, advance the peace and salvation of all the world" (*Haec Hostia nostrae reconciliationis proficiat, quaesumus Domine, ad totius mundi pacem atque salutem*).[32]

I might even venture a step beyond O'Collins's explicit insight and propose that the intercession before the Father offered by Jesus, the High Priest, is not in "words" (however heavenly) but

---

31. Gerald O'Collins, *A Christology of Religions* (Maryknoll, NY: Orbis, 2018).
32. Eucharistic Prayer III.

in his very person. His very being is to be Eucharist. Such realization may finally open toward a Christological-Eucharistic reading of reality itself, a Eucharistic ontology. It can also sensitize us in discerning *semina Eucharistiae*—seeds of the Eucharist—in all of history and creation.

The second recent book that I have found rich in possibilities for a mystagogy focused upon the headship of Jesus Christ is Rowan Williams's *Christ the Heart of Creation*.[33] The book is a creative retrieval and extension of the Church's classical Christology as it found metaphysical articulation in Thomas Aquinas. It proves a powerful antidote to the Christological reductionism that figures so prominently today. Besides Aquinas, Williams appreciatively engages with theologians like Calvin and Barth, Bonhoeffer, Przywara, and Farrer.

Williams begins with a salutary reminder: "Reflecting on the language of doctrine will not in itself do the job of persuading anyone to believe. What it may do is to give more depth and substance to imagining what it is like to believe and what new connections or possibilities are opened up by speaking and imagining like this."[34] Given the stunted imagination of secularity, this is already no small gain.

Then, in words that could serve as a résumé of Aquinas's teaching, Williams writes, "Now, since Christ's humanity is that of the Head of the Body of believers—since nothing impedes or limits his relation with and solidarity with those who are incorporated into his life through the Spirit—whatever he merits, whatever his human life makes possible in terms of relation to God, is by definition shared with that Body." And he continues, "His humanity is the ground of that 'kinship' with the human race that reaches its fullness in the life of the Church."[35]

---

33. Rowan Williams, *Christ: The Heart of Creation* (London: Bloomsbury Continuum, 2018).

34. Williams, xi.

35. Williams, 130–31.

Later, in appreciative dialogue with Bonhoeffer, he voices his persuasion that "the Christological transformation of humanity is the transformation of all our constitutive relationships as humans, so that they are now able to move more freely towards this maximal for-otherness"—thereby imaging Christ's total being for others.[36]

The newness of the constitutive relationships that define the members of the Body of Christ is such that

> their lives are linked to one another in a way that is not simply that of individual to individual, but in a comprehensive pattern of interdependence. . . . If the incarnate Word creates community in this unique way, every individual united with the Word becomes a point in a network of mutually defining and conditioning subjects in such a way that no individual's temporal or eternal well-being can be isolated from that of all others.[37]

One recalls the words of Benedict XVI in *Spe Salvi*:

> Our hope is always essentially also hope for others; only thus is it truly hope for me too. As Christians we should never limit ourselves to asking: how can I save myself? We should also ask: what can I do in order that others may be saved and that for them too the star of hope may rise? Then I will have done my utmost for my own personal salvation as well.[38]

There are no buffered selves in the Body of Christ.

Rowan Williams, as both theologian and pastor, has been fully engaged with the intellectual, artistic, and social issues of modernity. In *Christ the Heart of Creation*, he has articulated a

36. Williams, 204.
37. Williams, 249.
38. Benedict XVI, *Spe Salvi* 48, encyclical letter, November 30, 2007, vatican.va.

view of salvation in Christ that is both faithful to the great Tradition, yet innovative in its consideration of the headship of Jesus Christ and of the new relationships of which he is the source and center. And these relationships, though they attain sacramental fullness in the Church, aim at the transfiguration of all created reality.

However, though Williams stresses the ongoing transformative agency of Christ, he does not underscore in any notable detail the Ascension. Yet clearly it is the risen and exalted Lord who acts both in the Church and in the world as the heart of the new creation.

Therefore, I turn lastly to a liturgical theologian whose meditations on the Ascension form a fitting complement to both O'Collins and Williams.

The French Dominican Jean Corbon was one of the foremost liturgical theologians of the past century. As is well known, he played a major role in part 2 of the *Catechism of the Catholic Church*, "The Celebration of the Christian Mystery," and was the author of its fine part 4, "Christian Prayer." His book, *The Wellspring of Worship*, is a splendid mystagogical probing of the Church's liturgy and its source in the Paschal Mystery of Christ as the unique access to the communion of the Holy Trinity. For him, the Ascension is integral to the Paschal Mystery, not its postscript. Indeed, Ascension is the *telos* of Incarnation.

Corbon writes, "When the faithful gathered to manifest and become the body of Christ, they saw their Lord both as present and as coming. He is the head and draws his body toward the Father while giving it life through his Spirit." It is the ascended Christ, who is at the right hand of the Father, who sends his Spirit. For the Ascension is "the activation of the paschal energy of Christ 'who fills all things' (Eph. 4:10). It is the ever new 'moment' of his coming."[39]

Thus, Corbon gives further specificity to O'Collins's invocation of the agency of Christ the High Priest. In a passage as poetic as it is profound, he writes,

> The heavenly liturgy is the gestation of the new creation because our history is sustained by Christ who is now in the bosom of the Holy Trinity. It is there that the Lord of history is at every moment the Savior of his body and of the least of his brothers and sisters: he calls and feeds them, heals them and makes them grow, forgives and transforms them, delivers and divinizes them, tells them that they are loved by the Father and are being increasingly united to him until they reach their full stature in the kingdom.[40]

The mysteries of Ascension and Transfiguration breach the ultimately dehumanizing boundaries of the immanent frame and the buffered self and inaugurate the new creation. Contemplating their iconic representations in great works of Christian art furthers the graced realization that "if anyone is in Christ Jesus [there is] a new creation, the old has passed away, behold, the new has come!" (2 Cor. 5:17).

5. CONCLUSION: TOWARD A EUCHARISTIC MYSTICISM

The paschal energies emanating from the ascended Jesus Christ permeate the world. But they achieve privileged concentration in the Eucharistic celebration. The presence of the ascending Christ in the Eucharist is at once personal, corporate, and cosmic. For

39. Jean Corbon, *The Wellspring of Worship*, trans. Matthew J. O'Connell (Mahwah, NJ: Paulist, 1988), 36, 37.
40. Corbon, *Wellspring*, 42.

the one who is lifted up "draws all to himself" (John 12:32), so that Christ may be "all in all" (Col. 3:11).

In the Eucharist, the ascending Lord continues his saving work of transformation, sending his Spirit to effect communion, conforming us to his Eucharistic self, thereby extending his incarnational presence in the world.[41] Here, salvation as incorporation into Christ is most real and most actual.

Nonetheless, because our transformation is not yet complete, because we ourselves are often not really present, whether to ourselves or to others, our celebration of Christ's Real Presence "does not diminish awareness of his absence; it does not diminish but strengthens our longing for his coming in glory. Neither then does it invite us to suppose that our union with Christ is a union in which the cross is only behind us and not also before us."[42]

In the Church today, we are urgently called to a new experiential realization of the mystery we celebrate, in its height and depth and length and breadth. It is this experiential realization that I refer to as "a Eucharistic mysticism." A prime responsibility we hold, as theologians and pastors, is to promote a new Eucharistic mystagogy in which contemplation and action nourish one another, in the finest tradition of *contemplata aliis tradere*, both in the intellectual and the social sphere. And so we pray daily for the fulfillment of our hope, the Body of Christ come to full growth:

> Therefore, O Lord, as we now celebrate the memorial of our redemption, we remember Christ's Death and his descent to the realm of the dead, we proclaim his Resurrection and his Ascension to your right hand. And, as we await his coming in

41. Commenting upon the tripartite body of Christ—his ascended body, his Eucharistic body, and his ecclesial body—Anthony Kelly writes, "The different aspects or realizations of Christ's body are so interwoven, that one has a sense of a corporeal field of incarnational communication rather than of separable entities" (*Upward*, 87).

42. Farrow, *Ascension Theology*, 79. In *Upward*, chapter 5, "The Ascension and the Eucharist: Real Absence and Real Presence," Anthony Kelly contends, "Christ's ascension does not mean disembodiment"; rather, it is we who "are not yet fully embodied in him, as we are destined to be" (95). And such incorporation into Christ can never bypass the cross.

glory, we offer you his Body and Blood, the sacrifice acceptable to you which brings salvation to the whole world [*toti mundo salutare*].

Look, O Lord, upon the Sacrifice which you yourself have provided for your Church. Grant in your loving kindness to all who partake of this one Bread and one Chalice that, gathered into one Body by the Holy Spirit, they may truly become a living sacrifice in Christ—to the praise of your glory.[43]

43. Eucharistic Prayer IV. In *Ascension Theology*, Farrow writes, "If indeed Christ is present in his absence, present in a manner distinct from the parousia that is yet to come, he is present precisely in his freedom to include us in his offering and in his glory. He is present, that is, in his freedom to create by the Spirit a community of ascension and oblation, which is what the Church is" (66).

9. Resurrection and Real Presence

To Be in Christ Is to Live in Communion

Recently, I encountered a woman, a nun, who had spent the better part of a year living an almost solitary existence, a "desert" year given over to prayer and communion with God.

Speaking of her prayer, she surprised me by saying that a staple of her prayer life was the Creed; not merely because it formed a living link with the whole Body of Christ but because she prayed the Creed as, in its essence, a "love song." Once I thought about it, it made perfect sense. What we confess of God in the Creed are not dry propositions but divine praises. We proclaim God who creates out of goodness all that is visible and invisible. A review in *Commonweal* on the search for "dark matter" in the universe reminded us that "the entire visible universe is but a drop in the cosmic sea."[1]

In the Creed, we thank God, who, out of utmost compassion, sends the dearly Beloved to dwell in our midst; the Beloved who, for the sake of our salvation and well-being, offers himself in life and in death and is raised to new life.

In the Creed, we glorify God who establishes us in truth by the gift of the Holy Spirit; the Spirit who effects the communion of saints by *being* the forgiveness of sin and everlasting life. All these themes are but multiple variations on the one *cantus firmus*

---

* This essay was originally published as "Resurrection & Real Presence: To Be in Christ Is to Live in Communion," *Commonweal* 117, no. 7 (April 6, 1990): 210–13.

1. Chet Raymo, "It's Darker Than We Thought," review of *The Fifth Essence: The Search for Dark Matter in the Universe* by Lawrence M. Krauss, *Commonweal* 117, no. 4 (February 23, 1990): 118–19, at 118.

that is God's love: indeed, the one incomprehensible mystery of the triune God who is love.

Once made, the point appeared self-evident. Had not Johann Sebastian Bach shown as much long ago? For among the most sublime of his cantatas, the one which, in a sense, sums up all the rest, is the "Credo" of his Mass in B Minor: a "Credo" that is surely a cantata of love. The music and words sing out the wonder of creation and redemption, the alpha and omega of our origin and destiny: coming forth from love and called to love's wedding feast. Bach's "Credo" structures a cosmos and proclaims it a work of love. And the hinge of the whole is the Resurrection of Christ: "et resurrexit tertia die." The brilliance of Bach's trumpets underscores the tradition's conviction: "Christ, raised from the dead, will never die again; death no longer holds dominion over him" (Rom. 6:9). The trumpets herald the dark luminosity of Resurrection, recapitulating both visible and invisible, *visibilium et invisibilium*. For the appearances of the risen One provide sacramental glimpses into a world unseen, from which come healing, grace, and peace.

Without Christ's Resurrection, the universe of love is but wishful myth, well-meant illusion. The Creed, a hymn of love, hinges on the Resurrection. On this hinge swings wide the stone set before the tomb, opening an abyss before which the women stand and tremble. "He is risen; he is not here" (Mark 16:6). Joyful affirmation or terrifying revelation? Without doubt both; but both ever together—as Rudolf Otto speaks of the holy as ever evoking both dread and desire. "Maria" . . . "Rabboni": the ecstatic recognition, rejoicing at having been found, which is followed at once by the imperative, "Do not cling to me. . . . Go and tell" (cf. John 20:16–17). Here vision impels to mission; revelation serves transformation.

Resurrection faith stretches heart and mind to the breaking point, as they stagger under the unbearable lightness of being.

Is it any wonder that we frequently retreat before the mystery, reducing it to more manageable perspectives? And so, certain scholars contend, "He is risen into the kerygma"—betraying thereby their inordinate appetite for ideas. No resurrection there, only a ghostly apparition. Or, some ecclesiastical functionaries insist, "He is risen into the institutional church"—displaying, by the very contention, a rather petrified imagination. That would merely exchange one tomb for another. Or, others of more liberationist bent cry, "He is risen as the people"—manifesting their often havoc-wreaking innocence. A provocative resuscitation, perhaps, but no true resurrection. But against all infringement of the mystery, the angel stands adamant: "He is risen; he is not here!"

Traces may be found in "proclamation" and "people" and even, however implausible this may seem, in "institution." But these, in themselves, are but footprints left by the Beloved in his passage, as John of the Cross knew and suffered. They press us onward:

> Pouring out a thousand graces,
> He passed these groves in haste
> And having looked at them,
> With His image alone,
> Clothed them in beauty.[2]

For in the Resurrection of Jesus Christ, we confront new creation, transformed existence. As Sebastian Moore has written, "It's he that we are experiencing, but extraordinarily, in a way that takes us beyond ourselves, into a new world." Between the old and the new there is both continuity and discontinuity, identity in difference. All the meditation of the centuries-long tradition is but *lectio divina et continua* upon Paul's wonder-filled rhetoric in First

2. John of the Cross, *The Spiritual Canticle*, stanza 5, in *The Collected Works of St. John of the Cross*, trans. Kieran Kavanaugh and Otilio Rodriguez (Washington, DC: ICS Publications, 1979), 410.

Corinthians: "What is sown a perishable thing is raised imperishable. Sown in humiliation, it is raised in glory. Sown an animate body, raised a spiritual body" (15:42–44). Body, most certainly, but not merely resuscitated body: body transformed in the Spirit of God, imbued with God's power and glory. Body, assuredly: but in the full biblical sense of relational identity, no longer limited or thwarted, but diaphanous to Spirit. Body, indeed: but motile and incandescent, penetrating closed spaces and the confines of hearts. Paradoxical physicality: like "silent music . . . sounding solitude—*música callada . . . soledad sonora*" (as John of the Cross exclaims with eloquent stammer).[3]

Here, if anywhere, we encounter Real Presence. Presence so real as to be palpable—yet so discreet as to demand discernment. "Were not our hearts burning within us?" the disciples ponder at the close of Luke's narrative of the risen One's appearance on the road to Emmaus. It is the recognition-confession that Christian experience and discipleship will reiterate through the centuries.

A contemporary student of the New Testament writes, "The resurrection experience that gave birth to the Christian movement was the experience of the continuing presence of a personal, transcendent, and transforming power within the community."[4] This personal, embodied presence of the risen Christ defines the newness of the New Covenant, binding eyewitnesses and those to whom they testify into one body of love, at-oned in a common Eucharist: "Praised be the God and Father of our Lord Jesus Christ, who in great mercy has begotten us anew into a living hope by the Resurrection of Jesus Christ from the dead. . . . You have not seen Christ, yet you love him, and believing in him now, even without seeing, your joy overflows, a joy beyond all telling" (1 Pet. 1:3–8).

3. John of the Cross, *The Spiritual Canticle*, stanza 15.

4. Luke Timothy Johnson, *The Writings of the New Testament: An Interpretation* (Philadelphia: Fortress, 1986), 102.

There is simply no Christian faith without the density of Real Presence. If Christ be not raised, preaching and faith alike are useless, empty, vain. So Paul told the Corinthians; and there is no reason to retract his assessment today. For the Christian, the unique access to God is *through* Jesus Christ, God's Beloved and our Lord, who *lives* and reigns now. The living Christ *is* the presence of God in human flesh, the temple in whom all God's creatures can nest, the Bridegroom who is the unique Beloved of each. If Paul, in Romans 8, proclaims ecstatically the presence of love from which nothing can sunder—"neither death nor life, neither powers nor potentates, neither zenith nor abyss"—he makes patent that this presence is rendered real and irrevocable in the death and Resurrection of Christ.

The Christian life, the life of discipleship, *is* life in Christ, not metaphorically but really; not imitatively but participatively. What Baptism initiates, the life of discipleship realizes—not without cost. For the only way to Resurrection is the way of the cross; the only authentic mode of discipleship is the one that retraces the journey of the Lord—or, better, relives it, by living it in Christ. Perhaps no more moving contemporary witness can be found than that of Dietrich Bonhoeffer in his *Letters and Papers from Prison*. In his letter of August 21, 1944, Bonhoeffer achieves a realization that the disciple must ever appreciate anew, in each new circumstance of his or her life. "The key to everything is the [phrase] 'in him.' All that we rightly expect from God and pray for is to be found in Jesus Christ. . . . We must always live close to the presence of God, for that is newness of life; and then nothing is impossible for all things are possible with God."[5]

The new life in the living Christ is relational existence. The very identity of the Christian is to be in relation to Christ: "christened"—that is, "anointed"—through Christ with God's Holy

---

5. Dietrich Bonhoeffer, *Letters and Papers from Prison*, ed. Eberhard Bethge, trans. Reginald H. Fuller (London: SCM, 1953), 183.

Spirit. So intimate is this union with the living Lord that the Church's mystical tradition, from Origen through Bernard of Clairvaux to John of the Cross, found commentary upon the biblical Song of Songs to be the least inadequate way of expressing the unique love binding the Beloved to those he enlivens.

Yet it is also clear that this relation to Christ is not individualistic in any exclusive sense. Indeed, to be "in Christ" is, primarily, to live in communion: related to self and others through Christ, becoming members of one body. And the goal intended by Christ's redemptive love is the gathering of the whole Body, the "many" of the New Covenant in his Blood. This is the New Testament and the Patristic age fully appreciated. How can Real Presence not be foundationally inclusive? How can the new Temple in the Spirit, which is the risen Body of Christ, not embrace all the nations in its ampleness?

Not conflict but profound harmony issues from the confession of Christ as the unique Beloved of each and as Head of the entire Body of believers who draw their life from him. In the fourth Gospel's magnificent portrait of Jesus's hour of glory as his exaltation upon the cross, the consummation of the Good News is the pouring forth of the life-giving water and blood from the pierced side of Christ upon his mother and beloved disciple. These, the primordial witnesses and recipients of the new life in the Spirit, are inseparably particular individuals and representatives of the community: humanity regenerated.

Only the advent of modernity, articulated with devastating genius by Descartes, saw the propagation of an atomistic individualism that loosed the relational bonds between persons, even as it fragmented matter and spirit into separate and competing spheres. "Spiritual body," body transformed in Spirit, becomes an incomprehensible symbol in a Cartesian world, regulated by "clear and distinct ideas" that serve the purposes of power and control. Is it any coincidence that commentary on the Song of

Songs, as consummate and privileged evocation of the universe of love, soon ceases in a West avid for the subjugation of supposedly spiritless nature and peoples?

A Church founded on resurrection faith and nourished by Real Presence can only be an adversarial witness to this one-dimensional myopia of modernity. For the vision of the risen One is, as Paul exemplifies, ardent with expectation, opening a new horizon of hope for all creation. Christ, the New Adam become life-giving Spirit (1 Cor. 15:45), is himself the firstborn of a multitude of brothers and sisters (Rom. 8:29). The Resurrection of Christ thus marks a new beginning whose repercussions touch not only humanity but the entire created universe, now groaning and longing for the appearance and ministration of sons and daughters after God's own heart (Rom. 8:19). The Real Presence of Christ is, therefore, the principle and sustaining power of the realization of humanity's vocation to divine filiation and universal reconciliation. This corporate destiny is confessed with unsurpassed boldness in the Epistle to the Ephesians, whether by Paul himself or a disciple who had appropriated and extended Paul's mystical vision.

Remarkable, in the first chapter of Ephesians, is the author's insistent prayer for a sense of wisdom and discernment, a real apprehension (in Newman's terms) of the power of God revealed in the Resurrection of Jesus Christ from the dead. A power now at work in believers! And the purpose of that power is set forth, in chapter 4, with a depth we still scarcely fathom. It is nothing less than the building up of Christ's body, the realization of that one perfected person, who is Christ come to completion (Eph. 4:12–13).

The power in question, the power who is Holy Spirit, is—and this is crucial—persuasive, not coercive. Its manner is a bold if compassionate speaking of the truth (Eph. 4:15); and precisely by so doing, granting to all freedom and scope to grow into Christ, the alpha and omega of maturation in the Spirit. One need not naively deny that an untransformed world still falls under the illusory sway of principalities and powers. Though Christ's victory renders them ultimately impotent, they still make empty show of majesty and mastery. But their being, if not their immediate effect, is ultimately insubstantial. On those occasions when the program of truth-telling seems actually to have been translated into practice, and appeal is made to persuasion rather than coercion (as was the case with President Václav Havel of Czechoslovakia), one thrills to the promise the Paraclete, the Spirit of truth, offers ever anew.

The singular sense of union between the risen Christ and his disciples of every age provides the key to the distinctive patristic scriptural interpretation and pastoral practice and its continued relevance today. For the mystery, which Scripture illuminates, is, finally, the "whole Christ." And the making of the whole Christ is, at once, the unmerited gift of God and the urgent responsibility of believers. Pope Saint Leo the Great but recapitulates, in this regard, the common conviction of the undivided tradition of East and West:

> Beloved, it cannot be doubted that the Son of God assumed human nature so intimately that there is one single Christ in the one who was first-born of all creation, and also in all his saints. The head cannot be separated from the members, nor can the members from the head.

> That is why we daily celebrate the Lord's pasch with the unleavened bread of sincerity and truth. The leaven of our old malice is thrown away, and a new creature drinks deep and feeds upon the Lord himself. For our participation in the body and blood of Christ has this effect: it makes us become what we receive. It enables us, with our whole being, to bear him,

in whom and with whom we have died and been buried and risen again.[6]

The privileged place of encounter and exchange between the risen Christ and Christians remains the Eucharistic celebration. Here is enacted the *admirabile commercium*. Here, if anywhere, is celebrated Real Presence at its highest pitch. Liturgical celebration does not substitute for what the Spirit may be doing elsewhere but provides its norm and substantiation in Christ, some might even say, its transubstantiation.

I know of course (and have myself rehearsed) all the laments concerning tasteless liturgy, unhappy homilies, unmemorable music. And yet, for all the legitimate concern about the *opus operantis* (what *we* do as presiders, ministers, people), the primacy lies with the *opus operatum* (what *God* has done and is doing through the risen Christ). Can we dismiss, as only Orthodox exaggeration, what Alexander Schmemann urges: "The liturgy is, before everything else, the joyous gathering of those who are to meet the risen Lord and to enter with him into the bridal chamber."[7] Can faith in Resurrection and Real Presence entail any less?

That is why the full panoply of the Easter Vigil is required merely to initiate us into the Real Presence of the risen Lord, in the midst of the community which he constitutes and continues to found by the outpouring of his Spirit. This "Mother of Vigils," this unique "Mass of the Resurrection," is the measure and point of reference for every liturgical celebration, however modest. For the Easter Vigil shows that all creation is implicated in the coming to birth of Christians, by the anointing of the Holy Spirit, in the womb of the Church. Nothing is omitted: fasting and feasting, silence and music, darkness and light, water, oil, bread, and

6. Leo the Great, "Sermo 12 de Passione" 3.6–7. Translation based on an excerpt prepared by the Spiritual Theology Department of the Pontifical University of the Holy Cross for vatican. va: "Saint Leo the Great: Christ Lives in His Church."

7. Alexander Schmemann, *For the Life of the World: Sacraments and Orthodoxy* (Crestwood, NY: St. Vladimir's, 1973), 29.

wine. All body forth intimations of the Lord's transformed body, even as they conspire to effect the transformed embodiment of believers. Still, for all the splendid allusion and evocation, the issue remains, ultimately, one of faith. As John of the Cross insists, only the dark night of faith can be prelude to Easter dawn. And faith finally relies not upon rational demonstration but upon spiritual discernment.

The rest is in the living. But since it has long been my peculiar habit to meditate with the Bible in one hand and the *New Yorker* in the other, let me close this meditation in like fashion.

A 1990 issue of the *New Yorker* featured a remarkable poem by Czesław Miłosz entitled "Creating the World." Toward its end, the celestials address mortals thus:

> Oh, to have so little, nothing except feasts of love!
> How feeble your defense against the abyss!

And the poem's last stanza, summing up mortals' life on earth, reads,

> And the sun rises and the sun sets,
> And the sun rises and the sun sets
> While they go on running, running.[8]

Now, in counterpoint to this depiction of the human condition, a fugal variation upon a Johannine theme.

Early on the first day of the week, the sun having barely risen, Peter and the disciple whom Jesus loved came running to the tomb. Heart pounding, ears ringing with Magdala's message, they came running, running. Then, the one whom Jesus loved, in a final burst of desire, outstripped the other and reached the tomb first. The linen cloths, binding the dead, lay discarded, useless

---

8. Czesław Miłosz, "Creating the World," *The New Yorker*, February 26, 1990.

now. But the cloth that had covered the face of the Beloved was not found with the rest. It lay carefully folded in its own place apart. And love, taking all in at a glance, believed in the sun that never sets.

10. A Eucharistic Form of Life

In his pathbreaking *Grammar of Assent*, John Henry Newman famously distinguished between "notional apprehension" and "real apprehension." He then asserts that "theology properly and directly deals with notional apprehension; religion with imaginative."[1] It is important to note two features of Newman's reflection. First, it is not a question of either/or but, decidedly, of both/and. Both intellect and imagination, mind and heart, reason and affection must be engaged. Theology and religion are intimately, indeed indispensably, related.

Secondly, as the above quote indicates, "real apprehension" may also be designated "imaginative." For Newman, the passage from the merely notional to the real is mediated by the imagination by evocative images that captivate the heart. Hence the aesthetic has a crucial role to play in the cultivation of a robust spiritual life.

Thus, later in the *Grammar of Assent*, Newman makes appeal to the Church's liturgical life as the fruit of real and not merely notional apprehension. It is "the imagination and the heart" that, creating hymns like *Veni Creator* and *Veni Sancte Spiritus*, convert notional propositions about the divinity of the Holy Spirit into objects of real apprehension and assent.[2]

---

* This essay was originally published as "A Eucharistic Form of Life," *Nova et Vetera* (Winter 2023).

1. John Henry Newman, *An Essay in Aid of a Grammar of Assent*, ed. I.T. Ker (Oxford: Clarendon, 1985), 82.

2. Newman, Grammar, 94. See the remark by Paul Murray on Aquinas's sequence for the Feast of Corpus Christi: "In a work like *Lauda Sion* what offers sanction for belief is not simply the repetition of doctrinal statements, but the sharp and bright manner in which these state-

We are all familiar with the transforming effect on the young Francis of the image of the crucified in the church of San Damiano. And Teresa of Avila, after years of rather routine and rote religious life, experienced a renewed conversion through her encounter with a convent crucifix.

I dare say each of us can identify "images" (whether pictorial, sculptural, or musical) that have played a prominent part in the awakening and sustaining of our spiritual vision and commitment. Such vital, life-engendering images form an essential part of the religious life of every committed Christian.

But I think it important also to discern less wholesome images: images that are spiritually damaging, destructive, even demonic. There is the internet-fueled scourge of pornographic images, which both demean and addict. The image of the swastika unleashed legions of hatred in the past and still continues to enthrall some today. The human *imago Dei* has too often been perverted into *imago diaboli*, and images play a preponderant role in that degradation.

In this reflection I would like to offer a concrete instance of such a "negative" image that impacted me in a particularly profound way. As so often, mere happenstance led to the place and situation in question. But what I experienced there I count providential.

The place was the relatively small town of Litomerice in the Czech Republic, about forty miles northwest of Prague. A friend and I decided to drive out of Prague to savor something of the Czech countryside. As I recall, it was a sunny spring day, ideal for an excursion. Arriving at the town, we had lunch and then set out to explore. We soon came upon a Baroque church, in the Jesuit style, that we entered. However, instead of a quiet place of prayer, we found a scene of wanton destruction. We later learned that the

ments are made, the sheer memorability of the lines." *Aquinas at Prayer: The Bible, Mysticism and Poetry* (London: Bloomsbury, 2013), 231.

church had been converted into a warehouse during the Communist regime and left slowly to decay—part of the roof missing.

But the dominant image (awful, yet revelatory) was the sight of eight side altars lining the central nave. From each of them, the tabernacle had been gouged out, leaving mere emptiness, a gaping void. One sensed a truly malevolent action, opening upon a threatening abyss. Real Presence had been defiantly rejected. Absence prevailed.

The apocalyptic scene was heightened by an exhibition that had been mounted in the desecrated church. It depicted emaciated figures who had been imprisoned by the Nazis in the forced labor camp near the town (whose German name was Leitmeritz when it formed part of the Sudetenland). There were also letters and objects left by inmates of the nearby concentration camp of Theresienstadt. Recollections of those tortured under the Communist regime added to the desolation. The overwhelming sensation was that of a demonic inhumanity. The defacing of the altars was replicated in the defacing of the tortured and murdered human beings. As though the demonic intent was to obliterate all traces of the face of Christ.

What struck me, then, as revelatory was the nexus between the repudiation of presence represented by the violated tabernacles and the parallel violation of humanity. Of course, absence also assumes guises less stark, yet also deadening and deadly: loss of meaning and hope, resentment breeding hatred, desperation that turns destructive of self and others. I realized (in Newman's strong sense of the term) that one can fully appreciate and celebrate Real Presence only if one seriously comes to grips with its contradiction: real absence. The culture of death is fueled by a denial of presence, not only in its extraordinary manifestation in Litomerice, but in its all too ordinary appearances in our culture and our daily lives.

If this Dantean intuition resonates, then it suggests that the vocation of Christians and, especially, Catholics is to be stewards and witnesses of Real Presence in their lives and activities. To be so, they must be firmly rooted in faith in the Real Presence of Jesus Christ in the Eucharist. As Benedict XVI affirmed in his rich apostolic exhortation *Sacramentum Caritatis*, "Every great reform [in the Church] has in some way been linked to the rediscovery of belief in the Lord's Eucharistic presence among his people."[3]

A crucial dimension of that "rediscovery" must be the firm conviction of the unique agency of Christ in the Eucharistic celebration. He is the one priest as he is the one Savior. Indeed, salvation is the priestly work of Jesus himself, enacted once for all, and made present ever anew in the Eucharistic sacrifice. At a time when there is the persistent peril of "horizontalism" in our liturgical gatherings, the inversion of the community upon itself, Benedict's insistence is imperative:

> The Eucharist is Christ who gives himself to us and continually builds us up as his body. Hence, in the striking interplay between the Eucharist which builds up the Church, and the Church herself which "makes" the Eucharist, the primary causality is expressed in the first formula: the Church is able to celebrate and adore the mystery of Christ present in the Eucharist precisely because Christ first gave himself to her in the sacrifice of the Cross. The Church's ability to "make" the Eucharist is completely rooted in Christ's self-gift to her.[4]

This agency of Christ, his ongoing self-gift, is, paradoxically, made possible because of his Ascension to the Father's glory. The manifestations of this ongoing and multiform "giving" are manifold, as the book of Revelation witnesses in the letters to

3. Benedict XVI, *Sacramentum Caritatis* 6, apostolic exhortation, February 22, 2007, vatican.va.

4. *Sacramentum Caritatis* 14.

the churches. The risen, ascended Lord stands at the door of the churches and knocks (Rev. 3:20), bringing both judgment and healing. He does not exercise an absent lordship but present and active agency. And his presence and agency receive their fullest expression in the Eucharist. As Paul Griffiths rightly remarks, "The principal condition of the possibility of the Eucharist is exactly that Jesus has ascended. . . . After the Ascension, his flesh, veiled as bread, and his blood veiled as wine, can be touched and tasted everywhere and at once, without constraint by the metronome of time or the map grid of space."[5]

But this Real Presence of the risen, ascended Lord does not preclude but, rather, calls forth and enables, indeed, requires the participatory presence of those gathered to celebrate. The "full conscious, and active participation" of the congregation, desired and promoted by the council,[6] is most fundamentally our participation in the Paschal Mystery—the Death, Resurrection, and Ascension of Jesus Christ. By this participation in the Eucharist, we truly become the Body of Christ, living members of the living Head.

Indeed, Benedict XVI recalls that "Christian antiquity used the same words, *Corpus Christi*, to designate Christ's body born of the Virgin Mary, his Eucharistic body, and his ecclesial body. This clear datum of the tradition helps us to appreciate the inseparability of Christ and the Church."[7] In this regard, the Australian theologian Anthony Kelly perceptively comments, "The different aspects or realizations of Christ's body are so interwoven, that one has a sense of a corporeal field of incarnational communication rather than of separable entities."[8]

---

5. Paul Griffiths, *Christian Flesh* (Stanford, CA: Stanford University Press, 2018), 51.

6. Vatican Council II, *Sacrosanctum Concilium* 14, quoted in *Catechism of the Catholic Church* 1141.

7. *Sacramentum Caritatis* 15.

8. Anthony J. Kelly, *Upward: Faith, Church, and the Ascension of Christ* (Collegeville, MN: Liturgical, 2014), 87.

The *novum* of the Paschal Mystery inaugurates a new transformed order of relations constitutive of a new self. What Pascal calls the new *ordo caritatis* might fittingly be called the *ordo
Eucharistiae*. For Christians are nourished and schooled in the
Eucharist to "put on the Lord Jesus Christ" (Rom. 13:14) who is
our "hope of Glory" (Col. 1:27). Indeed, if our participation is
"full, conscious, and active," then "we all with unveiled faces, beholding the glory of the Lord, are being changed into his likeness
from one degree of glory to another" (2 Cor. 3:18). Thus, Saint
Paul exclaims with wonderment that "if anyone is in Christ he is
a new creation" (2 Cor. 5:17). In full harmony with this Pauline
vision, Benedict XVI, drawing upon his beloved Saint Augustine,
insists that, in the Eucharist, "Christ assimilates us to himself."
Consequently, "not only have we become Christians, we have become Christ himself."[9]

This "Christification," this incorporation into the Body of
Christ, is, of course, *in via*. As Gregory of Nyssa loved to insist, Christian life is both *telos* and *arche*: an ending that is ever
a new beginning. In this vein, Anthony Kelly rightly comments,
"Christ's Ascension does not mean disembodiment"; rather, it is
we who "are not yet fully embodied in him, as we are destined to
be."[10] We are not yet "fully embodied in him," fully transformed
into our new selfhood as members of Christ's Body. To put it
another way: *Jesus Christ is truly present in the Eucharist; it is we
who are not fully present to him, to ourselves, and to others.* To the
extent that we ourselves are deficient in our presence, we cannot
hope to be advocates and witnesses of Real Presence to the world.

Hence the need to engage in practices of presence, practices
that realize and enhance what *Sacramentum Caritatis* calls the
new "Eucharistic form of life."[11] It is the life to which we are
summoned each time the celebrant admonishes at the beginning

9. *Sacramentum Caritatis* 36.
10. Kelly, *Upward*, 95.
11. *Sacramentum Caritatis* 70–83.

of the Eucharistic Prayer, "Let us give thanks to the Lord our God!" and we consent by responding, "It is right and just!" Let us briefly consider, then, some practices by which we become more fully present to God, self, and others. Those I would underscore are attention, respect, reverence, adoration, and, permeating all, gratitude.

These practices need to be even more intentional in a secular culture that provides little external support to Christian faith. We need them to sharpen our "spiritual senses" in a culture where even our physical senses so often atrophy, dulled by sensory overload.

We might use the venerable image of a "spiritual ladder" to sketch briefly these indispensable practices.

The bottom rung of the ladder is *attention*. In a technological and media culture of countless distractions, we need to cultivate the discipline of paying attention, of being alert to the present moment with its challenges and possibilities. Without concentrated attention, presence is lessened and absence prevails. Indeed, attention is the prerequisite for dialogue. It fosters careful listening in whose absence conversation soon deteriorates into competing monologues.

A second rung of the ladder is *respect*. The word itself is suggestive. Its root meaning—*re-spicere*—is to look attentively. Not a quick passing glance, much less a looking down upon, a *despicere*, but a careful regard. Not the cell phone snapshot of some masterpiece of art as one dashes through a museum—pausing briefly for a selfie with the work of art dimly in the background: Mona Lisa and me!

Respect embraces care for the natural environment and even for material things. Saint Benedict in his *Rule* mandates a regard "for all the goods and utensils of the monastery as if they were sacred vessels of the altar, aware that nothing is to be neglected."[12]

---

12. *The Rule of St. Benedict in English*, trans. Timothy Fry (Collegeville, MN: Liturgical, 1980), 31.10–11.

By contrast, much of our "throwaway culture," so often de-cried by Pope Francis, not only quickly discards things deemed "out of fashion," but flippantly promotes actual abuse of the creation entrusted by God to human care.

A third rung is *reverence*. It bespeaks recognition of the in-violable dignity of persons and the sense of a holy presence em-anating from faces often weary and burdened. Such reverence is crucially needed in a late-capitalist society that too often spurns the poor, the elderly, the unborn. Once again, the *Rule of Saint Benedict* offers salutary, if radical counsel: "All guests who present themselves are to be welcomed as Christ"; indeed, "By a bow of the head or a complete prostration of the body, Christ is to be adored because he is welcomed in them."[13]

But reverence for persons also requires that others never be treated as things to satisfy one's desires, whether economic or sex-ual. In a Catholic Eucharistic form of life, both social and sex-ual ethics form a "seamless garment."[14] In truth, there is a much closer relation between them then is often admitted: both must address issues of power. And both are subjected to the lordship of Jesus Christ of whose Body Christians are members. The Apostle Paul provides the ultimate foundation for the Christian practice of reverence: "Do you not know that your body is a temple of the Holy Spirit within you, which you have from God? You are not your own; you were bought with a price. So, glorify God in your body" (1 Cor. 6:19–20).

Attention, respect, and reverence as "practices of presence" yield a twofold fruit. They heighten the presence of the subject, enriching his or her sense of self. But they also permit the pres-ence of others to stand forth, disclosing their inherent mystery.

13. *Rule* 53.1, 53.7.
14. Note the sections in *Sacramentum Caritatis* devoted to "The Social Implications of the Eucharistic Mystery" (89) and "The Sanctification of the World and the Protection of Creation" (92).

Thus, in both subject and object, the ground is laid for what we yearn for at our truest and deepest: communion of persons.

A final practice that is assuming greater importance, especially among young people, is that of *Eucharistic Adoration*. Like the young Gerard Manley Hopkins, they turn "with a fling of the heart to the heart of the Host."[15] In Adoration, Christ unveils the mystery of his presence and our own. To be present, in that reverential attention that is contemplation, to him who loves us and gives himself for us fosters our passage from the notional to the real in our relationship with Jesus, who is Lord, Savior, and friend.

To eyes being transformed in faith, all intimations of presence find in the Eucharist their recapitulation and fulfillment. Here, persons' true dignity and destiny stand revealed; they bear the form and face of Jesus Christ.

In this way, the Eucharist becomes a school in which we develop our spiritual senses, learning to be attentive, respectful, and reverential and to carry these attitudes into our daily lives and our everyday relations with others. Indeed, a Eucharistic form of life transcends the separation of "contemplation" and "action" by forming believers into "contemplatives in action" whose lives are founded upon and guided by the Apostle's injunction: "And be thankful [*eucharistoi ginesthe*]. . . . Whatever you do, in word or deed, do everything in the name of the Lord Jesus, giving thanks [*eucharistountes*] to God the Father through him" (Col. 3:15,17).

Becoming ever more fully conformed to the Eucharistic Christ, we allow his Real Presence to permeate our world.

---

15. Gerard Manley Hopkins, "The Wreck of the Deutschland," Poetry Foundation, poetryfoundation.com. Hopkins's poetry has helped so many to pass from a notional to the real apprehension that "the world is charged with the grandeur of God" and that "Christ plays in ten thousand places, lovely in limbs, lovely in eyes not his."

Fra Angelico, *Last Supper*

"Whatever you do, in word or deed, do everything in
the name of the Lord Jesus, giving thanks to God the
Father through him."
Colossians 3:17

PART II

Reviews

Soundings in
Contemporary
Theology

1. A Review of

Real Presences

by George Steiner

All good art and literature begin in immanence. But they do not stop there. Which is to say, very plainly, that it is the enterprise and privilege of the aesthetic to quicken into lit presence the continuum between temporality and eternity, between matter and spirit, between man and "the other." It is in this common and exact sense that poiesis *opens on to, is underwritten by, the religious and the metaphysical.*

—George Steiner

George Steiner, professor of English and comparative literature at Geneva, Extraordinary Fellow at Cambridge, polymath author of such studies in language and culture as *In Bluebeard's Castle* and *Language and Silence,* prolific reviewer for *The New Yorker,* has written an impassioned essay, both luminous and dense, brilliant and bothersome, suffused with references to the masterworks of Western culture from Homer to Picasso (with even a passing tribute to Edith Piaf), but whose single, ineluctable concern is the reality of God. Understanding of, yet unapologetic to, the cultured despisers of religion, Steiner declares his almost scandalous intent from the first page of his text: "Any coherent account of the capacity of human speech to communicate meaning and feeling is, in the final analysis, underwritten by the assumption of God's presence."[1] No wonder he anticipates bemused

*George Steiner, *Real Presences* (Chicago: University of Chicago Press, 1989). This book review was originally published as "Books: From Homer, to Picasso, to Piaf, to God," *Commonweal* 116, no. 19 (November 3, 1989): 596–98.

1. Steiner, *Real Presences*, 3.

incomprehension: for he writes out of the venerable tradition of the Word, the Logos, in an age which, he concedes, is that of the "afterword," the "epilogue."[2]

In Steiner's view, modern times represent a fundamental negation of the Logos tradition of the West, a breaking of the covenant between Word and world that had governed the aesthetic, intellectual, and religious sensibilities of Western culture since its origins in Israel and Greece. He maintains that this epochal repudiation fully dawned in Western consciousness toward the close of the nineteenth century and has culminated in our own day in the literary and philosophical movement known as "deconstruction." Like Hegel's celebrated owl, "it is at twilight, in the penumbra of epilogue, that this radical provocation has taken wing."[3] For if the Logos tradition confesses, "In the beginning was the Word," deconstruction declares, "There was no beginning . . . only the play of sounds and markers amid the mutations of time."[4] In deconstruction, we meet no mere "negative theology": a critical purification leading to a chastened affirmation. In it is displayed pure nihilism, in which the analogical imagination cedes to an equivocal cleverness, a "do-it-yourself hermeneutics" suitably tailored to the age of computerized consumption.[5]

In the face of the radical challenge deconstruction poses, Steiner mounts an argument whose purpose is to affirm that the "real presences" that we encounter in the classics of literature, art, and music anticipate and point to a Real Presence that subtends and sustains them. Much has been made in reviews of Steiner's book of his admission that, in these ultimate considerations, no "proof" is possible: that deconstruction's "real absence" is as feasible a proposal as the tradition's "real presence." However, I think that to leave the question there (as these reviews tend to do)

2. Steiner, 228.
3. Steiner, 116.
4. Steiner, 120.
5. See Steiner, 126.

misses the heart of Steiner's essay. For it is not a matter of demonstration but of discernment. What is at stake is an appreciation of the human, of its unique nature and responsibilities. What is at stake is the very character of the universe: whether it is hospitable to human endeavor; whether it affords the human a meaningful home. For Steiner, art's discernment and articulation of Logos encourage the wager of faith in the face of the threat of ultimate anomie. But it supports no irrational faith, no mindless leap.

In some respects, Steiner's procedure is reminiscent of that advocated by the great American philosopher and logician C.S. Peirce in his essay "A Neglected Argument for the Reality of God" (1908). Peirce distinguishes between argument and argumentation, contending that argument may proceed cogently and coherently without employing argumentation's more restricted and less fertile logical analysis. Argument's distinctive mode of thought is, for Peirce, the playful meditation, which he terms "musement."

Steiner's argument moves by such musement upon the great artistic creations of the Western tradition, not to impress by his erudition (which is astonishing) but to persuade by appeal to authoritative witnesses. And what these classics bespeak is the sacramentality of human existence, its spiritual seriousness and density. I would not hesitate to call Steiner's argument "mystagogic": he evokes the memory of the masterworks so that their embodied meanings might play forth intimations of transcendent mystery, of a source and destination beyond the range of the human.

Correlative to Steiner's insistence upon the objective givenness of the work of art and the fecund yet finite range of meaning it opens is his stress upon the subjective responsibility incumbent upon the one who encounters the classic expression. In one of the most sensitively compelling sections of the book, he limns an "ethics of reception," the stance of the receiving subject before the significant otherness of the work of art. The spiritual discipline of attention, respect, tact, and trust, which Steiner advocates, owes much to the sensitivities of Jewish thinkers like Martin Buber and Emmanuel Levinas; but it also calls to mind the monastic *lectio* in its radically contemplative sense of what is due the stranger, the other—in this case, the artist—who is to be welcomed as a guest and as a bearer of blessing.

Steiner sums up the requisite attitude in the word *cortesia*, that courtesy of heart that allows one to be touched by the other, to enter then into communication with the other, in the hope of realizing communion. Thereby, he repudiates modernity's postulate that the defining trait of the human is the will to power. Rather, with the Logos tradition, Steiner holds that more basic to the human is the will to interpret, the unrestricted desire to understand, which itself subserves the will *to* enter into relationship, *not* dominatingly, but for the sheer joy of being together. We are, Steiner insists, "monads haunted by communion."[6]

The book concludes with an evocation of humankind's messianic hope. Between the Good Friday of common human experience and the Easter Sunday of explicit Christian faith stands the in-between time: "the long day's journey of the Saturday," quickened by the poem, the painting, *the* song.[7] They serve as the promise of an integral word and the foretaste of a completed communion. "Without them, how could we be patient?"[8]

In this remarkable essay, the single note I find discordant is Steiner's view that artistic creation is "counter-creation": agonistic and rival to the primordial creation.[9] In this hypothesis, the artist enters the lists as maker confronting Maker, striving to bring forth a personal cosmos out of chaos in what verges upon a self-recreation. This almost Promethean insertion seems to me to fit poorly with Steiner's own argument, compromising its consistency.

6. Steiner, 140.
7. Steiner, 232.
8. Steiner, 232.
9. See Steiner's discussion beginning on 203.

For should not the artist be the prime practitioner of the ethics of reception? And is not an ethics of reception, at its heart, a Eucharistic ethics: receiving all, thankfully, as grace? Hence, in counterpoint to those strains of the tradition, cited by Steiner, that celebrate the artist as *alter deus*, another god,[10] I would invoke the more orthodox practice of Bach and Haydn. When, at the end of his musical composition, Bach inscribed "Soli Deo Gloria" and Haydn "Laus Deo," they seem not to have been concluding a cosmic competition or metaphysical rivalry. And they were certainly not being self-referential! The undeniably real presences of their musical offerings were grateful acknowledgments of the Real Presence who originates and sustains all things.

10. See Steiner, 208.

2. A Review of

And Now I See

A Theology of Transformation

by Robert Barron

I have reviewed many books over the past thirty years. I have learned from most, admired many, deeply appreciated some. But of relatively few was I moved to think: this is a book I would love to have written. Well, Robert Barron's *And Now I See* is a book I would love to have written. It is a simply splendid and enchanting work.

Many today trumpet the need, in the post–Vatican II Church, for a new integration of theology and spirituality, one that is pastorally sensitive and illuminating. Barron has actually produced such a work. It brings together in a perceptive and deeply pondered way material from the Bible and from the Church's dogmatic and theological traditions. But by imaginatively discerning truths of the tradition reflected in the affective literary forms of Dante, Faulkner, and Flannery O'Connor, Barron has sculpted these truths into new and relevant relief. By so doing, he has furthered the pastoral task envisioned by Cardinal Newman: to help the merely notional become real and concretely actual for a particular audience and situation.

Crucial to Barron's undertaking is his persuasion that the doctrines of the Church are, of their nature, mystagogic and transformative. By articulating the truth about God and the hu-

* Robert Barron, *And Now I See: A Theology of Transformation*, 2nd ed. (Park Ridge, IL: Word on Fire Academic, 2021). This book review was originally published in *Church* 15, no. 4 (Winter 1999): 51–52.

man person, they stretch the soul, salving its wounds. The implication, pressed home in diverse ways (to offset our stubborn penchant for denial), is that we stand in desperate need of healing. For, as Trent teaches, by propagation and predilection we dwell in a realm of spiritual blindness and must at last cry out with Bartimaeus: "Lord, let me see."

A singular merit of the book, therefore, is the depth of its depiction of our common human needfulness. The book's first part, "The Riven Self," unveils the plight of the *pusilla anima*: that self, ever intent on self-preservation and aggrandizement. To this end, Barron offers a masterful exegesis of Dante's *Inferno*, as a journey into the heart of darkness, to help us see the deadly power of human evil and of our complicity in it.

Only by realizing the true scope of our predicament can the call to conversion, at the heart of the Gospel take on for us real substance. For this metanoia entails much more than moral repentance. It initiates a new way of seeing, a new consciousness, indeed a new self, in every way counter to the false self of the *pusilla anima*. Barron calls this new self the *magna anima*, whose spacious hospitality images the infinite generosity of God.

The book proceeds to reflect upon the Christian understanding of this God who summons and supports us on the way of transformation. Its second part, entitled "The Uncanny God," expounds the Christian understanding of God in a spirit at once deeply biblical and traditional and impressively original. A major methodological theme in this section is the refusal to lapse into one-sided depictions of God's mystery. For these all too often only camouflage the desire to control and manipulate the mystery. Rather, in a series of variations, Barron skillfully orchestrates the both/and of the Catholic symphony: God's serenity and creativity, self-sufficiency and covenant-fidelity, lordliness and lowliness.

But once again, he elaborates this comprehensive vision of God's awesome intimacy not for the sake of detached, if appreciative, beholding but for the sake of soul-doctoring, of salvation. Living the creative tension of these polarities and refusing the temptation to sunder them expands the fear-ridden *pusilla anima* into closer configuration with God's Trinitarian plenitude. What begins to come to birth is a new, magnanimous self whose only measure is the infinite God.

Only in Christ, however, does the terrifying cost and scope of transformation become truly manifest. Hence the book's third part, "The Healing," presents the Christological heart of the matter: Jesus the anointed one, physician and healer of our souls. The Jesus whose portrait is here movingly sketched is far from the "warm fuzzy" of New Age piety. He appears as one whose compassionate medicine can, at first, taste bitter and thus is as apt to be spit up as swallowed. The cost of transformation is revealed in the light of the cross to be not less than everything, and the soul intent on self-preservation may understandably deem the price far too high.

To restore the original "shock therapy" of the overly familiar Gospel narratives, Barron re-tells a Flannery O'Connor story disclosing a human condition "worse than we have imagined" and "better than we could have hoped."[1] With our defensive battlements thus lowered, the figure of Jesus passes as through barred doors. The risen One is the true measure of the *magna anima*, the revealer and restorer of God's image in us. But the very unity of divinity and humanity in Jesus exemplifies to an unsurpassable degree the tension of seeming opposites that alone truly works human transformation. "He is the transfiguration of our frail humanity and he is the manifestation of God's frail divinity."[2] This manifestation and transfiguration find their consummation in the Paschal Mystery of Jesus's death and Resurrection.

1. Barron, *And Now I See*, 158.
2. Barron, 155.

In a contemporary theological context where the cross of Christ often seems marginalized, it is bracing to see Barron's robust confession of the soteriological centrality of the Paschal Mystery. "If God has spoken in Christ, it is from the cross; if there was a 'reason' for his coming, it was the Paschal Mystery of his dying and rising."[3] But as befits a theologian, he is not content only to confess the Church's faith; he seeks to provide some understanding of that faith. And he does so by offering one final sounding of the chaos that threatens the *pusilla anima* in order to appreciate fully the sole remedy commensurate with the need.

Barron expresses this so well that I cannot forebear quoting him at length:

> What most besets us, what stands most awfully between ourselves and God, what practically compels the curving in on self that is the essence of sin, is the fear of death. And hence it is into that fear that the Word of God journeys. All of Christ's sallyings forth into sickness, alienation, self-righteousness, and poverty are but preliminaries to the final assault on the stronghold of death itself. It is as though he moves first through the outer defenses—that is, the myriad effects of sin—before coming to the citadel: the origin of all sin which is the terror of dying.[4]

The full scope of transformation thus embraces death itself and makes of it the way to glory, transfiguring our most radical alienation into full communion. Of course, this is what we joyfully celebrate in the Eucharist. In the last analysis, then, Robert Barron has gifted us with a pastoral theology that is rooted in Eucharistic celebration and, in turn, enriches that celebration. What more could one desire?

3. Barron, 205.
4. Barron, 206.

3. A Review of

Faith Maps

Ten Religious Explorers from Newman to Joseph Ratzinger

by Michael Paul Gallagher, SJ

Michael Gallagher, professor of fundamental theology at Rome's Gregorian University, has written a gem of a book. In clear prose, laced with more than a touch of poetry, he presents the writings of ten prominent thinkers who explore the substance and challenge of Christian faith.

Besides Newman and Ratzinger, the "explorers" include not only theologians Karl Rahner and Hans Urs von Balthasar and philosophers Maurice Blondel and Charles Taylor but the short story writer Flannery O'Connor, among others. Despite obvious differences, what unites them all is the conviction that Christian faith must address, with theological and pastoral creativity, the distinctively new "sensibility" that characterizes contemporary men and women. For some today, "God is not so much incredible as unreal."[1]

Hence, it is often less a question of "ideas" and "reasons" than of what Charles Taylor calls the "social imaginary": "how people come to feel and interpret their lives at an intuitive level."[2] Central to this "imaginary" is the new sense of "self" that emerges with

---

* Michael Gallagher, *Faith Maps: Ten Religious Explorers from Newman to Joseph Ratzinger* (Mahwah, NJ: Paulist, 2010). This book review was originally published as "Spiritual Directors," *America: The Jesuit Review*, February 7, 2011, https://www.americamagazine.org/.

1. Gallagher, *Faith Maps*, 2.

2. Gallagher, 109.

modernity and assumes various protean shapes and misshapes in a now postmodern world. This rampant pluralism, however, all too often leads to incomprehension rather than communication, to fragmentation instead of authentic communion.

Besides theology, Gallagher has also studied and taught literature and thus brings to his theological explorations a keen attention to the oft-neglected aesthetic and affective dimensions of the life of faith and the doing of theology. Indeed, a major theme of the book is the need to engage the whole person, heart and mind, in the adventure of faith. For along with the undoubted benefits of modernity's "turn to the subject," there arises the specter of a "shrunken subject": one whose horizon is limited to the empirically verifiable and whose existence risks becoming "buffered," devoid of real relations. Hence a major challenge, as Newman insisted, is to engage and expand the imagination beyond its one-dimensional constrictions, in order to "imagine our lives grounded in a Love beyond all imagining."[3]

Each of the thinkers discussed seeks, in his or her distinctive way, to bring the riches of the Christian tradition into sympathetic and challenging engagement with this contemporary sensibility. Thus, O'Connor's unsettling shock therapy stands side by side with Taylor's measured appreciation of modernity's gains. Balthasar's beginning "from above"—with the unsurpassable beauty of the Father's surrender of his only Son—complements Rahner's committed probing of the human as always already called by grace.

All strive to awaken in the reader a sense of wonder and reverence before the manifestations of mystery in the everyday. To this end, they often draw generously upon poets, both classical and contemporary, who offer some glimpse of a reality "charged with the grandeur of God." Each of the faith-explorers respectfully seeks to show that these surprising intimations are not suppressed

3. Gallagher, 5.

but transfigured by the Good News of what God has done and is doing in Jesus Christ.

Gallagher himself embodies the imagination he cogently champions. He concludes eight of his ten presentations by assuming the "voice" of the thinker in question, directly addressing the contemporary reader. What might appear, at first blush, merely a "device" turns out to be an effective and affective way of summing up that thinker's vision and presenting it with art and insight.

In a final chapter, "Converging Pillars of Wisdom," Gallagher gathers together the insights he has so keenly appropriated along this journey of faith exploration. The brief eleven pages repay multiple readings and would, themselves, make a fine starting point for classroom or adult education discussion. The final pillar, "Doing the Truth," is a salutary reminder that, at its deepest, faith is, ineluctably, a way of life.[4] Gallagher quotes Wittgenstein's pointed observations regarding Christianity: "practice gives the words their sense"; ultimately, "you have to change your life."[5]

No wonder, then, that the theme of "transformation" figures so prominently in each of the faith maps presented. Encountering the Gospel's summons to "metanoia" presses the hearer of the Word toward the realization of a new self whose author and measure is Christ. And friendship with Christ is ever "viaticum": the food and drink that accompanies and sustains the Christian's journey of faith.

4. Gallagher, 156.
5. Gallagher, 157.

4. A Review of

Sacred and Secular Scriptures

A Catholic Approach to Literature

by Nicholas Boyle

Nicholas Boyle, professor of German literary and intellectual history at Cambridge University, has written a remarkable book. His point of departure is an essay of Marie-Dominique Chenu, OP, who suggested that literature may serve as a legitimate *locus theologiae*. But whereas Chenu's focus was the Bible, Boyle's distinctive proposal is that "the site of theology . . . is occupied by both sacred and secular scriptures."[1] Thus, his book explores, in a creative and stimulating way, both the distinction and overlap between these scriptures. In doing so, he elaborates a Catholic hermeneutical approach to literature.

Part 1 of the book, "The Bible as Literature," carefully lays the groundwork for his hermeneutic by a close and critical conversation with leading figures in the realm of biblical interpretation: Herder, Schleiermacher, Hegel, Frei, and Ricoeur. Though appreciative of their contributions, he finds that, with the significant exception of Hegel, they tend toward an individualistic construal of the interpretive task, negligent of the indispensable role of community and tradition. Hegel himself, whom Boyle finds most adequate on this score, nonetheless fails by his insufficient

---

* Nicholas Boyle, *Sacred and Secular Scriptures: A Catholic Approach to Literature* (Notre Dame, IN: University of Notre Dame Press, 2005). This book review was originally published in *Worship* 80, no. 2 (March 2006): 184–86.
    1. Boyle, *Scriptures*, 5.

regard for the originality of Jesus himself, as well as for the root-edness of the New Testament in the soil of the Old.

The scene is now set for the two key chapters of the book: Boyle's sympathetic and fruitful engagement with the thought of the Jewish philosopher Emmanuel Levinas.

At the heart of his approach to the Bible, Levinas postulates the Law as "ethical kerygma proclaimed in the name of the Un-nameable."[2] The revelation conveyed by the Hebrew Bible is that of the peremptory call to responsibility, inscribed upon the face of the other. Moreover, Levinas recognizes that such revelation cannot be circumscribed by a book but "exists in the tradition of reading it, in the process of interpreting it."[3] One finds in Lev-inas, then, a community and tradition-based hermeneutic that supports Boyle's own project of advancing "beyond Bibliolatry."

Where Boyle must, of course, part ways with Levinas is in the contention that Jesus Christ is the hermeneutical key to scriptures, both sacred and secular. The heart of a Catholic hermeneutic is the New Testament confession that the Word has become flesh and dwells in our midst. Drawing upon Levinas's sensitivity, the Christian interpreter dares to proclaim that the Word has become flesh. And the Catholic practitioner of *lectio divina* will recognize, with Gerard Manley Hopkins, that "Christ plays in ten thousand places / Lovely in limbs, and lovely in eyes not his / To the Father through the features of men's faces."[4] Respectful though he is of literature and text, Boyle is surely correct in his insistence that Christianity is not, in the final analysis, a religion of the book but of the person—the living Lord, Jesus Christ. Thus, in part 2 of the book, "Sacred and Secular," he asserts, by way of summary of his approach, "Where there is a boundary established between

2. Boyle, 81.

3. Boyle, 83.

4. Gerard Manley Hopkins, "As Kingfishers Catch Fire," Poetry Foundation, poetryfoundation.org.

what is within the Law and what is beyond it, Christ oversteps the boundary and seeks the incorporation of what was lost."[5]

Part 3, "Literature as Bible," applies Boyle's Christological hermeneutic to select works of secular literature, considering them as possible "prolegomena to the sacred scriptures."[6] In Goethe's *Faust*, Melville's *Moby Dick*, Austen's *Mansfield Park*, and Tolkien's *Lord of the Rings* (among others), he seeks to discern intimations of forgiveness, reconciliation, and communion. These secular classics represent not, certainly, the authoritative Word of God but rather the often-inarticulate groanings of the Spirit, an implicit prayer for redemption. They embody, perhaps, the inchoate realization that, as T.S. Eliot put it, "the hint half guessed, the gift half understood, is incarnation."[7] To a nonspecialist in the literature treated, Boyle's exercise of the analogical imagination offers readings that are acute and suggestive, even if they do not always fully persuade.

Closing this book, one will ponder for some time its implications, both intellectual and pastoral. One area that Boyle touches on but does not explore at length is that much of secular art and literature in the West has, since the Enlightenment, seemingly embarked upon "a deliberate repressing or forgetting of their Christian origins."[8] How, one wonders, do churches and Christian communities address a cultural context characterized more by amnesia than anamnesis? For example, among the classics discussed by Boyle one still finds a biblical literacy that can no longer be presumed. How do our liturgical celebrations, homiletic practices, RCIA programs, theology courses for undergraduates meet the daunting challenge this poses?

5. Boyle, *Scriptures*, 144.
6. Boyle, 142.
7. T. S. Eliot, *The Dry Salvages*, sect. 5.
8. Boyle, *Scriptures*, 144.

That Boyle does not directly address such issues is no criticism of his fine study; it rather pays tribute to the fecund stimulus it presents.

5. A Review of

Dante: A Brief History

by Peter S. Hawkins

In his encyclical *Deus Caritas Est*, Pope Benedict XVI explored the relationship between *eros* and *agape*, desire and self-gift, with pastoral sensitivity and theological depth. A few days before publishing the encyclical, the pope himself gave an important indication of his intent. He sought, he said, to express for our day something of what the great Italian poet Dante had achieved in his masterpiece, *La Commedia* ("Divina" added afterward by early admirers).

We are in the midst of a wonderful renaissance of translations and studies of *The Divine Comedy* in the United States. The past fifteen years alone have seen translations of one or all three of the poem's *Cantica* by such fine poets and scholars as Robert Pinsky, Robert and Jean Hollander, and Anthony Esolen (and that is not a complete list!). A number of colleges and universities continue the venerable tradition of *lectura Dantis*, the reading and exposition of a canto of the *Comedy* in a public forum. At Boston College, we have reached the midpoint of the *Purgatorio* in this seventh year since the inception of the monthly public readings.

Still, Dante remains daunting. If T.S. Eliot was right to say that Dante and Shakespeare divide the world of literature between them, there is no doubt that Dante requires the greater number of footnotes. We are thus most fortunate to have Peter Hawkins's *Dante: A Brief History* to guide our passage through

* Peter Hawkins, *Dante: A Brief History* (Malden, MA: Blackwell, 2006). This book review was originally published as "A Theologian in Verse," *America: The Jesuit Review*, May 7, 2007, https://www.americamagazine.org.

the dark descent, up the steep mount, and aloft on the wings of desire that at last attains its goal: union with the blessed Trinity.

Hawkins, a professor of religion at Boston University, previously authored a penetrating study, *Dante's Testaments: Essays in Scriptural Imagination*. His new book, in Blackwell's "Brief Histories of Religion" series, is more modest, but not less impressive.

Its accessible writing style, 5x7 format, and attractive contemporary art make it hospitable to beginners in Dante. But because it is the work of a seasoned scholar, the proficient in Dante will also delight in new perspectives and insights bountifully bestowed.

An introductory chapter on "Dante's Life and Works" leads to the central chapters that treat "Dante's Journey to God," "Dante's Beatrice," and "Dante's Religion." The book concludes with an excursion into "Dante's Afterlife," which ranges from Chaucer through Seamus Heaney to *New Yorker* cartoons. My favorite cartoon depicts a procession of lost souls passing through the portal of hell, above which is inscribed the well-known Dante verse: "Abandon All Hope, Ye Who Enter Here"—to which there's an addendum: "If you have already abandoned hope, please disregard this notice."[1]

Hawkins succinctly, but strikingly, contrasts Dante's hell and purgatory. "Hell [is] all about repetition-compulsion, an endless replay of the sinner's 'song of myself.'"[2] It is fitting that at hell's nadir we find not fire but Satan frozen immobile in ice. The promise of purgatory lies, instead, in dynamic movement, *moto spiritale*, "dedicated to change and transformation."[3] For here, the issue concerns "the rebirth of a soul free at last to be interested in others' souls and other things."[4]

---

1. Hawkins, *Dante*, 133.
2. Hawkins, 51.
3. Hawkins, 51.
4. Hawkins, 51.

Heaven celebrates, at last, the consummated at-one-ment of humanity in the communion of saints, imaging and nourished by the blessed communion of God's own Triune life. In *Paradiso*, sadly the least read of the *Cantica*, the poet summons the full measure of his genius to attempt the impossible: the verbal expression of the inexpressible. He conjures images of light, choreographs ecstatic patterns of dance, mints mind-stretching neologisms. Yet the struggle to forge an apt language is absolutely necessary. The task is no part-time avocation but God-gifted vocation. For Dante, as Hawkins reads him, "Poetry is the agent of the 'new life'; it is not the bridesmaid of theology, but the bride herself."[5] Dante scorns false modesty!

In the chapter on "Dante's Beatrice," the *eros/agape* theme comes fully to the fore. Hawkins wrestles, as we all must, with the figure of Beatrice and confesses that here, perhaps, "Dante was trying to do too much," endowing her with "a surfeit of meanings," thereby risking the loss of her person's meaning and mystery.[6] I register Hawkins's ambivalence and hesitate to challenge his considered view. Yet I wonder whether the very abundance of meaning, which he decries, hints at the surpassing mystery of Beatrice's person and the comprehensiveness of the salvation she mediates.

For, as Hawkins acknowledges in his very suggestive chapter on "Dante's Religion," the *Commedia* abounds with mediations of Christ, whose most prominent figures are Mary and Beatrice. And this, rather than signaling Christ's absence from the poem, proclaims his all-pervasive presence. Every instance of transformation Dante sets before us serves to refract, in the ongoing history of salvation, Christ's Paschal Mystery. Only thus can *eros* be transfigured, losing nothing of its humanity, but gaining everlasting life.

5. Hawkins, 57.
6. Hawkins, 92.

Instructed by Pope Benedict's encyclical, I would venture a contemporary application. We encounter today considerable discussion and writing about Catholic identity, about what is distinctive to the Catholic spiritual and intellectual tradition. Favorite terms mustered by way of response include "incarnational" and "sacramental." These concepts are, indeed, characteristic and crucial. But Dante's great poem impels the confession that flesh and blood can mediate grace only because God's eternal Word became flesh and blood, became incarnate. And the universe can be truly sacramental only if transfigured by what the tradition of the Christian East calls "Taboric" light.

Only by being thus transformed in Christ can created realities bear an incarnational and sacramental charge, purged of self-indulgent dross and sentimental fantasy. Only a transformative journey, such as Dante himself undertakes, will purify the erotic of its residual narcissism, freeing it to vibrate in harmony with "the Love that moves the sun and the other stars."[7]

In this splendid *vade mecum* to Dante, Hawkins argues that the fourteenth-century Italian poeticized in the conviction that he had a divine calling "to reform the world and transform the reader."[8] Dante can, of course, be approached simply as superb fabricator of words, rather than as inspired prophet. Nonetheless, Hawkins contends, "no one remains unchanged by an encounter with the *Commedia*."[9] And then, like the surgeon general, he warns, "There are consequences to picking it up."[10] *Caveat lector*!

7. *Paradiso*, xxxiii, 145.
8. Hawkins, *Dante*, 28.
9. Hawkins, 28.
10. Hawkins, 28.

6. A Review of

Theology for Pilgrims

by Nicholas Lash

I am a fan of Sancerre, the distinctive Loire Valley white wine: elegantly dry and a tad tart. I am also very much a fan of the distinguished English Catholic theologian Nicholas Lash. His writing also is distinctive: quite elegant and, at times, tart. One always savors it—but it is better if sipped slowly.

Lash's newest book, a collection of essays written over the last twelve years, bears the vintage-Lash title *Theology for Pilgrims*. The Christian community is embarked on a journey, with the paschal pillar of fire guiding our way. But darkness, both within and outside the Church, throws obstacles across our path.

One of the most compelling essays in the volume, "'An Immense Darkness' and the Tasks of Theology," vividly illustrates this contention. It presents a close reading and exegesis of Conrad's novel *Heart of Darkness*. Here, Lash provides one of his patented apothegms: "To learn to worship only God, only the holy and unmasterable mystery that is not the world or any part of it, is an unending task."[1]

This Rahnerian note is also sounded in the essay on "The Impossibility of Atheism." Lash parses the grammar of the word "God" as that which is worshipful, that upon which we set our hearts. From this vantage, the question is not *whether* we worship, as much as it is *what* we worship. For assertions about "God" are performative utterances, revelatory of a relation and a

* Nicholas Lash, *Theology for Pilgrims* (Notre Dame, IN: University of Notre Dame Press, 2008). This book review was originally published in *Worship* 83, no. 4 (July 2009): 382–84.
    1. Lash, *Pilgrims*, 103.

commitment rather than of a static state of affairs or some neutral object "out there." With his exquisite sensitivity to Christianity as a "school" in which mind and heart are purified, Lash declares, "Learning to use the word 'God' well is a matter of discovering that everything we have and are is given; that our existence is the finite form of God's self-gift, God's self-communication."[2]

Lash's austere spiritual vision finds a mooring in the short, abrupt ending of Mark's Gospel, where the Good News of Resurrection contends with the women's perduring fear. He, of course, does not dispute the Church's canonical quadriform Gospel. But he steadfastly refuses to tolerate any semblance of cheap grace. The essay "Fear of the Dark" offers almost a self-confession: "Whereas a theology that thinks along the dark grain of the world, insisting on treating with utmost seriousness the *solidity* of evil, may risk being mesmerized by darkness, a more exuberant insistence on new life imperishably sprung from womb and grave may risk sitting dangerously light to the sheer *weight* of the wounds and sorrows and injustice of the world."[3]

It is abundantly clear that Lash's own commitment is to wrestle with evil's solidity and to pay discriminating heed to the weight of the world's wounds. Hence, for all his insistence upon Christians as comprising a pilgrim people, it is not a pilgrimage that withdraws from the world but one immersed in the world, seeking to embody a way of justice and peace, in imitation of its incarnate Lord. To do so faithfully, the community needs substantive food for the journey, or, as another essay calls it, "Traveller's Fare."

Here, Lash insists that "sacraments are signs not disguises" and that what the Eucharist celebrates is Christ who gives himself as food and drink to nourish his ecclesial Body, fostering its growth in the Holy Spirit.[4] The Eucharist's ritual enactment

2. Lash, 26.
3. Lash, 191–92.
4. Lash, 194.

countenances no separation between sacrifice and meal, for, as Louis Bouyer affirms, "in antiquity the Eucharist was seen as the sacrifice of the Christians *because* it was the sacred meal of the Christian community."[5]

Lash then turns, in the essay, to consider article seven of Vatican II's constitution on the liturgy, *Sacrosanctum Concilium*, with the commendable aim of underscoring the multiple modalities of Christ's presence on our journey: in his Word, in his minister, in his assembled community, and especially (*maxime*) under the Eucharistic species. To my reading, however, he is so intent upon maximizing the diverse modes of Christ's presence that he risks minimizing Christ's presence under the Eucharistic species. This emerges, for instance, in the final section of the essay where he inveighs against a monastic author who, however ineptly, sought to raise up the "maxime" by reference to Eucharistic Adoration. Lash astringently dismisses the attempt as a case of that dread disease, "thingness," in which "reification rules."[6]

Well, perhaps. But a more benevolent treatment might engage the poor monk's concern and even enrich it by reference to the lovely poem with which Lash closes the essay. For of which other of Christ's presences can this truly be sung: "O sacrum convivium in quo Christus sumitur . . . et futurae gloriae nobis pignus datur"?[7]

By so doing, Lash, having served first the austere Sancerre, could have then complemented it with a mellower varietal: even (why not?) a Châteauneuf-du-Pape. Nonetheless, whether tart or mellow, Lash's finely crafted essays are very much worth the reading . . . or sipping.

---

5. Louis Bouyer, *Rite and Man: The Sense of the Sacred and Christian Liturgy*, trans. M. Joseph Costelloe (London, Burns & Oates, 1963), 83, cited in Lash, *Pilgrims*, 204–5.

6. Lash, *Pilgrims*, 207.

7. Cited in Lash, 208.

7. A Review of

The Personalism of
John Henry Newman

by John F. Crosby

One ought to never judge a book by its cover. However, some
covers are singularly appropriate to the subject matter of the
book. Such is the case here. The cover features a striking photo of the elderly John Henry Newman, pensive and far-seeing,
clothed in simple black cassock and coat, the trace of a smile on
the sculpted face. Each time one returns to *The Personalism of
John Henry Newman*, the cover beckons to a renewed personal
encounter with Father Newman.

Long-standing students of Newman will welcome Crosby's
fine study, while newcomers will find here a winning introduction to the thought of the great precursor of Vatican II. The book,
written in an engaging, almost conversational style, develops a
careful, cogent argument for Newman as a "personalist" thinker.
In making this case, Crosby, professor of philosophy at Franciscan University, suggestively places Newman in relation to thinkers like Kierkegaard and James, Scheler and Otto, Guardini and
von Hildebrand. Like Newman, these thinkers sought to overcome a constricted understanding of human experience, fruit of a
too narrowly defined rationalism, and broaden it to encompass
the affective and interpersonal realms.

Perhaps the book's crucial chapter is "Heart Speaks to
Heart"—the title, of course, taken from Newman's cardinalatial

* John F. Crosby, *The Personalism of John Henry Newman* (Washington, DC: The Catholic
University of America Press, 2014). This book review was originally published in *Theological
Studies* 76, no. 2 (June 2015): 355–56.

motto. Crosby highlights Newman's well-known assertion: "The heart is commonly reached, not through the reason. But through the imagination . . . persons influence us, voices melt us, looks subdue us, deeds inflame us."[1] In this chapter, then, Crosby mounts an argument for a more experiential knowing that engages the affections. He goes so far as to postulate the need, in philosophical anthropology, to speak not only of intellect and will but also of "heart" as the seat of distinctively human affectivity.

In this connection, one is reminded of the development in the Lonergan of *Method in Theology* of a new emphasis upon "feelings" and "intersubjectivity." Lonergan, who was early influenced by Newman, in his later writing drew upon the very authors important to Crosby: Scheler and von Hildebrand. Oddly, however, Lonergan receives no mention in the book.

In exploring Newman's "personalism," Crosby successfully eschews false dichotomies. He does not set heart in opposition to reason, or "real apprehension" to "notional apprehension." He strongly insists that one is not constrained to opt either for anthropocentrism or theocentrism but that one must affirm both. Indeed, the book's opening chapter underscores the critical importance of "Theocentric Religion." What recommends Newman is precisely his "rare comprehensiveness,"[2] his "inexhaustible plenitude."[3]

A further attractive feature of Crosby's exposition is his capacity to anticipate objections and to address them directly. Thus, he asks whether Newman's distinctive appeal to conscience is compromised by Freud's view of the role of the "superego" and provides an adequate philosophical rebuttal of that claim. He also quite rightly defends Newman's stress on interiority and the self-appropriation of the thinking, feeling, acting subject against

1. John Henry Newman, *An Essay in Aid of a Grammar of Assent* (London: Longmans, 1903), 92–93, cited in Crosby, *Personalism*, 47–48.
2. Crosby, *Personalism*, 144.
3. Crosby, 213.

the charge of "subjectivism," indeed, of setting the stage for "modernism." However, neither is Crosby an uncritical apologist for Newman. He concedes that Newman may not have held the material universe in sufficient regard and complements Newman, on this score, by reflections taken from the more articulated sacramental vision of Romano Guardini.

Though the book is primarily a philosophical study, the last chapter on "The Creative Principle of Religion" contains a final section entitled "A Personalist Approach to Revelation." Here, we encounter the Newman who anticipated *Dei Verbum*. Crosby draws upon the *Oxford University Sermons* and especially the great second sermon on "The Influence of Natural and Revealed Religion Respectively." Discussing this sermon, Crosby draws a telling contrast between Newman and Kant. He comments perceptively, "[Newman] sees God acting as living person in our midst, drawing us into dimensions of interpersonal life with God that could never be reduced to doing our universal duty."[4]

It seems an omission, then, that Crosby does not mention in this regard a phrase that Newman introduces in this very sermon. Speaking precisely of the personalist nature of revealed religion, Newman employs the term "method of personation."[5] The personal God reveals himself in history through the mediation of human persons, supremely in Jesus Christ. And, in this same sermon, Newman famously declares that "it is the Incarnation of the Son of God . . . which is the article of a standing or a falling Church."[6]

Thus, the theocentricity and anthropocentricity that Crosby rightly credits Newman for holding in creative tension find their capstone in Newman's Christocentricity. For, as a later sermon in the series celebrates, "The divinely-enlightened mind sees in

4. Crosby, 215 (emphasis removed).
5. John Henry Newman, *Fifteen Sermons Preached before the University of Oxford* (hereafter, *Oxford University Sermons*), 3rd ed. (New York: Scribner, 1872), 29.
6. Newman, *Oxford University Sermons*, 35.

Christ the very Object whom it desires to love and worship—the Object correlative of its own affections."[7] In these splendid *Oxford University Sermons*, we see revealed the Christological basis of Newman's personalism: heart truly speaking to heart.

7. Newman, 236.

8. A Review of

Truly Our Sister

A Theology of Mary in the Communion of Saints

by Elizabeth A. Johnson

Elizabeth Johnson, with accustomed verve and erudition, has written a passionate, insightful, yet problematic work. Its riches and pleasures are many. The chiseled prose frequently breaks forth into the pungent and poetic. The organization and argumentation bear abundant evidence of a fine systematic mind at work.

Further, the book embodies a rich store of information and resources, especially in the two areas that distinctively characterize Johnson's project. Firstly, it provides a primer of feminist hermeneutics and anthropology that in itself would be an excellent introduction to the field. Secondly, it offers a very helpful résumé of scholarship concerning the political, economic, cultural, and religious setting of first-century Palestine: indispensable background to a more realistic appropriation of the biblical witness.

Johnson cunningly employs these tools to reconfigure the Marian mosaic. She closely examines all the New Testament texts in which Mary appears, subjecting them to historical-critical and feminist analysis in order to recover tesserae suitable for a portrayal freed from the centuries-long grime of idealized encrustations and patriarchal disfigurement. What emerges from this restoration is a strong woman of the Spirit, firmly positioned within

*Elizabeth A. Johnson, *Truly Our Sister: A Theology of Mary in the Communion of Saints* (New York: Continuum, 2003). This book review was originally published in *Worship* 78, no. 6 (November 2004): 568–70.

the communion of saints, that cloud of witnesses in every age who have generously and courageously responded to God's grace, showing themselves to be friends of God and prophets.

Johnson's self-described "modest proposal" depicts Miriam of Nazareth with the unmistakable features of a Jewish woman of the first century, bravely confronting adversity and oppression, trusting in the liberating power of the God of Israel, and accepting the cost and adventure of such fidelity. No pallid, submissive Renaissance Madonna she, but the boldly subversive songster of the Magnificat, more truly our sister than our mother.

Of course, this is hardly a "modest" proposal at all. In the hands of so skilled and visionary an artisan, it represents a radical restoration, both compelling and controversial. The author, in truth, seems to acknowledge this, admitting that some will find the book "jarring."[1]

Thus, two lines of reflection are relevant. First, what principles govern the restoration? Secondly, what is highlighted and what left in shadow in the final portrait?

Johnson is extremely well versed in contemporary biblical scholarship, especially in the burgeoning field of feminist hermeneutics and anthropology. She employs both with great dexterity in her historical and imaginative reconstruction of "The Dangerous Memory of Mary" (chapter 10, which is the heart of the book). In setting forth the various strategies—corrective, critical, and reconstructive—honed by feminist hermeneuts, Johnson articulates their common goal: "To free up the word of God so that it stands in alliance with the flourishing of women."[2] A good measure of the book's power lies in her passionate and imaginative pursuit of this goal, as she polishes and positions the diverse tesserae of the emerging mosaic.

1. Johnson, *Our Sister*, xvi.
2. Johnson, 212.

But a question that the project perforce raises is what serves as ultimate norm for the undertaking? Does "human flourishing" itself stand under the judgment of divine revelation, or is revelation accommodated to the presumed imperatives of human flourishing as construed in a particular historical epoch? It is, ultimately, the Barthian question posed to this latest epiphany of the anthropological approach to theology, brilliantly pioneered by the father of modern theology, Friedrich Schleiermacher—a question that Johnson's ambitious reconstruction prompts one to ponder anew: Are we truly speaking of the *Holy* Spirit?

A second matter of concern stands related to the former. Johnson's powerful and persuasive reconstruction of the dangerous memory of Mary succeeds in re-positioning her within, not over against the Church: a precedent inaugurated and sanctioned by *Lumen Gentium*. But does the portrait presented, though qualified as "one approach," succeed in highlighting Mary's pre-eminent role within the Body of Christ, as mother of its Head? Is it sufficient to the Marian experience and discernment of the Church's Tradition to proclaim that "Mary is blessed among women and men who are themselves blessed"?[3]

Early on, the book issues this disclaimer: "It does not aim to present the full teaching of the church about Mary, which is amply available elsewhere."[4] Certainly, no one book can do everything. But by thoroughly bracketing the dogmatic and liturgical tradition of the Church regarding Mary's Immaculate Conception and Assumption, Johnson's reconfiguration of Mary into the communion of saints risks reducing her distinctive *figura*.

This impression is further reinforced by the discussion of the virginal conception, whose Catholic dogmatic understanding appears as but one possible interpretation of the scriptural data. The primary perspective that governs the reconstruction is to affirm

3. Johnson, 311.
4. Johnson, xiii.

"virginity as a symbol of female autonomy."[5] The author avers, "In this sense, the virginal conception is valuable in bearing a message of revolutionary female empowerment."[6] However, in a book whose purported thrust is to move reflection on Mary "from transcendent symbol to historical person,"[7] does this approach actually reverse the movement under different symbolic guise?

In sum, *Truly Our Sister* is an important and provocative manifesto. Much of the sentimental overlay has been removed from the mosaic of Mary and the dreary residue of Mariolatry has been effectively purged. But though the restored portrait shines forth in bold relief, one cannot but wonder whether some crucial colors have also been bleached in the process.

5. Johnson, 239.
6. Johnson, 239.
7. See Johnson, 95.

9. A Review of

The Priority of Christ

Toward a Postliberal Catholicism

by Robert Barron

Robert Barron, the author of *And Now I See* and *The Strangest Way* among other fine books, has now published his *magnum opus* to date. In his previous works, Barron imaginatively explored the Gospel's call to transformation, drawing upon both sacred and secular scriptures. Now, *The Priority of Christ* elucidates the ontological and epistemological suppositions and implications of transformation in Christ. Barron offers a compelling reading of several New Testament portraits of Christ and brings them into enriching conversation with later doctrinal and theological perspectives. He thus effects a renewed unity of biblical and systematic theology, which too often meander their separate ways. Finally, he examines the concrete living of the new life in Christ, embodied in four women saints of the nineteenth and twentieth centuries.

The radical newness of Jesus the Christ is the very fulcrum of the book. One can read it, therefore, as an extended meditation on the great Christological hymn in Colossians, especially the verses: "All things were created in him and for him. He is before all things, and in him all things hold together" (Col. 1:16–17). Here, scriptural witness gives rise to ontological claims—indeed, ultimately, to a Trinitarian ontology. In Barron's acute and, to my

* Robert Barron, *The Priority of Christ: Toward a Postliberal Catholicism* (Grand Rapids, MI: Brazos, 2007). This book review was originally published in *Worship* 82, no. 2 (March 2008): 188–90.

mind, cogent exegesis, the dominant trajectory of "liberal theology" fails to do justice to the sheer originality of Jesus, who in his person is the concrete universal, the eternal Word incarnate.

Hence Barron's approach is professedly "postliberal" (though in a sense that is closer to Balthasar than to Lindbeck). Barron does not indulge in "conservative" rant, however, but provides a careful exposition and respectful critique of figures like Rahner, Küng, and Schillebeeckx, as well as their forerunners Kant and Schleiermacher. His measured discernment is that whatever the real differences among them, their common "liberal" tendency is to reduce the originality and newness of Jesus by making him the supreme instance of a generic type: whether prophet, teacher, or savior. In the process, divine revelation risks being absorbed by human experience, Christology by anthropology, and religion by morality.

Barron's book counters these reductions by presenting an "iconic Christology" that draws upon both Scripture and Tradition, narrative and doctrine, theology and metaphysics, in a mutually illuminating "coinherence" (one of the author's privileged terms). He draws a compelling portrait of the one who is the Way, the Truth, and the Life. Doing so, he does not deconstruct but develops the (to some) scandalous ontological and epistemological implications of this claim.

Thus to "take on the mind of Christ," to undergo metanoia, is to see reality differently and distinctively: to exclaim, "And now I see!" It is, in brief, to see reality Eucharistically and relationally, originating from the God whose very "to be" is to be gift, self-donation. And the gifted response, impelled by this realization, is Eucharistic doxology and Eucharistic living: thereby according priority to Christ in all things. Such robust Christocentrism is neither constrictive nor sectarian but gloriously Catholic. It forms its practitioners to apprehend reality "most richly and thus, paradoxically enough, makes possible the most creative conversation with the non-Christian culture."[1]

The Balthasar-inspired title for the last part of the book is "The Display of the Christian Form: Ethics by Means of the Saints." Here, we see the form of Christ embodied concretely in Thérèse of Lisieux and Katharine Drexel, Edith Stein and Teresa of Kolkata. In them and in their companions in the communion of saints, "virtue ethics" reveals its ultimate Christological foundation and face.

One area I wish the author had engaged more fully is the liturgical enactment of this *canticum novum* which is the *totus Christus*. The Paschal Vigil's proclamation of Christ "yesterday and today, alpha and omega" to whom "all time belongs and all ages" would lend the substantial weight of the *lex orandi* to Barron's creative probing of the *lex credendi*. But that may provide matter for a sequel.

In the meantime, Barron has gifted us with an important work that opens exciting vistas for exploration and theological renewal.

1. Barron, *Priority*, 134.

10. A Review of

The Crucifixion

Understanding the Death of Jesus Christ

by Fleming Rutledge

Sixteen years ago, I reviewed appreciatively for *Commonweal* a book of sermons entitled *The Bible and the New York Times*. The title clearly played upon Karl Barth's noted dictum that the preacher "should preach with the Bible in one hand and the daily newspaper in the other." The incisive sermons revealed the preacher, Fleming Rutledge, an Episcopal priest, to be a deeply informed student of the Bible and a sensitive exegete of contemporary culture and society.

In her remarkable (indeed, monumental) new work, Rutledge further probes "the strange new world of the Bible" to its mysterious and scandalous depth in the Crucifixion of the Son of God. And she diagnoses the deepest need of the world (manifest not only in the daily newspapers but in the works of novelists and poets through the ages) as its often inchoate longing for redemption.

Though the book bears ample testament to the author's intimate familiarity with works of biblical and theological scholarship, her abiding concern remains pastoral. Not only the text but the footnotes as well bear generous witness to the author's own pastoral experience and discernment. Her pervasive concern is to support "a deepened commitment to preaching, teaching,

* Fleming Rutledge, *The Crucifixion: Understanding the Death of Jesus Christ* (Grand Rapids, MI: Eerdmans, 2015). This book review was originally published as "No Glib Gospel," *Commonweal* 143, no. 6 (March 25, 2016): 29–31.

praying."[1] Thus, the book is best approached through *lectio*: the slow, meditative savoring of its theological and spiritual richness.

The heart of the matter for the book (as for the New Testament itself) is the scandalous confession of a crucified Savior. Rutledge writes, "The cross, incomparably vindicated by the resurrection, is the *novum*, the new factor in human experience, the definitive and world-changing act of God, that makes the New Testament proclamation unique in all the world."[2] One might suppose this assertion to be self-evident were it not for the troubling marginalization of the cross in a good deal of contemporary theology, preaching, and pastoral practice.

Rutledge attributes some of this unholy neglect of Christianity's essence to the sensibilities of a therapeutic and consumerist culture that revels in feeling good about oneself, reacting warily to talk of "sacrifice." Another factor, contributing to the shunning of the cross, is its presumed association with an unhealthy passivity in the face of evil. Both attitudes, by evading the salvific scandal of the cross, conspire to reduce the Gospel to a one-dimensional moralism. Her urgent counterclaim argues that "the crucifixion is the touchstone of Christian authenticity, the unique feature by which everything else, including the resurrection, is given its true significance."[3]

Note that Rutledge accents not merely the "cross" but the "crucifixion": not merely the death but the horrendous manner of the death. The prolonged public choreography of crucifixion effects the utter dehumanization of the victim. Often enough, theologians will invoke the notion of *kenosis*: the self-emptying of God's Son. But paradoxically, the technical term can serve as a barrier to a true appreciation of the depths of degradation to

1. Rutledge, *Crucifixion*, 213.
2. Rutledge, 61.
3. Rutledge, 71.

which God has sunk to accomplish human salvation. Indeed, "it is in the crucifixion that the nature of God is truly revealed."[4]

Crucifixion unveils not only the abyss of God's love but also the depth of the alienation that must be addressed. "The crucifixion of Jesus is of such magnitude that it must call forth a concept of sin that is large enough to match it."[5] Rutledge time and again appeals to Paul to evoke the depths of the mystery revealed. "For our sake God made Christ, who knew no sin, to be sin, so that in him we might become the righteousness of God" (2 Cor. 5:21). And (not the least of the book's achievements) an entire chapter offers a spirited defense of Saint Anselm against the gross misinterpretations that have slandered this great theologian. Anselm's surpassing merit was to fathom the catastrophic disorder, the *pondus peccati*, the terrible weight of sin, that afflicts humankind and the necessarily radical remedy that alone can set it right.

Thus, the book is fundamentally an exploration of "soteriology," the Christian understanding of salvation, the salvation realized by Jesus Christ in his Incarnation and, supremely, in his Crucifixion and Resurrection. Rutledge structures the second part of her work in terms of the key "motifs" or themes through which the New Testament sounds the inexhaustible significance of God's salvific action in Jesus Christ. She expounds the motifs of Passover and sacrifice, ransom and redemption, *Christus Victor* and descent into hell, substitution and recapitulation.

She reproduces on a vast canvas the pattern that characterizes her sermons. The biblical theme is carefully set forth and examined and continually placed in relation to insights culled from classical works of literature and from historical events. Rutledge draws illuminating correlations with the quest for justice exemplified in the South African Truth and Reconciliation Commission and in the vision and practice of the civil rights movement in

4. Rutledge, 44 (emphasis removed).
5. Rutledge, 200.

the United States.[6] Both movements caution against "premature reconciliation," as though evil could be enacted with impunity.

Throughout, she inveighs against the sentimentality that reduces divine love to an attitude of "forgive and forget" or "God accepts us just as we are"—in effect sundering God's grace and God's judgment. She stresses that working out the relation between God's justice and God's mercy is "an essential task of Christian theology, preaching, and pastoral care" today.[7] Unless we do so, either merciless judgment or cheap grace will ensue.

Moreover, as she often cautions, the dividing line between the godly and ungodly cannot be facilely drawn. It does not pass only between "us" and "them"—for far too easily victims have turned into victimizers. "All have sinned and fall short of the glory of God" (Rom. 3:23). Each person, then, must take account of the power of sin to infiltrate and corrupt. Unsurprisingly, Flannery O'Connor figures among the novelists most cited in the book.

God's grace, therefore, does not exclude but enfolds judgment. God's love does not cancel condemnation of sin. But the Christian scandal is that God takes judgment and condemnation upon himself: "Wounded for our transgressions, crushed for our sins; upon him was the chastisement that made us whole—by his stripes we are healed" (Isa. 53:5). This is not the pound of flesh punishment inflicted by an angry Father upon a hapless Son. Redemption is the integral and integrating act of the Triune God whose love is compassion, suffering-with. Redemption is ultimate at-one-ment, beyond all division and estrangement.

Rutledge, while avoiding hardening the motif of "substitution" into an "explanatory theory" tinged with rationalism, considers it the *cantus firmus* undergirding the other motifs. It discloses how far God's grace truly extends . . . and its terrible cost. It proclaims a Savior who does not only act *on our behalf* but *in*

6. See Rutledge, 117f.
7. Rutledge, 114.

our place: "even unto death on a cross" (as the hymn in Philippians marvels). To take away the sin of the world, the Lamb of God who knew no sin, takes sin upon himself, becoming sin for our sake and in our place. He thereby justifies the unjust, rectifying sin's disorder at its root, transforming the world's pent-up hatred and murderous wrath into the new life of communion. For, ultimately, human hatred and wrath are an assault upon the Triune God who alone can propitiate and bring peace.

All this is God's doing in Christ, reconciling the world to himself. Yet we are not consigned to be inert bystanders, merely passive beneficiaries. We are called to grace-inspired participation in Christ. We are summoned to become members of Christ's Body, entering by Baptism into the New Covenant in his Blood. But this participation entails a "radical overhaul," for it is ever a Baptism "into his death" so that through his Resurrection we too might walk in "newness of life" (Rom. 6:4). As preacher and teacher in the Church, Rutledge vehemently counters the glib Gospel that we are acceptable "just the way we are." Rather, the Gospel of the Crucified compels her to assert, "Something has to transpire before we are counted as acceptable."[8] We must be crucified with Christ, so that we may be raised in him, by being incorporated into his Body.

It may be thought slightly perverse to wish that a rich volume of over six hundred fifty pages might be longer still. Yet I need to note what I take to be a salient omission from this splendid study. Having raised the crucial reality of "participation" and "incorporation" in Christ, it seems discordant that Rutledge makes no reference to the Eucharist. Her hesitancy in this regard may stem from a Barthian wariness with regard to "religion" as an idolatrous construct and with her reservations concerning the Eastern Orthodox focus on *theosis* or deification, which, she fears, risks blurring the distinction between Creator and creature.

8. Rutledge, 244.

Whatever the background reasons, the absence of attention to the *corpus mysticum* that is the Eucharist raises the question of the actuality of our humanity's incorporation into Christ. However transformed, is our God-given nature redeemed and saved, or is nature supplanted rather than perfected by grace? Are we, with our concrete histories and gifts, genuinely recapitulated in Christ and capacitated by his grace to act as real, if always dependent, collaborators? For it is, after all, by the Eucharist that our new identity in Christ is nourished and extended. It may be telling, in this regard, that the word "sanctification" does not appear in the very complete index of the book, nor is there any listing for "saints." Is our participation in Christ truly a present reality or only a future hope? Rutledge convincingly underscores the New Testament's "apocalyptic" horizon: God's redemptive intervention to rectify human and cosmic disorder. But does she do full justice to the eschatological "already" that is accomplished in the Paschal Mystery and made present in the Eucharist that believers share?

I trust the questions posed bear tribute to the challenging gift that Rutledge has provided. I can only echo the chant Augustine heard in the Garden: "Tolle, lege." Take up and read! Rutledge's volume wonderfully celebrates the triumph of redeeming grace: the crucified Messiah, Jesus, who is the wisdom and power of God.

11. A Review of

The Divine Ideas

Tradition in Christian Mystical Theology

by Mark A. McIntosh

Mark McIntosh, who died in October 2021 of ALS at the age of sixty-one, was an Episcopal priest and a remarkable theologian. He held the inaugural professorship in Christian Spirituality at Loyola University Chicago. I never met McIntosh, but as an appreciative reader of his work on Christian mystical theology, I have long felt a personal kinship with him.

McIntosh received his PhD from the University of Chicago, where he studied under David Tracy and Bernard McGinn and wrote his doctoral dissertation on Hans Urs von Balthasar. Among his writings, three deserve special mention: *Mystical Theology: The Integrity of Spirituality and Theology* shows the continuing influence of Balthasar but also the emergence of McIntosh's own distinctive voice. *Discernment and Truth: The Spirituality and Theology of Knowledge* explores the theological foundations of spiritual discernment and the transformative exigencies entailed by its truthful practice. *Mysteries of Faith*, addressed to a nonspecialized audience, is a gem of direct communication rich in theological and spiritual insight.

The topic of his last book, *The Divine Ideas*, might appear to be more recondite, yet it was written while the author contended with growing physical paralysis and with an acute sense of the

* Mark A. McIntosh, *The Divine Ideas: Tradition in Christian Mystical Theology* (Oxford: Oxford University Press, 2021). This book review was originally published as "Our True Identity," *Commonweal* 149, no. 5 (May 5, 2022): 57–59.

global threats posed by climate disruption, the pandemic, and misinformation. For McIntosh, immersion in the theological tradition concerning the "divine ideas" was not merely an academic exercise but a matter of burning actuality.

Mystical theology as McIntosh understands it is not a branch or subdivision of theology but rather a way of doing theology that keeps the inseparable connection of theology and spirituality to the fore. It presents the mysteries of the faith as realities into which we are invited to enter rather than just ideas we are able to entertain. For this reason, prayer and liturgy are part of the practice of mystical theology. In the words of the fourth-century mystical theologian Evagrius Ponticus, the one who is a theologian prays and the one who prays is a theologian. Mystical theology is therefore not the investigation of extraordinary physical and psychic phenomena but the cultivation, in mature Christian life, of a contemplative consciousness of the enlivening presence of God.

In *The Divine Ideas*, McIntosh marshals an array of Christian thinkers—from Origen and Augustine, through Maximus the Confessor and John Scotus Eriugena, to Aquinas and Bonaventure—who engaged with and transformed the Platonic philosophical tradition. For Platonists, the divine ideas constitute the permanent formal structures governing reality, of which the physical universe is only a derivative and passing reflection. Ideas, such as that of the good and of justice, are the ultimate measure of their shadowy earthly instantiations. Christian theologians, impelled by divine revelation, transformed this Platonic conception in two ways. Inspired by the doctrine of the Trinity, they viewed the Ideas not as subsistent realities but as intrinsic to divine knowing itself. Indeed, the very generation of the Word from the Father includes the archetypal "ideas" of all that God will create. "All things were made through the Word, and without him was not anything made that was made" (John 1:3). And because "the Word became flesh and dwelt among us" (John

1:14), the physical universe and bodily reality assume a unique dignity and luster. Rather than being depreciated as pale imitations of a far nobler reality, they became sacramental signifiers of an eternal truth and beauty. Here is how McIntosh recapitulates the Trinitarian and Christological revolution these theologians accomplished.

> The divine ideas teaching holds that the ideas of all creatures exist within the one eternal Idea that God has of Godself, namely within the eternal Word of God—and, conversely, that the one eternal Word who speaks the truth of every creature exists immanently within all creatures. . . . This means also that the incarnate Word, Jesus of Nazareth, bears within himself the deep truth of every creature.[1]

This is the complex fundamental theme that this book develops in a series of variations. McIntosh holds that the divine ideas tradition generates a "contemplative momentum."[2] The same thing could be said of his book, which explores ever more ample vistas. Let me sketch a few of these.

First, the book—and the tradition it retrieves—has a profound sense of the ongoing agency of the Blessed Trinity. It affirms not a deistic Supreme Being who withdraws into Olympian isolation, but the Triune God who creates *now*, forever speaking a life-giving Word and breathing forth the Spirit upon a beloved creation.

Second, a Christological grammar governs the Christian appropriation of the divine ideas teaching. The teaching is employed to elucidate the striking New Testament confession that Christ is "the image of the invisible God, the first-born of all creation" and that "in him all things hold together" (Col. 1:15, 17). McIntosh

1. McIntosh, *Divine Ideas*, 15.
2. McIntosh, 35.

writes that "God in Christ acts to restore the creation precisely by reuniting creatures with the knowledge of their true identity as it has always been known and loved in the eternal Word."[3] In Christ, the transcendent dignity of every human being stands revealed. He or she is a concrete expression of God's love, with a unique value and a distinct calling.

Third, the material creation exhibits "a rich depth of intelligibility" as the fruit of God's knowing and loving.[4] Creation's very being is sacramental. A richness of meaning lies embodied in the "ordinary." "Charged with the grandeur of God,"[5] creatures, both animate and inanimate, cry out, in Gerard Manley Hopkins's words, "What I do is me: for that I came."[6] McIntosh writes that for the divine ideas tradition, "the whole creation exists as a continuous event of communication and indeed communion—whose source is the eternal self-communication of the Trinity and whose goal is the fulfillment of creatures as they come more perfectly to share in this divine communion."[7]

The perfected embodiment of this divine communication and communion is the Resurrection of Jesus Christ. The "first-born of all creation" becomes the "first-born from the dead" (Col. 1:18), bringing creation home to its Source. Here, and in his other books, McIntosh shows a deep sense of the human plight and of our need for redemption. The divine ideas are luminous guides and goals, but they also bring into relief the illusions and addictions that are roadblocks to wisdom. Made for glory, we too often settle for fool's gold.

The death from which Christ saves us is far more than physical death. It is the very corroding of God's image in us through

3. McIntosh, 182.

4. McIntosh, 12.

5. Gerard Manley Hopkins, "God's Grandeur," Poetry Foundation, poetryfoundation.org.

6. Gerard Manley Hopkins, "As Kingfishers Catch Fire," Poetry Foundation, poetryfoundation.org.

7. McIntosh, *Divine Ideas*, 59.

fantasies of self-aggrandizement and hatred. These distortions of the generative divine ideas wreak havoc not only on individuals but on the whole human community and the rest of material creation. Sin falsifies divine communication and erects obstacles to the communion God desires. At its deepest, sin is refusal of Incarnation. For, in a sentence from Maximus the Confessor that McIntosh relishes, "the Word always and in all things desires to realize the mystery of his embodiment."[8]

With the Resurrection of Christ, God's life-giving Word stands fully revealed. Christians are those whose converted consciousness perceives the fulfillment of God's plan in the risen Christ and whose conduct seeks to further the restoration of all things in him. Immersed in Christ's Paschal Mystery in Baptism and nourished by the Eucharist, Christians are led "into a new communion with the divine ideas . . . a new perception of all reality from within the eternal divine knowing and loving of all things."[9] Moreover, the divine ideas tradition fosters the realization of the interconnectedness of all created reality.

Every life is constitutively relational, each imaging to every other its Triune Creator.

Significantly, McIntosh entitles the last chapter of his book "Beatitude and the Goodness of Truth." There, he struggles to give some expression to belief in "the life of the world to come." And, once more, his reflections are not notional but deeply, even poignantly, personal. In his preface, he frankly confesses, "As my physical incapacities became more challenging, I often wondered about the truth of my own life and how that truth might be grounded in a deeper reality."[10] And at the end of his exploration of the divine ideas tradition, he returns to the question: "What is the divine meaning inherent in our earthly struggle to fulfill the personal calling and gifts that comprise our embodied

8. Maximus the Confessor, *Ambiguum* 7.11, cited in McIntosh, *Divine Ideas*, 29.
9. McIntosh, *Divine Ideas*, 158.
10. McIntosh, viii.

existence—especially in light of the fact that we know ourselves to be mortal, that all we have loved and sought to achieve will need to be surrendered?"[11] With the help of that tradition, he ventures a response: "The self-sharing and self-communication through which we become who we are with others are meant to be life-giving and gracious moments of fulfillment, expressing in time the eternal self-sharing generosity of the Trinity within which our exemplar truth exists imperishably."[12] Thus, beyond the failures, the prideful refusals of communication and spurning of communion, our hope lies in "the Incarnation and Paschal mystery of the eternal Word [who] reconnects each creature with its truth in the Word and makes possible, through the self-giving love of Jesus Christ, the consummating self-donation of the creatures to each other and ultimately to God."[13]

As one immersed in the writings of mystical theologians from Evagrius to Merton, McIntosh wrestles in his works with the imperative to exorcise the false ego and put on the true self renewed in Christ. His book *Discernment and Truth* is, at heart, a study of the liberation of the ego from its illusions and addictions—liberation to the truth and freedom of the children of God. What the present work offers is the further insight that our true Christic self is already present in God's providential design for each of us in the Word that the Father utters from all eternity.

One might say that McIntosh has written, in this parting gift, an extended commentary upon Paul's exclamation: "For those whom God foreknew he also predestined to be conformed to the image of his Son, in order that the Son might be first-born among many brothers and sisters" (Rom. 8:29). This is the beatitude for which McIntosh longs: "As creatures are enabled in Christ to fulfill the relational nature of their identities, they are made whole again with God's knowing and loving of their truth, their divine

11. McIntosh, 200.
12. McIntosh, 200.
13. McIntosh, 201.

ideas; and this means that they are made one within the eternal event of God's knowing of Godself in the Word, and in this way come to share in the beatitude within which the Father knows all things in the Son within the eternal joy of the Holy Spirit."[14] May Mark McIntosh now know fully the One who has known and chosen him (and us) "before the foundation of the world."

14. McIntosh, 201.

Duccio di Buoninsegna, *Transfiguration*

"And we all, with unveiled faces, beholding the glory
of the Lord, are being transformed into his likeness,
from glory to glory."
2 Corinthians 3:18

PART III

Reflections

Soundings in the
Catholic Imagination

I. Soundings in the Christic *Novum*

A PATRISTIC MEDLEY*

Saint Irenaeus (130–202), bishop of Lyons during the last quarter of the second century, is often said to be the Church's first systematic theologian. In the fourth book of his magnum opus, *Adversus Haereses* ("Against the Heresies"), he expresses a conviction that lies at the heart of the Church's faith, yesterday and today: "Christ brought all newness in bringing himself"—*omnem novitatem attulit, semetipsum afferens*. And he adds, as an inseparable corollary: newness has dawned "to renew and give life to humankind"—*innovatura et vivificatura hominem.*[1]

I am persuaded that the witness of the New Testament is governed by this "logic" of newness and transformation. The absolute newness of Jesus Christ, the New Adam, bears, as its consequence, the radical newness of life to which disciples of Christ are called. To state the conviction in another way, "newness/transformation" is the very "grammar" of the New Testament, which its diverse assertions but illustrate.

The perennial importance of the early Fathers of the Church lies in their profound realization of this surpassing grace. In language redolent with the freshness of discovery, they draw upon this grammar in works both exacting and lyrical, intellectual and affective. They do so in closely argued treatises and soaring poetry.

---

* This essay was originally published as "A Patristic Medley," *The Catholic Thing*, May 17, 2020, www.thecatholicthing.org.

1. Irenaeus of Lyons, *Adversus Haereses* 4.34.1. The Patristic quotations in this essay are from the English translation of *The Liturgy of the Hours*.

They thereby belie any facile separation, much less disjunction, between the "doctrinal" and "pastoral." Their homilies are infused with doctrine and their essays spurred by pastoral concern. For the newness is Jesus Christ, and the new life is life in Christ.

I offer here some examples of their Spirit-inspired realization and proclamation of this newness.

The incomparable Saint Augustine of Hippo (354–430), preaching to his North African congregation on Christ's giving of a "new commandment," asks where this newness lies. And he responds: it is to love as Christ has loved. "Love one another, as I have loved you" (John 13:34). Christ's love is the newness to which every page of the New Testament bears witness. And it is inseparable from the "I" of Christ himself, who is God's love made flesh.

In a splendid homily on the Psalm "Sing to the Lord a new song," Augustine reminds his listeners, "We are urged to sing a new song to the Lord as new men and women who have learned a new song." Expounding the meaning of "new song," he riffs a set of variations on the theme of "new." "A song is a thing of joy; more profoundly, it is a thing of love. Anyone, therefore, who has learned to love the new life has learned to sing a new song, and the new song reminds us of our new life. The new man, the new song, the new covenant, all belong to the one kingdom of God, and so the new man will sing a new song and will belong to the new covenant."

One of Augustine's most striking insights into the Gospel's newness is that the New Adam is inseparably Christ and Christians. His term for this is "totus Christus," the whole Christ, Head and members. The insight is, of course, Pauline, but Augustine applies this to the Church's praying the Psalms. They are the prayer of the whole Christ; at times, the dominant voice is the Head's, at other times, members take the lead. But it is always the whole chorus singing, with Christ the Chorus Master, who guarantees proper rhythm and harmony.

Pope Saint Leo the Great (400–61), a generation later, will echo many Augustinian themes in his sermons on the liturgical seasons, though in a more modulated Roman style. His constant refrain is *etiam hodie*—"Today as well!" Christ's mysteries are not consigned to the past; they are actual in the today of faith, in the members of his Body.

Leo exults, "All that the Son of God did and taught for the world's reconciliation is not for us simply a matter of past history. Here and now we experience his power at work among us." Through Baptism and Eucharist, Christians participate in the new transformed life brought by Christ:

> The leaven of our former malice is thrown out, and a new creature is filled and inebriated with the Lord himself. For the effect of our sharing in the body and blood of Christ is to change us into what we receive. As we have died with him, and have been buried and raised to life with him, so we bear him within us, both in body and in spirit, in everything we do.

Leo often entreated his hearers, "Christian man and woman, recognize your great dignity!"

One theological-pastoral exploration of that dignity is found in a wonderful homily of the bishop of Ravenna Saint Peter Chrysologus (380–450). Though less well known than Augustine or Leo, Peter has the charism of concreteness and depth.

Commenting on Paul's exhortation to "offer your bodies as a living sacrifice, holy and acceptable to God" (Rom. 12:1), Chrysologus rhapsodizes, "How marvelous is the priesthood of the Christian, for he is both the victim that is offered on his own behalf, and the priest who makes the offering." Christ alone establishes the pattern by instituting the New Covenant. But he thereby constitutes Christian men and women as members of a priestly people, called to follow in Christ's paschal Way.

Thus, Peter can admonish his congregation, "Let your heart be an altar. Then, with full confidence in God, present your body for sacrifice. God desires not death, but faith; God thirsts not for blood, but for self-surrender; God is appeased not by slaughter, but by the offering of your free will."

The above is but a sampling of the rich variations the Fathers played upon the *cantus firmus* of newness and transformation in Christ. And they issue an invitation to proceed further. They urge their first hearers, and us their latter-day readers, to compose our own variations on the inexhaustible Good News, the mystery that is "Christ in you, the hope of glory" (Col. 1:27), as we are being transformed "from glory to glory" (2 Cor. 3:18).

COSTLY TRANSFIGURATION*

There's a New Testament verse that has always fascinated—and troubled—me. Yet I have rarely seen it commented upon. Paul exhorts the Colossians, "Do not lie to one another!" (Col. 3:9) The Apostle is not denouncing "garden variety" fibs or convenient mental reservations. Something much more serious is at stake. A fundamental falseness. Mere seeming rather than being. An inauthenticity and duplicity too often hidden even from oneself. Indeed, such willful self-deception is the "old leaven" that makes Pharisees of us all and that Paul exhorts us to "cleanse out" (1 Cor. 5:7).

The urgency and scope of the task is summed up succinctly by Paul in the very next verses he addresses to the Colossians. "You have put off the old man [*ton palaion anthrōpon*] with its practices; and have put on the new self [*ton neon*] who is being renewed in knowledge according to the image of its Creator"

* This essay was originally published as "Costly Transfiguration," *The Catholic Thing*, August 1, 2021, www.thecatholicthing.org.

(Col. 3:9–10). But since he has already proclaimed that Christ himself "is the image of the invisible God" (Col. 1:15), Paul is reiterating his insistent call to "put on the Lord Jesus Christ, making no provision for the desires of the flesh" (Rom. 13:14)—the very verse that spurred, at long last, Augustine's conversion.

And, of course, that movement from the old self to the new self has been initiated in Baptism. "All of us who were baptized into Christ Jesus were baptized into his death . . . so that, just as Christ was raised from the dead by the glory of the Father, so we too might walk in newness of life" (Rom. 6:3–4).

The whole of the Christian life, then, is the appropriation of what has already transpired in our Baptism but must now be realized fully in each of us until together "we all attain to the unity of faith and knowledge of the Son of God, to the one perfected humanity [*eis andra teleion*], to the measure of the stature of the fullness of Christ" (Eph. 4:13). One can sense the Apostle struggling to express the transformative newness to which Christians are called. The words tumble forth as he strains to provide some sense of the reality envisioned.

What's clear is that unlike the egoistic withdrawal of the old Adam, anyone incorporated into the New Adam, Jesus Christ, is fundamentally a self who lives the new life of communion. And foremost among the practices of that new self is "to renounce the lie and to speak truth to one's neighbor, since we are members of one another!" (Eph. 4:25)

One often hears that divine providence supplies the saint that the Church needs at a particular moment of its history. When Pope Francis canonized John Henry Newman on October 13, 2019, I had the privilege of being in Saint Peter's Square. And the special grace I received was to encounter a number of committed young people, who, seeing my Roman collar, asked me to hear their confession.

I asked each of them, "What brought you to Rome?" since four new saints were canonized that day. Each replied, "Newman." It was not the Newman who pioneered the theological discussion of the development of doctrine or who championed the indispensable role of the laity in the Church. It was Newman the spiritual guide, the preacher who sets before us the costly adventure of holiness, the path to transfigured life.

No accident, then, that the first of his great *Parochial and Plain Sermons* is entitled "Holiness Necessary for Future Blessedness" and that the text upon which it comments is from Hebrews: "Holiness, without which no man shall see the Lord" (Heb. 12:14).

Newman's sermons opened to his young English audience of the mid-nineteenth century vistas into the daunting beauty and challenge of the Christian life in the waning days of a domesticated established religion. But several of those sermons continue to challenge us all as we seek to find our way in the present societal and ecclesiastical decadence.

Sermons like "The Thought of God the Stay of the Soul," "The Cross of Christ the Measure of the World," and "The Yoke of Christ" offer a bracing regimen for cultivating that holiness to which Vatican II's *Lumen Gentium* summoned the Church. But perhaps one sermon is particularly apposite today: the sermon entitled "Unreal Words."

Newman begins this sermon with the timely reminder that Christ, being himself the Truth, "brought truth as well as grace."[2] But ever the realist, he concedes that when Christian profession becomes rote and the Church's rituals routine, religion becomes "a hollowness and a mockery, like the whited sepulchers of which our Lord speaks."[3] Then the life of Christians and the life of the Church becomes "unreal," devoid of vivifying substance. The professions and pronouncements no longer speak truth but a lie.

2. John Henry Newman, "Unreal Words," in *Parochial and Plain Sermons* (San Francisco: Ignatius, 1997), 977.

3. Newman, "Unreal," 985.

On this Feast of the Transfiguration of the Lord—a transfiguration to which Christ's disciples are all called—we need to make as honest an assessment of the Christianity of our day as Newman did the Christianity of his. We need to confess the lie embodied in our deeds: the infidelity of priests and people to their vows and promises, the scant transparency and accountability of leaders, the apostasy from or sacrilegious reception of the Holy Eucharist. The debasement of the language of faith.

And we need to hear anew and make real for ourselves Newman's great peroration to his sermon: "It is not an easy thing to learn that new language which Christ has brought us. He has interpreted all things for us in a new way; He has brought us a religion that sheds a new light on all that happens. Try to learn this language. Do not get it by rote, or speak it as a thing of course. . . . Time is short, eternity is long; God is great, man is weak; he stands between heaven and hell; Christ is his Savior; Christ has suffered for him."[4]

Saint John Henry Newman, pray that our words and acts not be unreal!

LOVING AND KNOWING JESUS*

In the foreword to the first volume of his *Jesus of Nazareth*, Benedict XVI reveals the deep theological and pastoral concern that inspired his labors. Owing to certain currents in biblical studies from the 1950s on, an impression has become widely diffused that "we have very little certain knowledge of Jesus and that only at a later stage did faith in his divinity shape the image we have of him."[5]

This theological challenge has immediate pastoral consequences. Benedict rightly discerns that this constitutes "a dramatic

---

4. Newman, 986.

* This essay was originally published as "Loving and Knowing Jesus," *The Catholic Thing*, October 4, 2020, www.thecatholicthing.org.

5. Pope Benedict XVI, foreword to *Jesus of Nazareth: From the Baptism in the Jordan to the Transfiguration*, trans. Adrian J. Walker (New York: Doubleday, 2007), xii.

situation for faith, because its point of reference is being placed in doubt: Intimate friendship with Jesus, on which everything depends, is in danger of clutching at thin air."[6]

Intimate friendship with Jesus is the very heart of the matter.

Benedict had already sounded a similar theme in his first encyclical, *Deus Caritas Est*. In a much-quoted sentence, he writes, "Being Christian is not the result of an ethical choice or a lofty idea, but the encounter with an event, a person, which gives life a new horizon and a decisive direction. Saint John's Gospel describes that event in these words: 'God so loved the world that he gave his only Son, that whoever believes in him should . . . have eternal life' (3:16)."[7]

This "encounter," by its very nature, is destined to grow into an abiding "friendship," as the Last Supper discourse in Saint John's Gospel makes clear. "No longer do I call you servants . . . but I have called you friends" (John 15:15). "Abide in me and I in you. . . . He who abides in me, and I in him, bears much fruit, for apart from me you can do nothing" (John 15:4–5).

I would like to explore three dimensions of "friendship with Jesus" that may serve us as we all seek to appropriate and deepen this call to friendship with the Lord.

First is what the liturgical and theological tradition speaks of as the "prevenient" love of Jesus. Friendship with Jesus Christ is not our initiative nor is it within our natural capacity. It depends utterly on the initiative of Jesus. "Love of Jesus" is, in the first instance, Jesus's love of us. Saint Paul is firm in his persuasion: "The Lord Jesus who loved me and gave himself for me" (Gal. 2:20).

Our love of Jesus is our grace-endowed and grateful response to his love of us even to death, death on a cross. I can still remember the deep affection with which, as a youngster participating

---

6. Benedict, *Jesus of Nazareth*, xii.
7. Benedict XVI, *Deus Caritas Est* 1, encyclical letter, December 25, 2005, vatican.va.

in the Stations of the Cross, I joined with many in professing, "I love you, Jesus my love, I repent of having offended you."

A second dimension of friendship with Jesus flows from this—namely, the love of Jesus gives rise to our knowledge of Jesus. My primary knowledge of the Lord is that of his love for me. To adapt Paul, I know "the Lord Jesus who loves me and gives himself for me." Real, not merely notional, knowledge of Jesus is the abiding fruit of love of Jesus. And the experiential setting for this knowledge is the Church's celebration of the Eucharist, where Jesus's loving self-gift is re-presented and made actual.

So, our knowledge of Jesus has its genesis as an affective, interpersonal knowledge. It is the type of knowledge to which Pascal points in his famous dictum: "The heart has its reasons which reason does not comprehend." It underlies John Henry Newman's conviction that "heart speaks to heart." One may call it a "participatory knowledge," the mutual knowledge that characterizes true friendship, as friends share one another's values, views, and virtues.

Of course, here we have an absolutely unique friendship and relation: Jesus remains ever the teacher and we the disciples, Jesus ever the Head and we the members of his Body. Thus, one comes to "know" Jesus more deeply the more one is conformed to him. "You are my friends if you do what I command you" (John 15:14). These "commands," however, are not obedience to external precepts, but adhering to a person, making one's own the vision and mission of Jesus, abiding in his love.

Paul, Apostle and mystic, brings out the depth of his identification with his Savior. "I have been crucified with Christ; it is no longer I who live, but Christ who lives in me" (Gal. 2:20). And all the great Christian spiritual masters have each, in his or her own fashion, echoed Paul's cry.

This "Christification," this being configured to Christ, begins in Baptism. But the seed planted there must be nourished so that the plant may grow sturdy. And then it must be further pruned and strengthened to withstand the "wickedness and snares" of world, flesh, and devil. Its full flowering will come only when the Lord gathers his beloved from the ends of the earth into the kingdom of the Father.

The third dimension of our friendship with Jesus is already adumbrated in the previous quote from Paul. As Paul and all the saints bear witness, growth in friendship with Christ entails an ever more generous embrace of his cross. In the Letter to the Philippians, Paul recounts his own experience of "cruciformity." He speaks of the life-giving loss of all he had formerly counted of worth, the prideful pomp of the "flesh": pedigree, accomplishments, death-dealing zeal for the ego-inflating cause. All unmasked as vanity in the revelatory light of "knowing Christ Jesus my Lord" (Phil. 3:8).

Yet, at the same time, Paul humbly acknowledges not yet being "perfected" (*teleios*), not yet fully transformed: "But I press on to make it my own, because Christ Jesus has made me his own . . . forgetting what lies behind and straining forward to what lies ahead" (Phil. 3:12–13). Only at the end of our journey shall we finally know and love even as we are known and loved.

This conviction undergirds and continually nourishes the excruciating, transfiguring adventure of our friendship with him who is Savior, Lord, ever-faithful friend.

CHRIST THE GIVER OF THE SPIRIT*

Many years ago, during my junior year of college, I read Hilaire Belloc's deliciously discerning book *The Path to Rome*. Written in 1902, it recounts his pilgrimage on foot (for the most part, at least) from his hometown in France to the Eternal City. Belloc embarked upon the journey because he had been enchanted by a

* This essay was originally published as "Christ the Giver of the Spirit," *The Catholic Thing*, June 5, 2022, www.thecatholicthing.org.

lovely statue of Our Lady that he discovered in his parish church. A work of beauty spurred and sustained his path to Rome.

The same year that I read Belloc, I too came upon a work of art that has guided and enriched my own journey. It has not been a physical trek of a thousand kilometers, but it has had its own small share of adventure. The image that has accompanied me for more than sixty years is that of a splendid stone carving in the Basilica of Saint Mary Magdalene in Vézelay, France.[8] One enters the twelfth-century church into a porch area to find, above the main entrance door, a monumental depiction of the risen, ascending Christ from whose outsized hands the rays of the Holy Spirit pour forth upon the Apostles.

This image of Christ the giver of the Spirit strikes me as particularly Johannine in inspiration. In my own pondering, it seems to draw upon three crucial passages of John's Gospel.

In chapter 7, John recounts Jesus's presence in Jerusalem for the Feast of Tabernacles, teaching in the temple and disputing with the Pharisees. On the last day of the feast, he solemnly proclaims that those who believe in him will receive living water. The narrator clarifies the meaning: "Now [Jesus] said this about the Spirit which those who believed in him were to receive." But then, in one of the Gospel's most enigmatic passages, John adds, "For as yet the Spirit had not been given, because Jesus was not yet glorified" (John 7:39). The Greek is starker still: "There was not yet Spirit!"

The reader is thus primed to anticipate an intimate nexus between Jesus's "glorification" and the bestowal of the Spirit. But the ongoing scandal of the Gospel (for Jew, Greek, and each of us) is that the hour of Jesus's glory is the hour of the cross. All the wondrous "signs" Jesus works in the course of the Gospel—from the wedding feast at Cana to the raising of Lazarus—are consummated and surpassed in his "hour of glory." Hence, we read at the

8. See the reproduction of this image at page xxvi above.

end of the Passion account, "Jesus said, 'It is fulfilled.' And, bowing his head, he handed over [*paredōken*] the Spirit" (John 19:30).

The fruit of this "handing over" of the Spirit—the deepest meaning of "tradition" in the Church—is further shown in the appearance of the risen One on "the evening of the first day of the week."

Jesus encounters his dispirited and fearful disciples, bringing peace and forgiveness. And "he breathed upon them, saying: 'Receive the Holy Spirit!'" (John 20:22) As an ancient prayer of the liturgy (prayed as the Prayer over the Gifts at Mass on Saturday before Pentecost) exults, "It is the Holy Spirit himself who is the forgiveness of sin!"

These three crucial passages—not yet Spirit, releasing the Spirit, sharing the Spirit—form the backdrop to the Vézelay sculpture and to our own appropriation of Pentecostal faith. The image evokes aesthetically what the Gospel realizes narratively: drawing the hearer or beholder into a life-giving relation to the living Lord, inviting him or her to abide in Christ, and, in the power of the Spirit, to share the Gospel for the life of the world.

The risen Lord's breathing of the Spirit, his in-spiriting his disciples, recalls the depiction in Genesis of the Lord God "forming man from the dust of the ground and breathing into his nostrils the breath of life" (Gen. 2:7). Tragically, beginning with Adam and Eve, life in the Spirit was rejected, and relation ruptured. But God's Spirit stood ever ready to repair the breach, inspiring friends of God and prophets until, in the fullness of time, God sent one who is more than friend or prophet, but the only begotten Son. Jesus, the Son of God's own heart, is not only bearer but bestower of the Spirit.

Thus, on the Eighth Day, the risen Jesus inaugurates the new creation, the true *novus ordo seclorum*. The entire New Testament is permeated with this sense of the new thing that God has accomplished through Jesus Christ, crucified by human beings but raised to new life and now seated at God's right hand.

But there is yet more. For humankind is not merely the recipient of God's creative and redemptive action. We are called to active engagement, to be participants in the very life of God. We are called to communion [*koinōnia*] with God and, inseparably, to communion with our brothers and sisters in the Spirit.

In his profound *Commentary on the Gospel of John*, Cyril of Alexandria underscores the ground and scope of Pentecostal transformation:

> Christ sends the Spirit, who is both the Father's Spirit and his own, to dwell in each of us. And that Spirit, being one and indivisible, unites those who are distinct from each other as individuals, and causes them all to be gathered into unity in himself.

Cyril continues:

> Joined to the Holy Spirit, our nature is transformed so that we are no longer merely human, but also sons of God, spiritual men and women, because we have received a share in the divine nature. We are all one, therefore, in the Father and the Son and the Holy Spirit. We are one in mind and holiness, we are one through our communion in the sacred flesh of Christ, and through our sharing in the one Holy Spirit.[9]

As Cyril perceives, the language of "Spirit" in the New Testament is a language of relationship and mutuality. It is a language of persons in relation: whether the persons of the Trinity—Father and Son related in the communion of the Holy Spirit—or of believers

---

9. Cyril of Alexandria, *Commentary on the Gospel of John* 11.11, quoted in *The Liturgy of the Hours*, vol. 2, *Lenten Season – Easter Season* (New York: Catholic Book Publishing, 1976), 889–91.

called to that fullness of personhood that is communion. Indeed, the God of Trinitarian love desires and inspires lovers who share God's own passion for communion.

NEWMAN AND DULLES: TWO WITNESSES TO CHRIST*

In the book of essays he compiled shortly before he died (*Evangelization for the Third Millennium*), Cardinal Avery Dulles issued a caution against a growing "soteriological pluralism" in contemporary theology. He was challenging the contention that though Christ may be, in some sense, normative for Christian salvation, such a claim should not be made normative for adherents of other religious traditions.

Dulles had also written a fine study entitled *John Henry Newman*. Though Dulles modestly disclaimed being "a Newman expert," he confessed that he had read Newman "over many decades" and had been "greatly influenced by his method and teaching."

A key area of convergence was that both advocated a critical stance toward what Newman called "Liberalism." In the famous speech that Newman gave in Rome in 1879 on the occasion of his being made a cardinal, he declared, "Liberalism in religion is the doctrine that there is no positive truth in religion, that one creed is as good as another. . . . It teaches that all are to be tolerated, for all are matters of opinion. Revealed religion is not a truth, but a sentiment and a taste."[10]

In explicit contrast to this, Newman, throughout his life, both as an Anglican and as a Catholic, espoused what he called "the principle of dogma." He meant by this that revealed religion enunciates truths that are objective—not mere sentiments nor

---

* This essay was originally published as "Newman and Dulles: Two Witnesses to Christ," *The Catholic Thing*, September 28, 2019, www.thecatholicthing.org.

10. John Henry Newman, "Biglietto Speech, Rome," in *Addresses to Cardinal Newman with His Replies*, ed. W.P. Neville (London: Longmans, 1905), 64, https://www.newmanreader.org/works/addresses/file2.html.

the fanciful wishes of individuals, but the fruit of real encounters with God as witnessed in the Scriptures and the Christian tradition.

For both Newman and Dulles, the Incarnation of the Eternal Word of God in Jesus Christ is the anchor of their faith and the abiding point of reference for spiritual life, preaching, and authentically Catholic theology.

In "The Influence of Natural and Revealed Religion Respectively," the second of his *Oxford University Sermons*, Newman speaks of God's economy of revelation as the "method of personation."[11] He declares that all the abstract principles of philosophy—Word, Light, Life, Truth, Wisdom—become personalized in Christ.

What otherwise can remain merely "notional" becomes "real" in him—concrete, vivid, enkindling affection and inspiring imitation. Newman sums up his persuasion in these words, with which Dulles would heartily concur: "It is the Incarnation of the Son of God rather than any doctrine drawn from a partial view of Scripture (however true and momentous it may be) which is the article of a standing or a falling Church."[12]

Thus, Newman speaks of "the Idea of the Incarnation" as the heart of the Christian faith vision. He means by "Idea" not merely a concept in the mind but a living and life-giving image that nourishes the heart and imagination as well.

And that concept and image is the reality of Jesus presented in the Gospels. As he insists in his (perhaps most profound theological work) *Lectures on the Doctrine of Justification*, "The true preaching of the Gospel is to preach Christ."[13]

11. John Henry Newman, *Fifteen Sermons Preached before the University of Oxford* (hereafter, *Oxford University Sermons*), 3rd ed. (New York: Scribner, 1872), 29.

12. Newman, *Oxford University Sermons*, 35.

13. John Henry Newman, "On Preaching the Gospel," in *Lectures on the Doctrine of Justification* (London: Longmans, 1914), 325.

For Newman, Jesus Christ is both utterly concrete and universally significant. In his late work *A Grammar of Assent*, he asserts, "All the providences of God centre in Christ."[14] And in *Lectures on Justification*, Newman declares,

> Christ came for this very purpose, to gather together in one all the elements of good dispersed throughout the world, to make them his own, to illuminate them with Himself, to reform and refashion them into Himself. He came to make a new and better beginning of all things than Adam had been, and to be a fountain-head from which all good henceforth might flow.[15]

And this not only for Christians but for all humanity.

For Newman, Christ is present not absent; he may be absent in the flesh, but he is truly present, through his Spirit, in faith. In his sermon on "The Spiritual Presence of Christ in the Church," Newman asks, "But why has the Spirit come? to supply Christ's absence, or to accomplish His presence?"

And he responds, "Surely to make Him present. Let us not for a moment suppose that God the Holy Ghost comes in such sense that God the Son remains away. No; [the Spirit] has not so come that Christ does not come, but rather He comes that Christ may come in His coming." And he concludes, "Thus the Spirit does not take the place of Christ in the soul, but secures that place to Christ."[16]

For both Newman and Dulles, this real and continuing Presence of Jesus Christ finds its fullest expression in the Eucharist. If their minds led each to acknowledge the fullness of Apostolic faith in the Roman Catholic Church, their hearts found fulfillment

14. John Henry Newman, *An Essay in Aid of a Grammar of Assent* (Oxford: Clarendon, 1985), 43.

15. John Henry Newman, "Righteousness Viewed as a Gift and as a Quality," in *Lectures on the Doctrine of Justification* (London: Longmans, 1914) 193.

16. John Henry Newman, "The Spiritual Presence of Christ in the Church," in *Parochial and Plain Sermons* (San Francisco: Ignatius, 1997), 1265–66.

of their ardent desire and affection in the Blessed Sacrament reserved in the humblest of Catholic churches and chapels.

Christ's Eucharistic presence is the paradigmatic instance of
"heart speaking to heart" (Newman's cardinalatial motto): the
heart of Christ addressing the heart of each disciple whom he
calls by name.

In a letter to a correspondent after becoming Catholic, Newman spoke of "the surpassing privilege of having a Chapel under
the very roof in which I live and Christ in it."[17] And he rejoiced in
"the extreme, ineffable comfort of being in the same house with
Him who cured the sick and taught His disciples, as we read of
Him in the Gospels, in the days of His flesh."[18]

Avery Dulles took as his own cardinalatial motto, "I know
him in whom I have believed," Christ, whom Dulles called, in
his last McGinley Lecture, "the Pearl of great price." For both
Newman and Dulles, the Incarnation of God's Eternal Word in
Jesus Christ and Christ's universal salvific significance is, indeed,
the article of faith upon which the Church stands or falls.

Given the turmoil and creedal confusion in the Church
today, their conjoint personal and theological witness to Jesus
Christ, as unique and universal Savior, is both gift and challenge.
For our pressing peril may be less *schism* than it is *apostasy* from
"the faith once and definitively delivered to the Saints."

KARL RAHNER: AN APPRECIATION AND CRITIQUE*

Robert Royal's fine book *A Deeper Vision: The Catholic Intellectual Tradition in the Twentieth Century* consists, by and large, of
a series of inviting and insightful essays on the great figures who

---

17. John Henry Newman, *Letters and Diaries of John Henry Newman*, vol. 11, ed. Charles
Stephen Dessain (Edinburgh: Thomas Nelson, 1961), 131.

18. Newman, *Letters*, 131.

* This essay was originally published as "Karl Rahner: An Appreciation and Critique,"
First Things, July 7, 2016, firstthings.com.

SOUNDINGS IN THE CHRISTIC *NOVUM*

brought that tradition into creative and challenging encounter with a culture that was fast forgetting its Christian roots.

Maritain and Gilson, de Lubac and Rahner, Balthasar and Ratzinger are treated with generosity and discernment, as are the poets and novelists of the Catholic revival in England and France: Chesterton, Belloc, Greene, and Tolkien; Péguy, Claudel, Bernanos, and Mauriac. Each essay sparkles with appreciation and delight. Yet Royal's is not an exercise in hagiography. As in all authentic discernment, one comes to recognize both light and shadow. Only thus can one learn and move forward.

I found particular resonance, for personal and professional reasons, in the pages dedicated to the great Jesuit theologian Karl Rahner. My own theological education began in the 1960s, at a time both propitious and problematic. I had the grace of studying at Rome's Gregorian University during the four sessions of Vatican II. I pursued my doctoral work during the ecclesial and cultural upheavals of the late sixties, with 1968 as the pivotal year of cultural revolution, political assassination, and ecclesial turmoil.

All through the sixties Karl Rahner was, by any measure, the dominant theological voice. He took a leading role in launching the journal *Concilium*, edited the multivolume *Sacramentum Mundi* (the one-volume abridgment of which was the ordination present of choice for about ten years), and produced a steady stream of dense articles that sought to further the *aggiornamento* motif of the council. These articles were quickly gathered into the many volumes of his *Schriften zur Theologie*, and, with increasing rapidity, translated into English as *Theological Investigations*.

Almost fifty years since I first read them, I still have vivid and grateful recollections of two of these articles: "The Concept of Mystery in Catholic Theology" and "What Is a Dogmatic Statement?" It would not be excessive to say that they provided me with a real sense of theological liberation. In the face of a more constricted neo-Scholasticism, Rahner enabled one to savor the rich amplitude of the Catholic dogmatic tradition that did not pretend to circumscribe mystery narrowly but evoked and pointed toward the true direction in which it was to be encountered, pondered, and celebrated.

Dogma, Rahner taught, is of its very nature mystagogic, and the theologian in the Church is called to be a mystagogue. But that requires that he or she be steeped in the Church's Tradition and nourished by the Church's liturgy and spirituality.

Hence Rahner's commitment to *aggiornamento* cannot be separated from his immersion in *ressourcement*—from his rootedness in Ignatian spirituality, his recovery of the Patristic tradition of the spiritual senses, and his ongoing wrestling with the thought of Thomas Aquinas. Only thus equipped can the theologian engage in fruitful dialogue with the modern world, seeking to illumine its joy and hope, suffering and affliction with the light of the Gospel.

Those of us who fell under the Rahnerian spell in the sixties and seventies reveled in his evocation of God's holy mystery, of God as "semper major," with its apophatic sensibility. "Si comprehendis, non est Deus," Rahner repeated with Augustine: If you think to have grasped God, it is not God whom you have grasped.

We also echoed with fervor his insistence upon the inseparability of the mystery of God and the mystery of man—his "anthropocentric turn" in theology. This promised to help repair the breach that, in neo-Scholasticism, separated theology and spirituality—a divorce also lamented by Hans Urs von Balthasar, who, like Rahner, was deeply rooted in the Ignatian spiritual tradition.

However, as the 1970s bled into the 1980s, students of Rahner assumed positions of importance in university and seminary schools of theology. More and more, they lacked the vital immersion in the Catholic theological tradition that had characterized Rahner himself. Too often, the hard-won and differentiated conclusions of the master became the facile and often clichéd starting points of the disciples.

Rahner's pregnant apophaticism, awe before the holy mystery, became an empty transcendentalism, without form or definition. It became the vague and distant mountain upon whose accommodating surface many salvific paths wended their winding way. Not "no other name" but "many other names under heaven."

This suggests what led me and others to take our distance from the Rahnerian enterprise while, like Robert Royal, remaining appreciative of much that he had accomplished. The crucial issue was the centrality of Jesus Christ. To his immense credit, Rahner always taught, faithful to the liturgical and theological tradition, that all grace is the grace of Christ. But when this was implicitly or explicitly denied by many who claimed to have learned from him, one could not but wonder whether Rahner's theological edifice was erected upon insufficient Christological foundations.

In 1970, a young theologian who had collaborated with Rahner during the council voiced his concerns in a series of probing questions. Royal cites him as asking, "Is it true that Christianity adds nothing to the universal but merely makes it known? Is the Christian really just man as he is? . . . Is it not the main point of the faith of both Testaments that man is what he ought to be only by conversion, that is, when he ceases to be what he is? Does not Christianity become meaningless when it is reinstated in the universal, whereas what we really want is the new, the other, the saving transformation?"[19]

Whether Rahner's theology allows him to respond adequately to these questions posed by Joseph Ratzinger would fuel a fascinating and lengthy discussion. But by placing the absolute newness of Christ and the transformation it demands at the very

19. Joseph Ratzinger, *The Ratzinger Report*, trans. Salvator Attanasio and Graham Harrison (San Francisco: Ignatius, 1985), 197, quoted in Robert Royal, *A Deeper Vision: The Catholic Intellectual Tradition in the Twentieth Century* (San Francisco: Ignatius, 2015), 219.

center of his theology, Joseph Ratzinger / Benedict XVI continues
to inspire and nourish the theology and spirituality of many of us.

JOSEPH RATZINGER: IN GRATITUDE*

Through successive waves of "downsizing" and the painful parting with many treasured books, I have carefully retained one volume: number 17 of the formidable series published before and
during Vatican II by Herder and Herder under the collective title:
Quaestiones Disputatae. The slim book, *Revelation and Tradition*,
contains three essays, one by Karl Rahner and two by Joseph
Ratzinger. As a seminarian finishing his studies in Rome during
the last session of the council, the attraction of essays by two of
the council's *periti* was compelling, and I willingly plunked down
twelve hundred lire, equivalent to the cover price of $1.95.

I was already somewhat familiar with some works of Rahner,
but this would be my first formal encounter with Ratzinger. Rahner's essay I found turgid; but Ratzinger's was not only pellucid—
it was illuminating. What it impressed upon me, as a young theology student, was an understanding of revelation as personal
communication and hence requiring for its realization the loving
and faith-filled reception by a subject. Three sentences were particularly "revelatory." Ratzinger maintained that "Revelation is
more than scripture to the extent that reality exceeds information
about it. . . . For revelation always and only becomes a reality
where there is faith." And, most significantly, "The actual reality
which occurs in Christian revelation is nothing and no other than
Christ himself."[20]

Already present in these observations was Ratzinger's commitment to the inseparability of theology and spirituality. Theology

---

* This essay was originally published as "What Benedict Saw," *First Things*, January 5,
2023, firstthings.com.

20. Karl Rahner and Joseph Ratzinger, *Revelation and Tradition*, trans. W.J. O'Hara (New
York: Herder, 1966), 35, 36.

as "faith seeking understanding" arises from a revelation, given and accepted, whose defining subject is Jesus Christ. Revelation, so understood, sounds an experiential, relational, and affective key—far richer than the narrowly propositional approach of the theology manuals. It is the understanding of revelation that is magisterially set forth in *Dei Verbum*, Vatican II's Dogmatic Constitution on Divine Revelation, in whose drafting Joseph Ratzinger played an important role.

My next serious encounter with Ratzinger came a few years later. I was a doctoral student at Yale in the tumultuous late sixties, slated to begin teaching at Saint Joseph's Seminary in Dunwoodie in fall 1970. Aside from the daunting prospect of teaching for the first time, there loomed the challenge as to what texts to use. The manuals had been discarded. Random articles proliferated, each probing in a tentative and exploratory fashion. None was suited to provide more than finger food, not the substantive fare needed by first-year seminarians.

Providentially (not for the last time), Ratzinger came to the rescue. His aid took the form of a book that has since become a theological classic, translated into twenty languages: *Introduction to Christianity*. It originated as lectures delivered in Tübingen in 1967, published the following year in German and translated into English in 1969—just in time to serve as the main text for my course at Dunwoodie. I venture to say it was probably the first use of the book in a seminary course in the United States. I taught the book my eight years at Dunwoodie and often thereafter in graduate seminars at Boston College. It is hardly an exaggeration to assert that the book has had a decisive influence upon many a student over the more than fifty years since it first appeared.

A few features of the book are worth highlighting since they remain importantly relevant even today. First, the clear-sightedness with which Ratzinger saw, within a few years of the council's close, the widespread betrayal of the council's foundational principles and governing affirmations. In the preface, dated summer 1968, he forthrightly contends, "The question of the real content and meaning of the Christian faith is enveloped today in a greater fog of uncertainty than at almost any earlier period in history." And he draws suggestively upon the folktale of "Clever Hans," who trades his lump of gold for ever less valuable objects until he is left with a cheap whetstone, to indict those theologians who have "gradually watered down the demands of faith."[21] A few years later, he would sum up the betrayal by lamenting that "they changed wine into water and called it 'aggiornamento.'"

Second, the book is structured as a theological-spiritual meditation upon the Apostles' Creed. The choice is significant, for its origin is the baptismal exchange wherein the neophyte commits to a transformed existence, renouncing those powers that diminish the human and confessing the life-giving belief in Father, Son, and Holy Spirit. Indeed, Ratzinger boldly sets forth his book's aim: "To help understand faith afresh as something that makes possible true humanity in the world of today."[22]

Third, the heart of the matter (and of the book), then, is its Christo-logic. Once again, his approach is fully theological and intensely personal. Perhaps nowhere is his Christological vision more incisively expressed than when he writes, "Christian faith is more than the option in favor of a spiritual ground to the world; its central formula is not 'I believe in something,' but 'I believe in you.' It is the encounter with the man Jesus, and in this encounter it experiences the meaning of the world as a person."[23] It is Jesus who grounds and enables transformed human existence: what the Tradition calls *theosis* or divinization.

21. Joseph Ratzinger, *Introduction to Christianity*, trans. J.R. Foster (San Francisco: Ignatius, 2004), 31.
22. Ratzinger, *Introduction*, 32.
23. Ratzinger, 79.

As always with Ratzinger, his reflection weds fidelity and creativity. The man had an abhorrence of prepackaged expressions, what John Henry Newman called "unreal words." In a biting comment written prior to Vatican II, the young theologian wrote, "Perhaps nothing . . . has done more harm to preaching than the loss of credibility that it incurred by merely handing on formulas that were no longer the living intellectual property of those who were proclaiming them."[24] And after the council, he lamented that often the malady remained the same, save that "dogmatic formulas" were now often replaced by "secular slogans," apodictically proclaimed.[25]

In *Introduction to Christianity*, Ratzinger sketched an approach to Christology that was faithful to the Church's millennial tradition yet painted in fresh interpersonal language. Jesus Christ is the New Adam, the *eschatos* Adam, who is defined by total relationality: the Son whose existence is *from* the Father, *for* the sake of men and women of every age. Jesus Christ does not merely institute the Eucharist. His total being is Eucharist: gratitude to the Father, self-gift for the many. And he continually consecrates his Church, by his loving sacrifice, as a Eucharistic people.

What was already evident in *Introduction to Christianity* is that the crisis of the post–Vatican II Church is, at its deepest, a Christological crisis. The transforming wine who is Jesus Christ is being diluted by invoking him as an inspiring model for sundry social causes, when not summarily dismissing him as a barely knowable figure from the first century of the "common era." It is this discernment that impelled Benedict to compose his trilogy *Jesus of Nazareth*. He expressed his pastoral concern poignantly in the foreword to the first volume: "This is a dramatic situation for faith, because its point of reference is being placed in doubt: Intimate friendship with Jesus, on which everything depends, is

---

24. Joseph Ratzinger, *Dogma and Preaching: Applying Christian Doctrine to Daily Life*, trans. Michael J. Miller and Matthew J. O'Connell (San Francisco: Ignatius, 2011), 57.

25. Ratzinger, *Dogma*, 57.

in danger of clutching at thin air."[26] It is only through a lived relationship with Jesus, who is Way, Truth, and Life, that we have access to the Trinity's love, in which all things live and move and have their being.

Since that first, long-ago encounter with the writings of Joseph Ratzinger, that young seminarian has become (how is it possible?) an octogenarian. I have taught courses on the theology of Joseph Ratzinger, written articles appreciative of his theological vision, profited personally from his spiritual wisdom. His homilies as pope have been, for me, sources of insight and renewed commitment to the following of Christ. And in my almost fifty-eight years of priesthood, his profound theology of the liturgy has been a polestar for my own.

In the foreword to the inaugural volume of his *Collected Works*, Benedict XVI wrote, "The liturgy of the Church has been for me since my childhood the central reality of my life, and . . . it became the center of my theological efforts."[27] Faced with the depth and richness of his liturgical writings, it is a sad testament to the captiousness and theological superficiality of many of his critics that they reductively charge him with favoring the celebration of Mass with the priest's back to the congregation. Aside from the empirical fact that the Masses Benedict celebrated in Saint Peter's Basilica were always *coram populo*, his concern was less physical position than spiritual orientation.

What is at stake, of course, is Christological: the unique and universal significance of Jesus Christ. As I have written, in contemporary Church life and theology, it can too often seem as if we are a "decapitated body," a self-referential gathering that proceeds (in the words of Cardinal Cantalamessa) "etsi Christus non

26. Pope Benedict XVI, foreword to *Jesus of Nazareth: From the Baptism in the Jordan to the Transfiguration*, trans. Adrian J. Walker (New York: Doubleday, 2007), xii.

27. Joseph Ratzinger, foreword to *Collected Works: Theology of the Liturgy* (San Francisco: Ignatius, 2014), xvi.

daretur"—"as though Christ were not given."[28] In clear contrast to this, Ratzinger insists, in his splendid *The Spirit of the Liturgy*, that "what matters is looking together at the Lord. It is now not a question of dialogue but of common worship, of setting off toward the One who is to come. What corresponds with the reality of what is happening is not the closed circle but the common movement forward."[29]

For this humble worker in the vineyard of the Lord, so attuned to the rhythms of the liturgical year, it is certainly providential that his baptismal liturgy was celebrated on the Vigil of Easter and his funeral liturgy on the Vigil of the Epiphany. The Epiphany always had a special attraction for the theologian pope. It unites the hopes of Israel and the nations. It integrates the light of faith and that of reason. Among the memorable homilies of Pope Benedict, those for the Epiphany have a special luster.

In the homily he preached on the first Feast of the Epiphany of his pontificate, Benedict XVI said,

> The Church is holy, but made up of men and women with their limitations and errors. It is Christ, Christ alone, who, in giving us the Holy Spirit, can transform our misery and constantly renew us. He is the light of the peoples, the *lumen gentium,* who has chosen to illumine the world through his Church. "How can this come about?," we also ask ourselves with the words that the Virgin addresses to the Archangel Gabriel. And she herself, the Mother of Christ and of the Church, gives us the answer: with her example of total availability to God's will—"*fiat mihi secundum verbum tuum*" Lk 1:38—she teaches us to be a "manifestation" of the Lord, opening our

28. Raniero Cantalamessa, *The Power of the Cross: Good Friday Sermons from the Papal Preacher* (Elk Grove Village, IL: Word on Fire, 2023), 320.

29. Joseph Ratzinger, *The Spirit of the Liturgy*, trans. John Saward (San Francisco: Ignatius, 2000), 81.

hearts to the power of grace and faithfully abiding by the words of her Son, light of the world and the ultimate end of history.[30]

If the music of Mozart always delighted Ratzinger by the depth of its humanity, the music of Bach strengthened him by its sublime witness and call to faith. Hence it is more than fitting that I was listening to Bach's *Christmas Oratorio* when news came of Benedict's death. The fourth cantata, that for New Year's Day, ends with a soft prayerful choral:

> May Jesus govern my beginning,
> May Jesus ever remain at my side.
> May Jesus direct my feelings,
> May Jesus alone be my desire.
> May Jesus be in my thoughts.
> Jesus, let me never waver.

How consonant with his entire life's journey and vision that, as Joseph Ratzinger lay dying, his final words would be, "*Signore, ti amo.*"

A BODILY FAITH[*]

Cardinal Robert McElroy of San Diego recently published a long and provocative article in *America* magazine.[31] It has already garnered both grateful praise and pointed criticism. Count me among the critics.

---

30. Benedict XVI, "Homily on the Solemnity of the Epiphany," January 6, 2006, vatican.va.

* This essay was originally published as "A Bodily Faith," *First Things*, January 31, 2023, firstthings.com.

31. See Robert W. McElroy, "Cardinal McElroy on 'Radical Inclusion' for L.G.B.T. People, Women and Others in the Catholic Church," *America*, January 24, 2023, americamagazine. org.

The article is about the current synodal process underway in the Catholic Church. McElroy calls, among other things, for the "radical inclusion" of LGBT people in the Church and the dismantling of "structures and cultures of exclusion" that alienate them. And, though he insists that "a synodal culture demands listening . . . that seeks not to convince but to understand the experiences and values of others," clearly, in his article, the cardinal aims primarily to convince.

Among the "structures and cultures" that serve effectively to exclude, Cardinal McElroy singles out the Church's traditional moral teaching regarding human sexuality. And, though he insists that the issue of exclusion is "pre-eminently a pastoral question, not a doctrinal one," the thrust of his essay evidently seeks to change Church teaching regarding human sexual activity. That the cardinal is forthcoming on this matter is both illuminating and troubling. For, in the article, he clearly aligns himself with those in Germany and even in Rome who espouse a view that another cardinal, the late George Pell, deemed "noxious."

Two of McElroy's proposals are indeed radical. He laments the traditional teaching that "all sexual sins outside of marriage constitute objectively grave sin." And regarding LGBT individuals in particular, he holds that "the distinction between orientation and activity" is divisive, distinguishing "those who refrain from sexual activity and those who do not." Thus, presumably, this teaching is to be voided or, at least, avoided since it can appear "pastorally" insensitive and even demeaning.

Cardinal McElroy's severe indictment is that the result of the traditional teaching has been "to focus the Christian moral life disproportionately upon sexual activity." It has thereby obscured "the heart of Christian discipleship," which is "relationship with God, the Father, Son, and Spirit rooted in the life, death, and resurrection of Jesus Christ."

Now, I certainly concur with the cardinal in affirming that relationship with the Triune God, realized and enabled through the Paschal Mystery of Jesus Christ, is indeed the heart of discipleship. Where we differ, I suspect, is in our discernment as to what full, conscious, and active participation in the life, death, and Resurrection of the Lord entails.

To indicate, at least briefly, its scope and cost, I turn to the Church's first and foundational mystagogue, the Apostle Paul. Unlike "Gnostic" mysticism that flees the material and corporeal, Pauline mysticism is decidedly somatic in nature (*sōma* is the Greek word for body).

In the Letter to the Colossians, Paul gives expression to the Church's defining kerygma. He seeks to strengthen the hearts of his fellow Christians by assuring them that in Christ are "all the treasures of wisdom and of knowledge" (Col. 2:3). And the foundation of this conviction is the apostolic faith that, in Christ, "all the fullness of divinity dwells bodily [*sōmatikōs*]" (Col. 2:9). This proclamation of the *novum* of Christian faith, the absolute uniqueness and significance of Jesus Christ, permeates the Letter to the Colossians—as it does, in myriad forms and expressions, the entire New Testament. But this confession is not merely a subject of joyful contemplation. It is also an urgent call for transformation.

The entire third chapter of Paul's letter is devoted to setting forth the "grammar" of such transformation: putting off the old self with its deadly and death-dealing practices and putting on the new self that is constantly being renewed (Col. 3:9–10). Such transformative practice is the fruit of true participation in the radicality of Christ's Paschal Mystery. "For you have died and your life is hidden with Christ in God" (Col. 3:3). And, since you have been "raised with Christ, seek the things that are above where Christ is seated at the right hand of God" (Col. 3:1).

This "logic" of transformation permeates the Catholic spiritual tradition—from the New Testament, through Origen, Gregory of Nyssa, Dante, Teresa of Avila, and John of the Cross, to Thomas Merton, Ruth Burrows, and Erik Varden in our own day. These figures do not minimize the cruciform "yoke" of discipleship or the costliness of grace; but they take to heart the promise of the Savior that his "yoke is easy and his burden is light" (Matt. 11:30). And they are united in their conviction that this spiritual transformation is—integrally and inescapably—bodily.

How can it be otherwise, since the risen, ascended Lord is bodily transformed in the Spirit: *sōma pneumatikon* (1 Cor. 15:44)? Hence, Paul exhorts the early Christians (and us), "I implore you, brothers and sisters, through God's mercy, to present your bodies [*sōmatika*], as a living and holy sacrifice, well pleasing to God. This is worship according to Logos. Neither be conformed to this world; but be transformed [*metamorphousthe*] by the renewal of your discernment" (Rom. 12:1–2, my translation). Here, then, is the Apostle Paul's "pastoral program," and it should serve as the prologue for Vatican II's much heralded and little heeded "universal call to holiness."

And so, I suggest that prior to any talk about "enlarging the tent," Catholics and particularly their bishops should strive to realize anew whose "tent" it is, and the doxological end it serves. If it is the tent where God's glory dwells, then Paul's imperative must apply: "You are not your own; you were purchased for a price. So, glorify God in your body!" (1 Cor. 6:19–20). As ever for Paul, the "body" is both the body of individual Christians and the ecclesial Body of Christ into whom they are incorporated, initially by Baptism and ever more fully in the Eucharist. But each must seriously examine him or herself, that each may discern the condition of the body: for those "who eat or drink without discerning the body eat and drink judgment upon themselves" (1 Cor. 11:29). As is evident in Paul, this discernment concerns both sexual and social conduct. For both reveal the self we are becoming or failing to become.

This is not rigidity; it is simply the cost of discipleship. Nor is it elitism, for even Paul confesses that he is not yet "perfected," but, as he exclaims, "forgetting what lies behind, I strain forward to what lies ahead, towards the goal"—which is life in Christ, being fully appropriated by Christ (Phil. 3:12–16). So, though the forecourt may be the catechumenal "field hospital," the tent itself is the new temple, the living Body of Christ, where those who have been initiated into Christ's death and Resurrection enter to worship the living God.

Indeed, as Cardinal McElroy rightly insists, the call to relationship with God, in and through the Paschal Mystery of his beloved Son, is the heart of Christian discipleship. What this elderly *presbuteros* (pardon the redundancy) asks of him and his fellow bishops (those ordained to oversight, to *episkopē*) is that they embrace and foster what Paul himself proclaimed and strove to realize: "the glory of this mystery, who is Christ in you, the hope of glory. Therefore, we proclaim Christ, warning everyone and teaching everyone in all wisdom, that we may present everyone perfected [*teleion*] in Christ" (Col. 1:27–28).

A Church that neglects to exhort and instruct about the sins of the body, be they sexual or social, risks losing its Christological center and the fullness of the transformation to which Christ calls us.

II. Artistic Soundings

Exactly forty years ago, I had the wondrous experience of discovering the Scuola Grande di San Rocco in Venice. The Scuola di San Rocco is one of the numerous lay confraternities founded by rich patrons during the Middle Ages and Renaissance to support charitable outreach to the poor. "Scuola" also refers to the majestic building that served as meeting room and chapel for the brotherhood. And it houses the splendid series of paintings, created over a period of twenty years, by the Venetian genius Jacopo Robusti, best known as Tintoretto (1518–94). He undertook this herculean task—sixty paintings, of extraordinary size and complexity—"to demonstrate the great love that I bear for the saint and our venerable school, because of my devotion to the glorious Messer San Rocho."

It is scarcely possible to take in the sweep of Tintoretto's vision in a single visit. But even a first encounter overwhelms with a sense of almost tangible artistic originality wedded to profound religious faith and devotion. No wonder the sometime artist and full-time adulator of Michelangelo, Giorgio Vasari, could say (perhaps begrudgingly) of Tintoretto that he had "the most extraordinary brain that the art of painting has ever produced."

But for those for whom a trip to Venice may prove a *ponte* too far, the National Gallery in Washington has mounted a superb exhibition to commemorate the five hundredth anniversary of the artist's birth. The exhibition will run through July 7; and admission is free!

* This essay was originally published as "Tintoretto's Enlightenment," *The Catholic Thing*, June 2, 2019, www.thecatholicthing.org.

Forty-six paintings reveal the depth and breadth of Tintoretto's art: religious scenes, of course, together with mythological episodes, where the naked human body is as celebrated as it was by Michelangelo, who was an admired exemplar for Tintoretto. Remarkable portraits—including two stunning self-portraits—anticipate Rembrandt and Velázquez. The first self-portrait dramatizes the assertive and determined young artist; the other depicts the chastened, almost transfigured old man. Together, they serve not only to bookend physically the exhibition; they unveil a moving spiritual journey: what Dante called "un moto spiritale."

One painting at which I lingered long, even contemplatively, is the artist's portrayal of the Baptism of Jesus. The theme is a commonplace in Venetian art, where the Jordan evokes associations with the circumambient sea. But there is nothing commonplace about Tintoretto's rendition of the scene in this late painting, an altarpiece for the Church of San Silvestro in Venice.

The gracious interaction between the Lord and his herald resembles a spiritual *pas de deux*. The artist's kinetic choreography verbalizes in motion Jesus's humble acquiescence that "all justice must be fulfilled" (Matt. 3:14–15); while John's generous gesture acknowledges that Jesus "must increase, while he himself must decrease" (John 3:30). The light radiating from Jesus illumines John, who still stands partly in darkness, bearing witness that "the true Light has come into the world" (John 1:9). Without doubt, we have here a striking foreshadowing of Caravaggio's "tenebrism."

Fine as the range of artworks on exhibition is, one critic has pronounced that the final self-portrait of the seventy-year-old master would alone merit a journey to Washington. It is this portrait that the painter Édouard Manet proclaimed "one of the most beautiful paintings in the world."

The painter stands before us devoid of artifice; exposed; a palpable presence. But presence of what? One viewer sees here only sadness and suffering, resignation. Yet I think this too passive a reading of a man of such surpassing genius. Another discerns fear in the features of an old man approaching death. This too fails to do justice to one of so passionate a faith, far transcending a merely cultural Christianity. A third, much closer to the mark, sees a face "mysteriously cognizant." But cognizant of what?

Might I suggest, cognizant of truth: truth beyond the masks and defenses we daily assume.

It is said that the young philosopher Edith Stein spent an entire night of awe reading the life of Teresa of Avila. At dawn, she closed the book and remarked simply, "This is truth." That night marked the beginning of her spiritual transformation, culminating in *The Science of the Cross* and her willing sacrifice for her people.

I thought of Saint Teresa Benedicta of the Cross as I contemplated Tintoretto's self-portrait. The man who painted the Light that shines in the darkness painted himself enlightened: purified of illusions—illusions of fame and fortune, of rivalry and revenge.

This "beautiful painting" bears no trace of the superficial or the sentimental. In all his spiritual journey, Tintoretto was cognizant of the poor, both as a member of the confraternity dedicated to their service and in the commissions he undertook, often accepting minimal fees from simple associations of laborers. Now he has himself become poor, shorn of pretense and superfluity. And never was his inner self so richly portrayed.

THE GLORY OF SAINTS PETER AND PAUL*

"Taking every human design into captivity to the obedience of
Christ." (2 Cor. 10:5)

Michelangelo Buonarroti always insisted that he was a sculptor, not a painter. That he had imbibed stone dust with the milk of his wet nurse. That his sculpting only released the form, the design,

* This essay was originally published as "The Glory of Sts. Peter and Paul," *The Catholic Thing*, June 29, 2021, www.thecatholicthing.org.

"il concetto," already embedded in the block of marble that he worked with such passion. That he painted only under constraint and enforced obedience to a succession of popes, from the imperious Julius II to the more amiable Paul III.

It was Paul who conceived the project of constructing and then decorating the chapel that bears his name: Cappella Paolina. It was to serve as Chapel of the Blessed Sacrament and the place where the cardinals would gather prior to entering conclave in the adjacent Cappella Sistina. And he charged Michelangelo, the greatest artist of an age of great artists, to decorate the chapel walls with depictions of the founding saints of the Roman Church: Peter and Paul.

Michelangelo had recently finished the incomparable and revolutionary *Last Judgment* in the Sistine Chapel and yearned to return to the work that had haunted him for a lifetime: the grandiosely designed and hubristically undertaken tomb of Julius II. But once more, he acquiesced to the wishes and dictates of a pope.

Thus, over a period of seven years, the master toiled on what were to be his last paintings: *The Conversion of Saul* and *The Crucifixion of Saint Peter*, concluding his labors in his seventy-fifth year.

Though Pope Paul himself seems to have been well pleased with his artist's achievement, the paintings themselves were met with incomprehension and even disapproval. The alluring celebration of physical beauty of the young Michelangelo's creations—in the monumental *David* and in the depictions on the ceiling of the Sistine Chapel—now yields to the seeming disharmonies of spiritual drama.

The *Conversion of Saul* represents the first act of the theo-drama. The ascended Christ is the center of radiating energy. No remote figure, he enters our world as disruptive grace. Christ's mighty right arm hurls the proud Pharisee to the earth and also suffuses the prone figure with new mysterious light. At the same time, the gesture of Christ's left arm directs the soon-to-be-apostle to Damascus where a new identity and mission await him.

But the dramatic narrative suggests yet more. For beyond Damascus lies Rome and the Vatican Hill. Indeed, the very chapel where the viewer stands is testimony to the drama's denouement. By the ultimate surrender of self in the shedding of his blood, Paul consecrated the very ground on which the chapel stands and spread the faith that viewers of the painting, clergy and laity alike, profess.

There remains one more piece to the drama, intriguing, if controverted. Contrary to the prevailing tradition, Michelangelo portrays the blinded Saul as an elderly man. Indeed, some have contended that the figure bears notable resemblance to portraits of the elderly Michelangelo himself.

Leo Steinberg, in his perceptive and provocative essays (published posthumously as *Michelangelo's Painting*, edited by Sheila Schwartz), treats at length Michelangelo's last paintings. Of the *Conversion of Saul*, he writes, "The artist is like the protagonist of his picture in past pride and selfhood, and in longing to undergo the apostolic ordeal—wanting only the assurance of grace. . . . His self-projection into the role of Saul is a petition."[32]

Michelangelo worked on his last painting, the *Crucifixion of Saint Peter*, from 1547 to 1549. Paul III scampered up a ladder to the scaffold to view the fresco in October 1549. Within a month, the aged pontiff was called to render an account of his stewardship.

What the pope beheld was the massive figure of the man, whose ministry he inherited, affixed to a cross raised, as he requested, upside down. By a prodigious feat of will, the crucified Peter lifts his upper body, turns and fixes his gaze upon the viewer.

---

32. Leo Steinberg, *Michelangelo's Painting*, ed. Sheila Schwartz (Chicago: University of Chicago Press, 2019), 285.

Two observations help underscore Michelangelo's striking achievement. First is the fact that he portrays the crucifixion of Peter and not the consigning of the keys. It appears that Christ giving the keys to Peter was the originally intended subject, as befits a chapel associated with a papal conclave. Though there is no sure evidence, indications are that it was the artist himself who proposed the changed theme. That the pope acquiesced was an evident sign of his affection and esteem for the artist.

The second crucial observation is that Michelangelo's depiction of Peter's crucifixion broke in a radical way from the iconographic tradition, which portrayed the event circumspectly, the cross already embedded in the ground. Prior portrayals offer little sign of the physical and spiritual energies in play (never separable for Michelangelo), either on the part of the antagonists or, especially, on the part of the protagonist himself.

Michelangelo's Peter is no passive victim, but active participant, who in his death bears witness to and proclaims the crucified Lord who turns the world upside down. The ancient world, the viewer's world, the artist's world on the verge of being transformed.

In a brilliant analysis of the painting, Leo Steinberg discerns a diagonal that descends from the Roman captain in upper left pointing to Peter, through the transverse beam of the cross, to terminate at the outsize figure of the elder striding out of the frame and into our present.

We recognize a clear resemblance between the figure in the fresco and that of Nicodemus in the great, unfinished *Pietà* that Michelangelo began to sculpt at night, after days of toil in the Cappella Paolina. The erudite but uncomprehending Nicodemus comes to Jesus by night and is instructed of the need to be "born from above of water and the Spirit" (John 3:1–8). In the *Pietà*, he now embraces the crucified-living Christ—some even suggest in a posture of giving birth.

Significantly, both the figure of Nicodemus and the elder in the fresco bear the features of the artist.

Whether working in stone or paint, concept and design were for Michelangelo never abstract ideas but somatic realities. And the artistic embodiment ultimately involves and implicates the artist personally. Whether in his last paintings or his last *Pietàs*, the supreme, excruciating art is to allow the Christ form to emerge from the recalcitrant marble of the self. To bring the self's purposes and designs into alignment with those of Christ.

A PILGRIMAGE TO ORVIETO*

Though I once lived in Rome for four years and have had the good fortune to return numerous times, I had never visited the lovely town of Orvieto, only an hour or so away by train. Happily, I recently had occasion to remedy that grievous fault.

The town traces its origins to Etruscan times and is situated upon a high bluff that commands the surrounding region of southern Umbria. It is reached by a funicular that provides sky-borne access to the town and further charms the pilgrim. For indeed, it was a pilgrimage that we were on—brief, but rich and grace-filled.

I traveled with a young priest, newly ordained, who, though himself Italian, had also never visited Orvieto. Part of the attraction of coming was that here, during his time teaching theology at the Dominican priory, Thomas Aquinas composed the office for the newly established Feast of Corpus Christi. The wonderful poem-hymns *Pange, lingua* and *Lauda, Sion* issue from the heart of the "Poet of the Eucharist," as Thomas has been called.

The former poem hymns the glorious Body and precious Blood poured out for the salvation of the world. The latter closes by lauding the living Christ: "You who feed us mortals here below,

* This essay was originally published as "A Pilgrimage to Orvieto," *The Catholic Thing*, November 2, 2018, www.thecatholicthing.org.

make us fellow-guests, coheirs, and companions, with the saints in heaven." Both present experience and future hope are central to Thomas's celebration of the Eucharist.

The great scholar of Saint Thomas, Jean-Pierre Torrell, OP, writes of Thomas's achievement in these hymns: "Full of the memory of the Passion, the celebration is entirely turned toward the eschatological achievement, since it is the pledge, the *pignus*, of future glory."[33]

The highly intellectual Aquinas of the *Summa theologiae* exhibits in these prayer-poems not only intellectual desire but intense affective yearning. Perhaps nowhere is this union more harmoniously and concisely expressed than in his antiphon for the *Magnificat*:

> O sacred banquet! in which Christ is received,
> the memory of his Passion is renewed,
> the mind is filled with grace,
> and a pledge of future glory is given us.
> Alleluia.

It is more than fitting, therefore, that in the magnificent yet spare Duomo of Orvieto, the Blessed Sacrament Chapel houses the relic of the Eucharistic miracle of Bolsena: the blood-tinged corporal that strengthened the Eucharistic faith of a German pilgrim priest. Though no sure connection has been established between the institution of the Feast of Corpus Christi and the supposed miracle, their proximity in time and place, together with the office composed by Aquinas, show how popular piety, liturgical

---

33. Jean-Pierre Torrell, *Saint Thomas Aquinas*, vol. 1, *The Person and His Work*, trans. Robert Royal (Washington, DC: The Catholic University of America Press, 1996), 135.

celebration, and theologically substantive poetry can conspire to proclaim Christ's Real Presence.

But another "miracle" awaits the pilgrim visiting Orvieto. For in the other chapel of the cathedral, the so-called "Cappella Nova," are the extraordinary frescoes by the early Renaissance painter Luca Signorelli. His great depictions of the *Preaching of the Antichrist*, of the *Last Judgment*, and of the *Resurrection of the Flesh* clearly inspired Michelangelo's own masterpieces in the Sistine Chapel.

The depiction of the Antichrist is an astonishing imaginative feat: the figure bears close resemblance to Christ, yet in subtly distorted fashion. And as he mouths the words that the devil is whispering into his ear, he lures his hearers into the very vices that degrade the flesh.

By contrast, the Signorelli fresco that displays the *Resurrection of the Flesh* is a glorious affirmation of human dignity and destiny. To stand contemplating the resurrected bodies of the just is to revel in man's and woman's true freedom, expressing itself in unbounded joy and generous communion. The newly resurrected are shown shaking off the skeletons of confinement and emerging upright into the new creation. They assist one another in their ascent and embrace each other in chaste and life-giving fellowship.

Along the borders of his great frescoes, Signorelli has painted figures of literature, both classical and more contemporary. One in particular seems singularly appropriate: Dante Alighieri appears, composing his *Commedia*, appropriate not only for his poetic exploration of *Inferno* and *Paradiso* but also for his genial insight into the constitutive features of both conditions. The monumental "egos" of *Inferno* dwell in searing isolation, while the joyful inhabitants of *Paradiso* exult in mutual praise and communion.

Dante intuits that the resurrection of the flesh is not an optional "add-on" to a self-sufficient soul but is intrinsic to the self's personal fulfillment and beatitude. For the body sacramentalizes the self with its identity-forming relationships. The affective desire of the saved souls for the resurrection of the flesh finds expression in the words Dante places in the mouth of Solomon in the "Canto of the Sun." Solomon speaks of the surpassing glory that will accompany the resurrection of the flesh. And the whole choir of holy ones by their "Amen!" voice their yearning to be fully clothed with their resurrected bodies.

Then, in some of the most poignant lines in the whole *Commedia*, Dante comments,

> Forse non pur per lor, ma per le mamme,
> per li padri e per li altri che fuor cari
> anzi che fosser sempiterne fiamme.

> Not perhaps for themselves alone, but for their mothers,
> for their fathers, and for others whom they loved
> before they all became eternal flames.[34]

Remembering Signorelli's penetrating vision, and with Solomon's words still resounding in our hearts, the new priest and I celebrated the Eucharist together in the Chapel of the Blessed Sacrament. For me personally, a particularly moving moment of the celebration came as I heard him, in the *memento* for the dead, speak the names "Giulia e Francesco"—my mother and father.

On this All Souls Day, we pray for the resurrection of the body and life everlasting, not only for ourselves, but, with tender love, for "our mothers and fathers, and all who are dear to us."

---

34. Dante Alighieri, *Paradiso* 14.64–66, in Dante, *Paradiso*, trans. Robert Hollander and Jean Hollander (New York: Anchor, 2008), 375.

CARAVAGGIO: BETWEEN DESPAIR AND HOPE*

Claims of a "once in a lifetime opportunity" to see the works of a popular artistic genius rightfully merit skepticism. But when they come from an acknowledged authority like Keith Christiansen, curator of European paintings at New York's Metropolitan Museum of Art, one pays heed. When I read his enthusiastic review in the December 12, 2004, *New York Times* of "Caravaggio: L'Ultimo Tempo 1606–1610," on display at Naples' Capodimonte Museum, I knew this was a singular opportunity.

Since my student days in Rome in the mid-1960s, I have been enchanted by Michelangelo Merisi da Caravaggio (1571–1610). The church of San Luigi dei Francesi, which houses his great cycle of the calling, inspiration, and martyrdom of Saint Matthew, has become a regular pilgrimage stop on my visits to Rome. In addition, Rome's splendid Galleria Borghese, founded by one of Caravaggio's patrons, features several outstanding paintings of this revolutionary artistic genius, including two of the last he completed.

These two, joined with sixteen others painted in Naples, Malta, and Sicily during Caravaggio's fearful flight from Rome (under papal sentence of death for having killed a rival), comprised the astonishing collection at the Naples exhibition. Though the exhibit will travel to the National Gallery in London, still, as Christiansen rightfully insisted, Naples was the place to see it "because in Naples the paintings resonate as nowhere else."[35] Since I was in Rome in early January, a two-hour train ride to Naples and a two-hour waiting line at Capodimonte allowed entrance into the tragic world of a tormented man and extraordinary artist.

The Capodimonte galleries were crowded but with little sense of rush. An almost contemplative air pervaded. Often, the

---

* This essay was original published as "Tortured Genius: The Miracle of Caravaggio's Art," *Commonweal* 132, no. 5 (March 11, 2005): 27–28.

35. Keith Christiansen, "The Bounty of Caravaggio's Glorious Exile," *New York Times*, December 12, 2004, nytimes.com.

paintings were hung one to a wall, offering ample space to focus, to view from different angles, to linger, and to return. Caravaggio's style seems to have changed as he absorbed the particularities of the places to which his exile drove him. The rough and tumble of Neapolitan streets give way to the confined, weary world of the island domain of the Knights of Malta, only to pass into the almost impressionistic figures and dreamlike spaces of Sicily. Each new stay pressed out of the painter singular compositions. One finds in the paintings no formulary Baroque Madonnas, no prettily ornamental angels or idealized saints. One learns, rather, to see the ordinary, the everyday, anew, as it reveals its dignity and depth of mystery. Caravaggio's stunning interplay of light and darkness seems to intimate a ceaseless struggle between encroaching despair and impossible hope. His paintings' intensity and pathos feel rooted in overwhelming personal experience.

While the exhibition was devoted to Caravaggio's *Ultimo Tempo* (final period), its climax might be styled *L'Ultimo dell'Ultimo Tempo*. For reasons not fully clear, in late summer 1609 Caravaggio returned to Naples, probably hoping to obtain a long-desired papal pardon that would allow him to return to Rome. He remained there until midsummer the following year. Not yet assured of pardon, he set out for Rome but was arrested on route and delayed for several days, causing him to miss the ship carrying his belongings. This precipitated a final feverish rush to the small seaport where he died, possibly of malaria, on July 18, 1610. One of his first biographers, Giovanni Baglione, a fellow painter and hostile competitor, penned these barbed words at the conclusion of his life of Caravaggio: "*Morì malamente, come malamente avea vivuto*": "He died as badly as he had lived."

Another more compassionate contemporary, Giulio Cesare Gigli, captured the artist's tragic ambiguity when he exclaimed, "Such was the great Michelangelo Caravaggio, a miracle of art, a wonder of nature, though buffeted by unhappy fortune."

Caravaggio's final sojourn in Naples illustrates both poles of this judgment. During the approximately ten months of his second stay in Naples, Caravaggio, always a prolific artist, created at least a half dozen masterworks. These last surviving pictures manifest a new concentration and interiority, a mélange of light and darkness that is no merely stylistic device, however striking, but wells up from within the personages depicted. At the same time, the violence that marred so much of his personal life continued. On October 24, 1609, the painter was assaulted outside a Naples tavern, nearly killed, and left disfigured. His plight is summed up by two of his final works: *David with the Head of Goliath* from Rome's Galleria Borghese, and *The Denial of Saint Peter* from New York's Metropolitan Museum of Art—both prominent in the exhibition.

Few paintings in the Western tradition evoke so great a sense of dread as Caravaggio's *David with the Head of Goliath*. In what was to be one of Caravaggio's last works, the adolescent David holds the bloody, decapitated head of the giant, gazing on it with a mix of fascination and pity. This portrayal alone would make the painting memorable, but what makes it unforgettable is that the battered giant's head is Caravaggio's own, vacant eyes still staring, mouth agape.

The painting was intended as a gift to Cardinal Scipione Borghese, an inducement to intercede with his uncle Pope Paul V for *grazia*, clemency, to be shown the beleaguered, near-despairing Caravaggio. Contemplating the painting, the words of one of Gerard Manley Hopkins's "Terrible Sonnets" spring to mind: "No worst, there is none. Pitched past pitch of grief, / More pangs will, schooled at forepangs, wilder wring."[36]

What, perhaps, forestalls total despair in the painting is that the pitying David is, according to some scholars, a representation

<hr>

36. Gerard Manley Hopkins, "No worst, there is none. Pitched past pitch of grief," Poetry Foundation, poetryfoundation.org.

of the young Caravaggio. His look of compassion is the lone sign of hope in the scene, one that unites the wounded humanity of both executioner and victim in a common yearning for redemption.

The Denial of Saint Peter portrays another dramatic scene, Peter's betrayal of his Lord. Three figures are frozen in a decisive, life-transforming moment: the accusing maidservant, the threatening guard, and the shamed, stricken Apostle. In the background, the dying embers of a fire cast their physical light; but the foreground discloses the faces on which spiritual darkness and light contend. Christiansen, in his notes for the exhibition catalogue, remarks upon the Neapolitan "rhetoric of gesture" at play in the painting.[37] The hand of the soldier and the two hands of the servant signify the threefold accusation and denial; the in-folded hands of Peter tellingly express both denial and repentance.

One is also drawn into the drama of the eyes, as they dance in counterclockwise motion, a *moto spiritale*: the soldier's menace, the woman's denunciation, Peter's grief-filled realization of guilt. The Apostle stands slightly apart, confronting the inescapable imperative of decision. Entering meditatively and imaginatively into the biblical narrative, as the spirituality of the Catholic Reformation exhorted, applying it to the "today" of faith, one can journey with Caravaggio to the crossroads of despair and hope. In this *ultimo tempo*, the ways of Peter and his apostolic twin Judas cross and ultimately diverge.

Michelangelo da Caravaggio set out for Rome in hope. He died before receiving confirmation that the pope's *grazia* had been accorded him. One can only pray he died not *malamente*, as his critic contended, but in the light that darkness does not overcome.

When I ponder the "miracle of art" of these two paintings, so wonderfully contextualized in the Naples exhibit, I recall another of Hopkins's late poems. Its complex title almost conjures Caravaggio: "That Nature is a Heraclitean Fire and of the comfort

37. Christiansen, "Bounty."

of the Resurrection." Two verses sum up the struggle between despair and hope that permeates Caravaggio's last paintings: "All is in an enormous dark / Drowned." But, "Across my foundering deck shone / A beacon, an eternal beam."[38]

SOLI DEO GLORIA: ON BRAHMS AND MACMILLAN*

Austrian-born conductor Manfred Honeck is the father of six and a devout Catholic. He attends Mass several times a week and prays before each concert. Since 2008, he has been the music director of the Pittsburgh Symphony Orchestra. His tenure has been renewed four times, and now extends through the 2027–28 season.

Honeck's remarkable success is due not only to the freshness and originality he brings to familiar orchestral masterpieces but to his willingness to listen to the perspectives of his orchestra members. It might be said that he strives for a "musical synodality," sharing the same goal that Bach affixed to all his musical scores: "Soli Deo Gloria."

I first came to know of Honeck and his outstanding orchestra through a *New Yorker* article that I read two years ago, in which Alex Ross, one of America's finest music critics, asserts, "After listening to the Pittsburgh Symphony's recent recording of the Bruckner Ninth Symphony for the tenth or eleventh time, I began planning a trip to Pittsburgh, in the hope of understanding how such a formidable achievement had come about."[39]

I, too, was struck by Honeck's striking interpretation. His attention to detail and ability to clarify various musical textures while also drawing them into a coherent whole are masterful.

38. Gerard Manley Hopkins, "That Nature Is a Heraclitean Fire and of the Comfort of the Resurrection," Poetry Foundation, poetryfoundation.org.

* This essay was originally published as "Soli Deo Gloria," *First Things*, April 11, 2022, firstthings.com.

39. Alex Ross, "The Pittsburgh Symphony's Savage Precision," *The New Yorker*, February 10, 2020.

Though by no means tutored in the finer points of musical analysis, I resonated with Ross's assessment of the achievement: "savagely precise in detail, and almost scarily sublime in cumulative effect, it gives notice that the right orchestra and the right conductor can unleash unsuspected energies in familiar works."[40]

The Bruckner Ninth is only one of several splendid recordings by Honeck and the Pittsburgh Symphony. Some of them have been nominated for Grammys, and one received the award in 2018. The sound quality of each recording is superb, and each is accompanied by Honeck's extensive and illuminating notes in which he outlines his understanding of and approach to the score.

The orchestra's most recent release is an astounding performance of Brahms's Fourth Symphony, accompanied by a recent composition by the Scottish composer James MacMillan. What was said of Honeck's Bruckner recording applies equally to this one. As one critic confessed, "Does someone who already owns four different recordings of Johannes Brahms' Symphony No. 4 really need another? Yes . . . there's magic happening here."[41]

But the "magic" is no facile entertainment, no retreat into some bucolic world. Brahms's Fourth probes what Charles Taylor calls secularity's "immanent frame" with unromantic honesty, evoking a world at once painfully beautiful and utterly desolate.

In the first movement, we seem to enter upon a centuries-old conversation. Weariness erupts at times into belligerence, and then subsides into moments of tenderness, only to end in what sounds like a cry of anguish. A second movement of intense lyricism, colored by nostalgia, follows, but peters out in futility. Promethean struggle marks the third movement: a steady drumbeat of progress that collapses into acrid dissonance.

40. Alex Ross, "Pittsburgh Symphony."

41. Richard Ray, "'Clarity' in Honeck's New Brahms Recording Makes It a 2021 Standout," CPR Classical, November 19, 2021, https://www.cpr.org/2021/11/19/clarity-in-honecks-new-brahms-recording-makes-it-a-2021-standout/.

But the fourth movement takes the symphony beyond even these forebodings. Paradoxically, the movement is based upon a melody Brahms borrows from Bach. The theme from Bach's Cantata 150, "I long for thee, O Lord," unfolds in thirty variations. Here, tenderness and terror vie as the music displays an impassioned search for resolution. But the lyrical flute solo is overwhelmed by the martial outbursts of horns and percussion. Is it only a fevered imagination that hears the tramp of goose-stepping armies?

Like the critic cited above, I have four other recordings of the Brahms Fourth. But none (even that of the legendary Carlos Kleiber) approaches the sheer desolation that Honeck conjures in the final notes. Shuddering, one carries away the apocalyptic sense of humanity crushed.

As previously mentioned, the riveting recording of Brahms is followed by a composition by James MacMillan. The *Larghetto for Orchestra* was composed in honor of Honeck's tenth anniversary with the Pittsburgh Symphony.

Larghetto for Orchestra is no mere "filler" on the disc but integral to Honeck's vision. Developed from an earlier a cappella setting of Psalm 51 by MacMillan, the "Miserere," it appears as a graced collaboration between Catholic conductor and Catholic composer. The Fourth Symphony's anguish, bordering on despair, yields to the Psalm's cry for mercy. The forlorn notes of the brass instruments are tempered by soft echoes of Gregorian chant; the darkness of night tinged by a dawning of hope.

Listening to the entire recording—the harrowing Brahms giving way to MacMillan's intimations of transcendence—I thought of Dante and Virgil emerging from the darkness of hell into purgatorial day. Though I would not dare deviate from Bach's *Passions* for Good Friday music listening, I cannot think of a more appropriate recording than Honeck's for Holy Saturday: the day we profess that Christ descended into hell, bearing his cross of mercy and renewal to redeem repentant sinners.

BRUCKNER'S GETHSEMANE*

In the 1950s, the symphonies of Gustav Mahler became a staple of orchestras throughout the world, thanks in large part to the fervent advocacy of Leonard Bernstein. The works of Mahler's older contemporary Anton Bruckner, though regularly performed in central Europe by conductors such as Herbert von Karajan and Bernard Haitink, were relatively neglected in the United States.

This may have been due in part to the support given to Bruckner's music by the Nazi regime (which came to power more than thirty years after Bruckner's death). But it was due also to the extraordinary demands placed on the listener by the complex structure and contemplative nature of Bruckner's symphonies. Typically lasting an hour or more, the works of this organist-composer are sonic cathedrals, often incorporating moments of silence, as though inviting the listener to appropriate what she or he has just heard.

The neglect of Bruckner in North America is happily coming to an end. The Austrian-born conductor Franz Welser-Möst has emerged as a foremost Brucknerian and has regularly performed Bruckner symphonies at Carnegie Hall with the Cleveland Orchestra. He and the orchestra have recorded a number of the symphonies on DVD, making them accessible far beyond the confines of the concert hall.

Another advocate of Bruckner's symphonies is the Argentine-Israeli pianist and conductor Daniel Barenboim. Barenboim has championed the symphonies through numerous recordings and concert performances over the years, especially with the orchestra of the Staatskapelle Berlin, of which he is

* This essay was originally published as "Bruckner's Gethsemane," *First Things*, January 31, 2017, firstthings.com.

music director. His commitment to Bruckner reached its high point this past week, in a performance of all nine symphonies at Carnegie Hall—the first time all the symphonies have been played in one series in the United States.

This prodigious feat is all the more astonishing in that Barenboim conducts these monumental works entirely from memory. In addition, most of the concerts included a Mozart piano concerto with Barenboim as soloist.

I had the privilege of attending the final concert, which also featured the radiant Twenty-Third Piano Concerto in A Major of Mozart. It is rare that Mozart will function as a "crowd warmer"—but so it was in this case. The sellout audience had clearly come for the Bruckner Ninth in D Minor, the same key as Beethoven's monumental Ninth Symphony, which exerted such a spell upon Bruckner. The devoutly Catholic Bruckner dedicated his last symphony to "the dear God," and prayed in his final illness that the Lord would allow him to finish his masterwork. In the event, his prayer was not granted. Yet in a deeper sense, the three movements he lived to complete could hardly be surpassed. The sublime and harrowing third movement makes any further statement, this side of heaven, redundant!

With the certainty of falling far short, let me at least seek to explain why.

The notoriously insecure and obsessive Bruckner knew any number of disappointments and setbacks, both personal and professional, in the course of his life. His works were slow to gain acceptance among the musical elite of nineteenth-century Vienna, who favored Brahms over the allegedly "Wagnerian" Bruckner. Then, just as he seemed to be finding a more favorable reception by the acclaim that greeted his Seventh Symphony, his monumental Eighth was rejected by the very conductor whom Bruckner considered his "spiritual father." The composition of the

Ninth was delayed, as the harried composer revised the Eighth and compulsively revisited some of his earlier symphonies.

In the midst of psychological turmoil and an increasingly frail physical state, Bruckner labored to complete the Ninth. The third movement opens with a promise of becoming one of those signature "Adagios" that characterized his mature work. A sweeping opening melody seems to confirm the promise, only to be counterpointed by another theme that, through a series of ever more frenzied repetitions, threatens to overwhelm that promise to the point of annihilation.

As I listened to Barenboim drive the orchestra to the limits of its sonic capability, Simone Weil's sense of a soul-threatening "affliction" came to mind. And then there came, unbidden, the image of Jesus's anguish in the Garden of Gethsemane. An incessant pulsing rhythm conjured beads of sweat and dripping blood. The movement builds to an astonishing, dissonant climax that sounds like a primal wail of suffering humanity. I am aware of nothing in music that can match this naked cry of despair—echoing the lament "Dear God, let this chalice pass."

And then the propulsive disharmony fades and the tortuous movement transforms into a sigh of peace.

Is the ending of the movement a fatalistic resignation before the terrible abyss? Or is it a faith-filled surrender to the God whom Bruckner had served his entire life? Each listener will hear Bruckner's testimony differently. But for me, on a Sunday afternoon, it spoke eloquently of transfiguration. As though the long passion was endured and intimations of resurrection had, at last, dawned.

PRAYING WITH BEETHOVEN'S *MISSA SOLEMNIS**

In book 10 of his *Confessions*, Saint Augustine explores the mystery of memory. At one point, he exclaims, "Great is the power of

---

* This essay was originally published as "Praying with Beethoven's *Missa Solemnis*," *First Things*, March 22, 2022, firstthings.com.

memory, a thing, O my God, to be in awe of, a profound and immeasurable multiplicity; and this thing is my mind, this thing am I."[42]

Among the "immeasurable multiplicities" we remember are events deeply significant, even life-changing; other recollections are seemingly trivial, of little import. And part of the mystery of memory is that events and persons suddenly appear, unbidden, sometimes after decades of forgetfulness. I recently remembered an incident, decidedly trivial, from more than sixty years ago: while riding a bus to a Fordham Glee Club concert, I was reading a book by the once well-known psychiatrist Karl Stern. What strangely remained embedded in my memory was Stern's passing remark that Beethoven's *Missa Solemnis* was a transcendent masterpiece. I noted it, and promptly forgot it.

Over the years, though I came to appreciate and enjoy so much of Beethoven's music, somehow the *Missa Solemnis* remained beyond my ken. To me it seemed excessively showy and hyperbolic, with little genuine religious sensibility. Not that I didn't try to appreciate it. I bought a recording by Leonard Bernstein, but it did nothing to disabuse me of my initial unfavorable impressions. Later, I purchased John Eliot Gardiner's swift, no-nonsense version. I remained unmoved. I even attended one of the rare live performances. Yet after every attempt I found myself returning with relief to Bach's Mass in B Minor.

Recently, however, I came upon the newly remastered version of the 1966 recording of the *Missa Solemnis* by Herbert von Karajan. It is available both on CD and Blu-ray audio disc. The resulting recording has extraordinary clarity of sound. There is flow and coherence to von Karajan's interpretation; the various parts of the Mass, however different in musical form and rhetoric, weave together seamlessly. And the stellar soloists—Gundula Janowitz,

---

42. Augustine, *Confessions* 10.17, trans. F. J. Sheed (Park Ridge, IL: Word on Fire Classics, 2017), 249.

Christa Ludwig, Fritz Wunderlich, and Walter Berry—achieve a remarkable integration as one voice singing praise to God. The result is stunning and, yes, seamless.

What is especially striking about the performance is its prayerfulness. Von Karajan's rendition allowed me to experience the *Missa Solemnis* as prayer for the first time—prayer in many registers. The exuberance of the "Gloria" would make Balthasar blush. During the "Et vitam venturi saeculi" of the "Credo," an extended fugue swells to a choral affirmation of mystery, before ending with the soloists' rapt "Amen." The baritone's plangent "Miserere" during the "Agnus Dei" is said by some to be an expression of Beethoven's own anguish over the turmoil of his life; a little later, the intrusion of martial music threatens to overwhelm a plaintive "dona nobis pacem"—before yielding to a transcending hope.

In my opinion, the keystone of this vast musical arch is, fittingly, the central section of the "Credo." Here, we are graced with an "Et incarnatus" whose tenderness rivals Mozart and a "Passus et sepultus" whose utter grief conjures Bach. But the resplendent "et HOMO factus est," declaimed in D major, is all Beethoven. Here, the composer of the "Eroica" symphony, the passionate advocate of human dignity and liberation in the opera *Fidelio*, is fully on display.

Catholic composer James MacMillan has spoken of Beethoven's lifelong "search for justice," which in this Mass "is tempered with a profound knowledge of divine mercy." He calls the *Missa Solemnis* "one of the most deeply Catholic works ever written." I would add that I find it a magnificent affirmation of Catholic humanism, accenting at its midpoint the good news, both scandalous and salvific, that God became man.

Originally intended to adorn the festivities for the installation of Beethoven's pupil and patron Archduke Rudolf as archbishop of Olmütz in March of 1820, the Mass was not completed until 1823. Beethoven considered it his greatest work, though the Ninth Symphony and the last quartets were still to come.

In the chorus straining to encompass the entire diapason of sound, from piano to fortissimo, one hears clear intimations of the great choral conclusion to the Ninth Symphony. Indeed, the range from lamentation to exultation surpasses even that masterpiece. One can only imagine how the choristers, challenged to the utmost, might have echoed the complaint of the violinist who thought a passage in one of Beethoven's string quartets was too taxing. To whom the maestro replied gruffly, "When I composed that passage, I was conscious of being inspired by God Almighty. Do you think I can consider your puny little fiddle when He speaks to me?"

In the *Missa Solemnis*, Beethoven's titanic subjectivity seems chastened by suffering and transformed by his engagement with the graced objectivity of liturgical text and tradition. His diaries and notebooks reveal that he had the text of the Mass carefully translated so he could study it closely, and that he explored the religious music of Palestrina and Handel, Haydn and Cherubini in constructing his own approach. The framework that the Mass provided did not constrict him but inspired and oriented his creativity. At the head of his score, he inscribed the words "From the heart—may it go to the heart."

And so, I have finally come to appreciate and affirm what Dr. Stern tried to teach me during that dimly remembered bus ride sixty-three years ago. But then, I've always been a slow learner.

III. Liturgical Soundings

THE CATHOLIC IMAGINATION: SONGS OF ANGELS, ANIMALS, AND MEN*

The great twentieth-century Protestant theologian Karl Barth once opined, "Though before the Throne of God the angels undoubtedly play Bach, among themselves they surely play Mozart." Emboldened by Barth, I suggest that, though the Most High may favor Palestrina, the angels have a soft spot for Victoria.

Tomás Luis de Victoria (1548–1611), born in Avila, was active in Rome during the height of the Catholic Reformation. He knew and was influenced by Palestrina. However, to this lay listener, Victoria's music seems at once more melodic and more affective than Palestrina's chaste counterpoint. Among Victoria's many motets, his setting of the responsory for Matins of Christmas Day stands out.

> O magnum mysterium et admirabile sacramentum, ut animalia viderent Dominum natum jacentem in prasepio. O Beata Virgo, cujus viscera meruerunt portare Dominum Jesum Christum. Alleluia.

> O awesome mystery and wondrous sacrament: that the animals behold the new-born Lord, lying in a manger. O Blessed Virgin, whose womb was worthy to bear the Lord Jesus Christ. Alleluia.

---

* This essay was originally published as "Songs of Angels, Animals, and Men," *The Catholic Thing*, December 18, 2022, www.thecatholicthing.org.

I know no other piece of music that, in less than five minutes, manages to convey such a wondrous sense of awe and reverence culminating in fervent joy. Some years later, Victoria composed a complete Mass based on motifs from the motet. The recording of motet and Mass by David Hill leading the Westminster Cathedral Choir is quite fine.

But of late, it has led me to think more meditatively of those "animalia." Our manger scenes traditionally feature at least an ox and a donkey; the more elaborate find space for shepherds with lambs and sheep. And at the appropriate time, camels and kings make their required appearance. I own a simple yet lovely set from Bolivia that fittingly includes a llama.

These simple creatures mirror the Old Testament's prophetic hope for the restoration of all creation at the Messiah's coming. As we heard on the Second Sunday of this long Advent, Isaiah foresaw a messianic age when the wolf will show hospitality to the lamb, calf and young lion will happily converse, and lion and ox sit down to an amicable supper—all emerging unscathed and refreshed!

In the time before that final consummation, the Christian contemplative gaze will espy anticipations and intimations. Tertullian recognized that "birds, when they awake, rise toward heaven and in place of hands lift their wings which they open in the shape of the cross, chirping something that might seem to be a prayer."

And the eighteenth-century poet Christopher Smart celebrated his cat Jeoffry, who "at the first glance of the glory of God in the East he worships in his way."[43] The fact that Smart wrote these lines while confined in a home for the mentally unstable may well say more about his custodians than about him. Smart tellingly reminds his keepers that he stands "under the same

---

43. Christopher Smart, "Fragment B2," in *Jubilate Agno*, ed. W.H. Bond (New York: Greenwood, 1969), 116.

accusation / With my Saviour, / For they said, / He is besides himself."[44] Happily, if belatedly (Smart's poem "Rejoice in the Lamb" was not discovered until 1939), Benjamin Britten has set it to music to moving effect.

But the Catholic imagination ranges well beyond beasts wild and tame, beyond humans, however "sane" (for we all stand in need of the Savior's sanation). It breaks through secularity's stifling "immanent frame" to catch the melody of angelic choirs whose singing glorifies the Lord. So, Luke recounts the angelic apparition to the shepherds announcing the Good News of the Savior's birth. Not surprisingly, the angels cannot contain their joy and burst into song: "Glory to God in highest heaven; and on earth peace to men of good will!" (Luke 2:14).

Nor could one imagine for a moment Gabriel traveling all the way to Nazareth only to pronounce prosaically, "Hail, full of grace." Clearly, he sang out (or at the very least chanted) the words, so musical in the original: "*Chaire, kecharitōmenē!*" (Luke 1:28). And could he, though appearing in a dream, do any less for Joseph? Especially when intoning, with all reverence, the sweet name "Jesus" (Matt. 1:21). After all, the revelation of the Savior's Name is not a mere matter of fact but a happening of stupendous joy.

And what shall we say of that wearisome journey of Mary and Joseph to Bethlehem—eighty some miles over four anxious days? How did they hasten the time and dispel fear? By singing, of course. The Psalms undoubtedly. But also more recent compositions: Zechariah's lilting "Blessed be the Lord, the God of Israel who has visited his people to set them free" (Luke 1:68). And surely Mary hummed her own heartfelt "My soul magnifies the Lord, and my spirit rejoices in God, my Savior" (Luke 1:46).

---

44. Christopher Smart, "Selections from Rejoice in the Lamb," in *Poems*, ed. Robert Brittain (Princeton: Princeton University Press, 1950), 113.

All these many voices, of angels, animals, women, and men, conspire together. Each one's song but a sounding of that *magnum mysterium* that today's Gospel for the Fourth Sunday of Advent proclaims, "Emmanuel: God is with us!" (Matt. 1:23). The voices harmonize, forming one exultant hymn both intimate and intense, scandalously particular and comprehensively Catholic.

In many a parish church on Christmas Day, an intrepid choir will essay Handel's "Hallelujah Chorus." Often, the sopranos will strain to reach the high notes, while basses struggle to plumb the depths. But they will all sing out lustily, knowing that theirs is but the earthly echo of the angelic choir. And that long before Handel imagined aurally the earthly tones, it was already being sung in heaven—in tune, and in perfect harmony.

SAVORING BERNARD AND BACH DURING ADVENT*

My impression (certainly subject to correction) is that most parishes still retain the "four-hymn" format at Sunday Mass. A growing number, however, seem to be adopting a chant version of the Introit or Entrance Antiphon of the Mass, whether in English or in Latin. In my view, much is gained by that practice. Not only does chant serve to foster a meditative opening to liturgical worship; the "Introit" itself is integral to the day's liturgy, setting its doxological tone.

Thus the "Introit" for this Third Sunday of Advent boldly hymns the Pauline injunction: "Rejoice in the Lord always; again I say, rejoice. Indeed the Lord is near" (Phil. 4:4).

Those of a certain (my) age remember the designation of Advent's Third Sunday as "Gaudete Sunday"—a welcome reminder that Advent's expectant austerity is a joyful austerity. A salutary reminder more urgent in this time of Covid-enforced austerity, both physical and spiritual.

* This essay was originally published as "Savoring B&B During Advent," *The Catholic Thing*, December 13, 2020, www.thecatholicthing.org.

Yet the perennial challenge, whether in times of stress or (ever relative) security, is to appropriate personally the new life that Jesus offers, that Jesus is. In terms so central to Saint John Henry Newman's preaching and writing, how are we to pass from a merely "notional" to a "real" understanding and experience of the saving truths of the faith? In the case of the Entrance Antiphon of today's liturgy, how make real for ourselves that the Lord is truly near and that abiding in him is cause of exceeding joy?

Newman suggests that the passage from notional to real is facilitated by the "imagination." Think of Saint Ignatius's procedure in his *Spiritual Exercises*. He recommends placing ourselves imaginatively in the Gospel scene as a participant or onlooker. By exercising our senses of sight or hearing, touch or smell, the scene becomes vivid, our meditation more personal and affecting.

Though Newman does not define what he means by "imagination," he typically associates it with the affections, the heart, especially within the setting of a concrete encounter between persons. No surprise, then, that he chose as his "motto," when he was made cardinal, *Cor ad cor loquitur*—"Heart speaks to heart."

Two persons have been speaking to my own heart in a special way this Advent season. Though separated from each other by 600 years and from us by even more, they are cherished "mystagogues"—guides into the mystery of Advent and the still greater mystery of the Lord's Incarnation. The two are Saint Bernard of Clairvaux (1090–1153) and Johann Sebastian Bach (1685–1750). A spiritually inebriating B&B.

Focus upon the "heart" as the seat of human affectivity is prominent in both Bernard and Bach. They appreciate that unless the heart is touched, roused, enkindled, religion remains merely a dry and dutiful practice. So they set their poetic and musical genius to stir into flame the embers of devotion that may lie dormant.

For neither of them does affection connote sentimentality. Both, in different ways, rouse the heart without deprecating the head. Though Bernard is fond of speaking of the "sweetness" of Jesus—"Jesu dulcis memoria"—it is an invigorating, never a saccharine sweetness. He exclaims in the "Twentieth Sermon" on the Song of Songs, "Your affection for your Lord Jesus should be both tender and intimate, to oppose the sweet enticements of sensual life. Sweetness conquers sweetness as one nail drives out another."[45] A "sweetness" hard as nails!

Bach twice composed Advent cantatas based on Luther's hymn "Nun komm, der Heiden Heiland"—"Come now, Savior of the Gentiles." In the first, he offers a lovely aria for soprano who sings softly, "Open fully, my heart, for Jesus comes to enter in." In the second rendition, ten years later, the bass intones his conviction, "The hero comes forth from Judah. He runs his course with joy to redeem us the fallen." And Christ the hero wrings from the human heart the joyous choral refrain: "O wunderbarer Segensschein"—"O wondrous sign of blessing."

But Bernard and Bach employ all their gifts of poetic and musical rhetoric to lead us yet deeper. The goal of the diapason of Advent affections they sound is to promote a renewed realization of the intimate union uniting Christians with their Lord. Both chant a spousal mysticism that joins Christ and Christian in loving embrace. In his "Seventy-fourth Sermon" Bernard assumes the persona of the bride in the Song of Songs and pledges, "As often as he slips away from me, so often will I seek him . . . begging him, with a burning desire of the heart to return. I will beseech him to give me the joy of his salvation and return to me."[46]

Bach, in a third Advent cantata, "Schwingt freudig euch empor"—"Soar joyfully aloft"—provides the tenor with a tender

45. Bernard of Clairvaux, *On the Song of Songs*, vol. 1, trans. Kilian Walsh (Collegeville, MN: Cistercian, 1971), 150.

46. Bernard of Clairvaux, *On the Song of Songs*, vol. 4, trans. Irene Edmonds (Collegeville, MN: Cistercian, 1980), 92.

aria, accompanied by oboe d'amore, to declaim: "As the bride is enchanted to behold the bridegroom, so the heart seeks Jesus." And the chorus ecstatically celebrates the wedding feast: "Sing, dance, rejoice, exult, thank the Lord!"

In his fine book *Bach's Major Vocal Works*, Markus Rathey sums up well Bach's synoptic vision. Bach gives voice, in surpassing musical genius, to "the love story between Christ and humanity, bridegroom and bride . . . the longing and waiting for the beloved, his arrival, the loving gaze, the kiss."[47]

And a discerning commentator on Bernard's *Sermons on the Song of Songs* writes, "The name of Jesus is constantly on his tongue, in his heart and on the tip of his pen. The name of Jesus is light, nourishment and medicine for the poor human heart."[48] Saint Bernard himself rhapsodizes, "Only one who has shared the experience can know what it is to love Jesus."

So, we return to the Introit for the Third Sunday of Advent, enlightened and enchanted by Bernard and Bach, enabled to appropriate more deeply the glad tidings it proclaims. Why rejoice? For the Lord is indeed near! How near? In our very heart—heart speaking truly to heart.

SECOND PETER: FROM PERIPHERY TO CENTER[*]

The daily lectionary has recently offered two passages from the Second Letter of Peter—certainly one of the least known of the New Testament books. Indeed, it seems to have entered the New Testament canon, belatedly, by the skin of its teeth (or parchment). Some credible scholars date it as late as 130 AD, though others place it toward the end of the first century. So both in

---

47. Markus Rathey, *Bach's Major Vocal Works: Music, Drama, Liturgy* (New Haven, CT: Yale University Press, 2016), 202.

48. M. Corneille Halflants, introduction to Bernard of Clairvaux, *Song of Songs*, vol. 1, xx.

* This essay was originally published as "Second Peter: From Periphery to Center," *The Catholic Thing*, June 10, 2018, www.thecatholicthing.org.

terms of its history, its lectionary use, and its impact on the lives of clergy and laity alike, Second Peter seems decidedly peripheral.

Which is regrettable—especially today. For, I think, we urgently need to heed its message. Which is what? Happy you asked!

Second Peter presents itself as the testimony of the Apostle Peter to communities threatened by "false teachers" who are importing "destructive heresies," even to the point of "denying the Master who bought them" (2 Pet. 2:1). Of particular concern to the author is their denial of the eschatological heart of the Christian message. Jesus Christ will return as Lord and Judge of the living and the dead.

Moreover, this denial has present consequences. A salient conviction of the author is that conduct derives from doctrine. Change the doctrine, and wayward conduct, both adulterous and covetous (2:14), will follow in its wake.

Thus, the word "remember" serves as a leitmotif in the letter. The author, speaking in the name of the Petrine tradition, urges remembrance of the true doctrine handed down from the Apostles, the right way of life in steadfast expectation of the *parousia*, the coming of the Lord. Its seeming delay is due to God's forbearance and mercy, not to any change of salvific plan and promise (3:9).

Remarkable, and too little appreciated, is Second Peter's high Christology. The opening greeting unites "Simon Peter, slave and apostle of Jesus Christ," with all who share the faith "in the righteousness of our God and Savior, Jesus Christ" (1:1)—one of the few New Testament passages that explicitly designates Jesus as "God."

No doubt, the thrust of the letter's teaching is to affirm the sureness of the Lord's eschatological coming and the decisive day of universal judgment. Famously, Second Peter predicts the transformation of all created reality and the promise of "new heavens and a new earth in which righteousness dwells" (3:13).

Yet a close reading also reveals intimations of "realized eschatology." Not merely the still to come but the already present. The Greek word *parousia* suggests both presence and coming. The one who is coming is also the one who is really present among the faithful, the source of their life and hope.

In this regard, it is noteworthy that Second Peter evokes the memory of the Lord's Transfiguration—the only explicit reference outside the synoptic Gospels. He writes, "We did not devise cleverly concocted fables when we made known to you the power and presence/coming (*parousia*) of our Lord Jesus Christ. For we were with him on the mountain when he received honor and glory from God the Father, and we heard the voice from the heavens: 'This is my Son, the Beloved, in whom I am well pleased!'" (1:16–18)

The Transfiguration testifies to the powerful presence of the Lord, prefiguration and pledge of Christ's final epiphany.

Thus, what is at stake for Second Peter is not less than Christianity's defining belief. He is concerned with "eschatology," because the Gospel proclaims that Jesus Christ is himself the *eschatos*: God's definitive Word, God's revelatory presence among us. This presence will, indeed, be consummated at the end time but is already operative in these present days of grace. God has no other Word of grace and of judgment than his beloved Son.

Jesus Christ, for the New Testament, is the new paradigm of humanity, whether confessed as "Son of Man," "New Adam," or "Word made flesh." Second Peter was ultimately accepted into the canon because it corresponds to this Christological measure.

Throughout, the letter exhorts its readers to "knowledge of the Lord." Such knowledge and the way of life it inspires guide believers to "become sharers in the divine nature" (1:4). This bold assertion, so foundational to the Orthodox spirituality of *theosis* or divinization, has tainted Second Peter in the eyes of liberal Protestant exegetes and theologians.

For notwithstanding the letter's insistence on "holy living" (3:11), the seer of the Transfiguration is more the mystic than the moralist. Of course, holy living matters; but it is ever living according to the pattern of the Holy One.

Toward the end of the letter, the author speaks of "waiting for and hastening the coming (*parousia*) of the day of the Lord" (3:12). It is no passive waiting. One might ask, then, "How does one hasten the coming of the Lord?" And the response seems to be by "growing in the grace and knowledge of our Lord and Savior, Jesus Christ" (3:18). For the author of Second Peter, divinization is Christification.

Jesus Christ's life-bestowing coming in our present and our growing conformity to him presage and prepare his future *parousia*. He initiates the new creation now.

John Calvin voiced reservations about the letter's attribution to the Apostle Peter. Nevertheless, he exclaimed, "I have a dread of repudiating it."[49] We, too, should dread to repudiate it. Rather, we should take pains not to relegate it to the periphery of our spiritual discernment. It represents priceless testimony to the Christic center of our faith.

"FOR ME TO LIVE IS CHRIST!"*

N.T. Wright—Anglican bishop, professor, prolific New Testament scholar—has written more books than many of us have time to read. Happily, he often follows a major work with a shorter, more accessible book. This reflects his conviction that biblical scholarship is for the sake of the life of the Church, that

---

49. John Calvin, *The Epistle of Paul the Apostle to the Hebrews and The First and Second Epistles of St. Peter*, trans. William B. Johnston (Grand Rapids, MI: Eerdmans, 1963), 325.

* This essay was originally published as "'For Me to Live Is Christ!'" *The Catholic Thing*, December 9, 2018, www.thecatholicthing.org.

the pastoral is not extracurricular but the curriculum, the nour-ishing of the disciples on the Way.

Wright's latest book (at least last I looked) is *Paul: A Biogra-phy*. In many ways, it is the culmination of a decades-long wres-tling with the vision and mission of the Apostle to the Gentiles. Of particular significance is Wright's concluding summary chap-ter: "The Challenge of Paul." He is persuaded that the origin and goal of Paul's life and mission was always Jesus.

> Jesus as the shocking fulfillment of Israel's hopes; Jesus as the genuinely human being, the true "image"; Jesus the embodi-ment of Israel's God—so that without leaving Jewish mono-theism, one would worship and invoke Jesus as Lord within, not alongside the service of the "living and true God." Jesus, the one for whose sake one would forsake all idols, all ri-val "lords."[50]

I cite this conviction because I think it offers rich and needed con-text for the brief passage from Paul's Letter to the Philippians that serves as the second reading for this Second Sunday of Advent.

Paul never wrote an impersonal, dispassionate letter. But Phi-lippians may well be his most personal and passionate. He tells them how he longs for them "with the affection of Christ Jesus" (1:8), using the word for visceral emotion the synoptics use in speaking of Jesus's deep compassion. The whole of today's reading expresses Paul's joyful prayer for those who share communion of life with him in the Gospel. Indeed, the passage actually begins at verse 3—inexplicably omitted from the lectionary reading—with the crucial word "*Eucharistō*": "I give thanks to my God for my every memory of you!"

Paul's bond with the Philippians is of the closest and most intimate because he and they are united in a shared common life

---

50. N.T. Wright, *Paul: A Biography* (New York: HarperOne, 2018), 400.

in Christ Jesus. He himself exults, as he will confess later in the letter, that "to live is Christ" (1:21), echoing his passionate cry in Galatians: "I have been crucified with Christ: it is no longer I who live, but Christ who lives in me. And the life I now live in the flesh, I live by faith in the Son of God, who loved me and gave himself for me" (Gal. 2:20).

All this only confirms Wright's contention that it is the person of Jesus who is the very heart of Paul's life and proclamation, "not just as the label to put on an idea, a theological fact, if you like, but as the living, inspiring, consoling, warning, and encouraging presence, the one whose love 'makes us press on,' the one 'who loved me and gave himself for me,' the one whom to know, Paul declared, was worth more than all the privileges that the world . . . has to offer."[51]

Further, this new life in Christ Jesus is inexhaustible and unending. Thus, Paul's prayer for the Philippians (and for us) continues: "that your love may increase ever more and more in knowledge and discernment so that you may be pure and blameless for the day of Christ" (1:9–10).

Nor does Paul exclude himself from the imperative of continuing growth in the knowledge and love of him who is the source of their salvation and the goal of their striving. He will confess later in the letter, "Not that I am myself yet perfected (*teteleiō-mai*)" (3:12); but he strives, as he exhorts them to do, to "know Christ and the power of his resurrection, to share in Christ's suffering, becoming conformed (*summorphizomenos*) to his death, so as to attain the resurrection from the dead" (3:10–11).

This new being, this new life, this ongoing transformation in Christ is the Apostle's fervent desire for those whom he evangelized and for whom he prays unceasingly.

But, in all this, has Paul, perhaps unwittingly, substituted his own Gospel for the simple Good News of Jesus? Has he

---

51. Wright, *Paul*, 401.

subverted Jesus's radical message of social reform into an individualistic "mysticism"—pie in the sky for the oppressed? Is Paul, in effect, the founder of "Christianity," traducing thereby his ancestral faith?

The questions may seem to have about them the musty whiff of nineteenth-century German "higher criticism"; but spruced up and repackaged, they reappear in various guises and disguises even at academic conferences and in "progressive" Catholic publications.

Aeons ago (that is, before Vatican II!), the Jesuit theologian John Courtney Murray gave a series of lectures at Yale, published under the title *The Problem of God*. Perhaps to the surprise of his ecumenical audience, Murray stated that the really crucial question is, "What think ye of *homoousion*?" Guerilla sniping between advocates of "one in being" and partisans of "consubstantial" can be mindless evasions of the decisive and defining question.

For underpinning all Paul's prayers and desires is the absolute conviction that comes to expression in the Christological hymn he sings together with his beloved Philippians: "Though he was in the form of God . . . Jesus took on human form . . . even to death on a cross . . . at the Name of Jesus every knee shall bend . . . Jesus Christ is Lord!" (Phil. 2:6–11)

This hymn of praise and worship (together with the hymns in Colossians 1:15–20 and John 1:1–14) is far closer to Nicaea's *homoousion* than we are often ready to admit. But if we dare not confess it, whatever is Advent for? Whose coming do we truly, in wonder, await—if not Emmanuel: God himself with us in the Father's only-begotten Son, Jesus.

HOPKINS' PASCHAL PRAYER:
"THOU MASTERING ME GOD!"*

With these hammer-driven words, Gerard Manley Hopkins hurls heavenward his anguished confession of faith. With them, the frail, pale convert and Jesuit scholastic launched a revolution in English poetry. With them he plunges deeper into his lifelong wrestling with "(my God!) my God"—as he will exclaim ten years later in one of his "Terrible Sonnets."[52]

The occasion for breaking his seven-year poetic fast was, of course, the news of the drowning of five Franciscan nuns exiled from their German homeland. Invited by his superior to write a brief commemorative poem in their remembrance, Hopkins forged his thirty-five-stanza Pindaric ode. Its first stanza sounds the theme of "The Wreck of the Deutschland" and almost seems to presage the dark days and nights that he will come to experience intimately those last years before his death in Dublin at age forty-five.

> Thou mastering me
> God! giver of breath and bread;
> World's strand, sway of the sea;
> Lord of living and dead;
> Thou hast bound bones and veins in me,
> fastened me flesh,
> And after it almost unmade, what with dread,
> Thy doing: and dost thou touch me afresh?
> Over again I feel thy finger and find thee.[53]

* This essay was originally published as "For Lent: 'Thou Mastering Me God!'" *The Catholic Thing*, February 14, 2018, www.thecatholicthing.org.

52. Gerard Manley Hopkins, "Carrion Comfort," Poetry Foundation, poetryfoundation. org.

53. Gerard Manley Hopkins, "The Wreck of the Deutschland," Poetry Foundation, poetryfoundation.org.

The God whom Hopkins espies with devotion and dread, the "Lord of living and dead," is no faceless deity (in which an increasing number of his Victorian contemporaries believed), but Christ himself. True to Ignatius's *Spiritual Exercises*, which so shaped him, Hopkins confesses Christ's sustaining and transforming presence in all of creation, especially in the human being, created to praise and glorify the Creator.

In one of the poem's most lyrical stanzas, he sings,

> I kiss my hand
> To the stars, lovely-asunder
> Starlight, wafting him out of it; and
> Glow, glory in thunder;
> Kiss my hand to the dappled-with-damson west:
> Since, tho' he is under the world's splendour
> and wonder,
> His mystery must be instressed, stressed;
> For I greet him the days I meet him, and bless
> when I understand.[54]

Pindar's odes celebrated the triumph of some hero of the great Greek athletic competitions at Olympus or Delphi. Hopkins's ode chants the victory of Christ, "hero of Calvary," who triumphs in defeat and reveals the terrible beauty of the cross. But this Paschal Mystery must be continually "instressed, stressed." For as the renowned Hopkins scholar Paul Mariani puts it, the mystery is "the stress of Christ's own love for the human race in spending himself on the cross."[55]

If Ignatius provided the method for conforming Gerard Manley Hopkins more closely to Christ's form, Duns Scotus (whom Hopkins extols in another poem as "of realty the

---

54. Hopkins, "Wreck."

55. Paul Mariani, *A Usable Past: Essays on Modern and Contemporary Poetry* (Amherst, MA: University of Massachusetts Press, 1984), 130.

rarest-veinèd unraveller") helped him perceive the Christic pattern and depth of all creation.[56] The Word is encoded in every particularity. Every "haecceitas" bespeaks him: "*Ipse*, the only one, Christ, King, Head." All creatures, seen through a Christic lens, display their own unique particularity and infinite worth.

It has often been remarked that "The Wreck of the Deutschland" is structured in eight-line stanzas whose rhyme scheme is ABAB-CBCA. Less commented, to my knowledge, is the theological significance of this choice. Pondering the poem as a whole, the reader comes to realize that Hopkins heralds the awe-filled wonder of new creation in Christ. Eight is the symbol of the eighth day inaugurated by Christ's Resurrection from the dead. It assumes concrete form in the octagonal shape of ancient baptismal fonts.

Hence, the poem's heroine, a stalwart Franciscan nun, steadfastly invokes Christ as she submits to the baptism of the flood: "The cross to her she calls Christ to her, christens her wildworst Best." She shares (as we all are called to do) the defeat and victory of "Our passion-plungèd giant risen." Like Paul, she makes up in her own flesh "what is lacking in the sufferings of Christ for the sake of his body the Church" (Col. 1:24) And thus the Word, the Form of forms, once more transfigures human flesh.

Manifesting still further theological richness, the rhyme scheme propels the poem's forward movement by its Trinitarian and Incarnational rhythm. Thus, the first stanza's rhymes—me/sea/thee/bread/dead/dread/flesh/afresh—disclose the "double-naturèd name" (flesh, afresh) as "Mid-numberèd he in three of the thunder-throne" (me/see/thee; bread/dead/dread).

Rooted in Ignatian spirituality and illumined by Scotist ontology, Hopkins effectively counters a reductionism prevalent among our present-day "spiritual, but not religious" brethren. Far too often they advocate an "incarnationalism" bereft of the Incarnation;

---

56. Gerard Manley Hopkins, "Duns Scotus's Oxford," Poetry Foundation, poetryfoundation.org.

and extol "sacramentality" while eschewing the sacraments. Hopkins gives short shrift to such sentimental and unsubstantial romanticism.

Margaret Ellsberg has recently edited selections from Hopkins' poems, letters, and journals and provided sensitive commentary in her attractive and accessible *The Gospel in Gerard Manley Hopkins*. She perceptively identifies the doctrine of transubstantiation as the pole star of Hopkins' spiritual journey, the fecund source of his poetry.

Ellsberg writes, "One could say that Hopkins practiced transubstantiation in every poem. By mysterious talent, he changed plain element into reality sublime."[57] The analogy is alluring, though it inevitably falls short. There is only one salvific sacrifice, that of Christ himself. Still, there is true participation in that sacrifice, whether by exiled nun or exiled poet, that gives God glory. For God's praises are played even on frail and faulty instruments that become more finely tuned *ad majorem Dei gloriam*, as the believer time and again flees "with a fling of the heart to the heart of the Host."

And so "The Wreck of the Deutschland" builds to its final magnificent crescendo and heartfelt prayer:

> Let him easter in us, be a dayspring to the
> dimness of us,
> be a crimson-cresseted east,
> More brightening her, rare-dear Britain, as his
> reign rolls,
> Pride, rose, prince, hero of us, high-priest,
> Our hearts' charity's hearth's fire, our thoughts'
> chivalry's
> throng's Lord.

57. Margaret Ellsberg, introduction to *The Gospel in Gerard Manley Hopkins*, ed. Margaret Ellsberg (Walden, NY: Plough, 2017), 8.

Yet this Easter supplication, in our earthly exile, *in hac lacrimarum valle*, will always be accompanied by Hopkins's Lenten plea in his "Terrible Sonnets": "Mine, O thou lord of life, send my roots rain."[58]

POST-PENTECOSTAL DEPRESSION*

Having celebrated with music and incense the glorious Pentecostal feast, I suddenly found myself unceremoniously dumped into "The Ninth Week in Ordinary Time." Or at least that is what my iBreviary announced, in a decidedly low key, when I opened it.

Immediately, there came to mind the story related by Peter Hebblethwaite in his biography of Paul VI. On the Monday after Pentecost 1970, the pope, preparing to celebrate Mass, was surprised to find that green vestments had been set out. Puzzled, he asked: Where were the red vestments for the Octave of Pentecost? He was dismayed to learn that the Pentecostal Octave had been abolished on his authority. A modest beginning of the Reform of the Reform might well restore the Pentecostal Octave so that we might *lente ac suaviter*, relish and digest the feast.

Until that blessed day comes round, we have at hand, happily, an antidote to depression: Johann Sebastian Bach's sublime Pentecost cantatas. There are four for Pentecost or Whit Sunday, three for Whit Monday, and two for Whit Tuesday.

John Eliot Gardiner has recorded all of Bach's cantatas for the liturgical year in a series of splendid albums on the *Soli Deo Gloria* label. Not only are the performances excellent, but each album contains Gardiner's own comments on the cantatas. These are not only musically informative but theologically insightful.

---

58. Gerard Manley Hopkins, "'Thou art indeed just, Lord, if I contend,'" Poetry Foundation, poetryfoundation.org.
* This essay was originally published as "Post-Pentecostal Depression," *First Things*, December 6, 2017, firstthings.com.

Cantata 68 for Whit Monday is titled "Also hat Gott die Welt geliebt" ("God so loved the world"). It contains a rollicking soprano aria, "My faithful heart, rejoice, sing, be glad." As so often, Bach took an aria he had composed for another occasion and seamlessly adapted it to its new setting and purpose. Gardiner says of the aria that "it is surely one of Bach's most refreshing and unbuttoned expressions of melodic joy and high spirits."[59] Just the thing to counter the drabness of "Ordinary Time."

But Bach, astute student of the liturgy and of human nature, did not simply end the piece with the last words sung by the soprano. Instead, he added an instrumental coda, including two more instruments in the ensemble, almost as if (as Gardiner says) Bach felt "the singer's words were inadequate to express the full joy at the coming of the Holy Spirit."

Exactly. Call it a "coda" or an "octave"—we need more than merely ordinary time. We need festal time, to express our full joy at the coming of the Holy Spirit.

MERCY AND METANOIA*

Packing to move is both bane and boon. And doing so after a thirty-year residence ups the ante considerably! Yet amongst the non-discarded papers and articles saved for some never quite materialized future use, one stumbles across real treasures, even from what may seem unlikely places.

Burrowing through the umpteenth folder, I came upon a 1989 document from the Congregation for Catholic Education: "Instruction on the Study of the Fathers of the Church in the Formation of Priests."

59. John Eliot Gardiner, introduction to "Cantatas Nos 34, 59, 68, 74, 172, 173 & 174," Hyperion Records, https://www.hyperion-records.co.uk/dc.asp?dc=D_SDG121.

* This essay was originally published as "Mercy and 'Metanoia,'" *The Catholic Thing*, September 11, 2016, www.thecatholicthing.org.

Despite the bland title and restricted audience being addressed, it was a refreshing reminder of the riches of the Church Fathers' approach to the theological task—an approach the document states to be "unique, irreplaceable and perennially valid."[60] I'd like to highlight some of what it evoked in me, which I think particularly relevant in our current ecclesial and theological climate.

First, the "place" of theology was, for the Fathers, "in medio ecclesiae," in the midst of the Church—with privileged status accorded the liturgical assembly. Here, theology was inseparably pastoral and spiritual. How could it be otherwise since, at its heart, theology was the unfolding of the riches of the mystery of Christ. Its ultimate goal is "that Christ may dwell in your hearts through faith; that you, rooted and grounded in love, may have strength to comprehend with all the holy ones, what is the breadth and length and height and depth, to know the love of Christ that surpasses knowledge, so that you may be filled with all the fullness of God" (Eph. 3:17–19).

Second, their theology was resolutely Christ centered, "entirely centered on the Mystery of Christ, to whom all the individual truths are referred in a wonderful synthesis," as the Congregation's document states.[61] And it continues: "Everything in their pastoral action and teaching is brought back to charity, and charity to Christ, the universal way of salvation."[62]

Irenaeus's persuasion that "Christ brought all newness in bringing himself" (*omnem novitatem attulit, semetipsum afferens*)[63] was the common conviction of the Fathers. This joyful, exuberant affirmation of the Christic *novum* permeated their preaching and

---

60. Congregation for Catholic Education, introduction to *Instruction on the Study of the Fathers of the Church in the Formation of Priests* (Washington, DC: United States Catholic Conference, 1989), 3.

61. Congregation for Catholic Education, *Instruction*, 15.

62. Congregation for Catholic Education, 24.

63. Irenaeus of Lyons, *Adversus Haereses* 4.34.1. All of the remaining Patristic citations in this essay are from the English translation of *The Liturgy of the Hours*.

writing. It is, significantly, echoed by Pope Francis in *Evangelii Gaudium* 11.

Hence, there is a decidedly "mystical" flavor to the theology of the Fathers. Most of them showed a keen appreciation for reason, for the contribution to theological reflection of Greek culture and philosophy. But, as the congregation's document suggests, they drew especially upon "their affective existential knowledge, anchored in intimate union with Christ, nourished by prayer and sustained by grace and the gifts of the Spirit."[64]

Third, then, their vision of the Good News of Christ was radically participatory. They reveled in the joy of the mystery that is "Christ in you, the hope of glory." And with Paul, they insist that their prime pastoral-theological task was to admonish and teach so as to "present everyone perfect (*teleion*) in Christ" (Col. 1:27–28).

This "Christification" is the end, the *telos*, of their preaching, teaching, and theologizing. And it requires conversion/metanoia and ongoing transformation. They accompanied their hearers *suaviter ac fortiter*, "tenderly and boldly," because they knew intimately the goal of the journey. As Augustine would phrase it, the way and the goal are the same—Christ who is the Way, the Truth, and the Life (John 14:6). And we are called to become members of Christ, making up the *totus Christus*, the whole Christ, so central to Augustine's preaching and theology.

The newness of Jesus Christ, who, through his Paschal Mystery, has inaugurated the new creation, must be reflected in his Body, the Church. Augustine plays magnificently upon this theme in one of his sermons: "We are urged to sing a new song to the Lord, as new men who have learned a new song. . . . Anyone, therefore, who has learned to love the new life has learned to sing a new song, and the new song reminds us of our new life. The new man, the new song, the new covenant."

64. Congregation for Catholic Education, *Instruction*, 20.

Fourth, as Augustine's language displays, the Fathers often rise to the level of poetry in their rhapsody for Christ and the salvation he brings. Ephrem the Syrian exults, "We give glory to you, Lord, who raised up your cross to span the jaws of death like a bridge by which souls might pass from the region of the dead to the land of the living. . . . Your murderers sowed your living body in the earth as farmers sow grain, but it sprang up and yielded an abundant harvest of men and women raised from the dead."

Lovers of Jesus, they did not shy from singing their songs of love.

For the Fathers, God's wondrous mercy in Christ is a supreme gift but also a daunting task. The pearl of great price requires the selling of all to make it one's own. Moreover, the Fathers were supreme "pathologists" of the spiritual life. They were keen discerners of the myriad desires, deceptions, and deceits that impede or poison the new life. They knew the many false notes that distort the harmony of the new song.

Thus, even as they celebrated the mercy of the Father and the turning, the *conversio*, the metanoia, of the Prodigal Son, they realized that the elder brother lurks in each of us, all too apt to lash out ferociously. They carefully scrutinized Galatians 5, on the fruits of the Spirit and the works of the flesh. And they took to heart Paul's admonitions both with respect to themselves and the people to whom they were wed, with whom they journeyed.

In their light, then, we hear today's Gospel of the Prodigal Son (Luke 15:11–32) and wonder: Will mercy at last meet metanoia? Will the elder brother welcome the Father's love and—having converted—enter rejoicing into the Father's house to join the feast? Will we?

"HOW LOVELY IS YOUR DWELLING PLACE, O LORD OF HOSTS"

1. A few years ago at a gathering of Boston College students who were discerning a vocation to the priesthood, one student asked me, "When did you know you wanted to be a priest?"

Like others of my generation, I replied that since grammar school the idea had been firmly in my mind. But I went on to say that it was not only an idea in my mind but a movement of the heart as well. And that movement of the heart was called forth by a prayer that was in my old Latin and English Missal. Actually the prayer was a psalm, Psalm 84, and its opening line is "How lovely is your dwelling place, O Lord of Hosts."

It is the beauty of the Lord's house that beckoned and continues to beckon.

2. I have been graced for almost thirty years now to live and celebrate Mass here at Sacred Heart Church. Those of us who worship here weekly, as we dutifully perform the Sunday ritual of shepherding children into pews, locating the hymn in the book, struggle to remember "consubstantial with," may tend to take for granted the beauty of this church. But visitors always remark on its loveliness: "How lovely is your dwelling place, O Lord of Hosts."

Visitors notice, of course, the intricate ceiling, and are struck by the loveliness of the stained glass, created by Mayer and Company, Munich and New York, in the first years of the twentieth century. They and we often do not have time to consider the windows carefully: the remarkable detail, the sense of depth, the splendid composition of scene each window portrays.

Allow me to spend a moment to share some of that beautiful detail with you, parishioners and guests.

---

* This is a homily given at Sacred Heart Church in Newton Centre, MA, on September 20, 2015, at a Mass of Thanksgiving for the fiftieth anniversary of Fr. Imbelli's ordination to the priesthood.

One feature that I find intriguing is the prominent place of Saint Joseph: a strong, manly presence in six of the seven windows on my left / your right. He is not a secondary figure relegated to the background but is Mary's partner in guarding and guiding the young Jesus.

In the sixth window, depicting the Holy Family of Nazareth, the adolescent Jesus is shown in Joseph's workshop, contemplating the carving of a cross he has made, while Joseph and Mary gaze wistfully at him.

Being Italian, window eight is a particular favorite of mine (the first on your left in the rear): the wedding feast at Cana. When you have the opportunity, spend some time examining it.

Note the profusion of wine pouring into the containers, with the fellow on the right smacking his lips as he holds up a goblet filled to the brim with Chianti Classico. Note also the befuddled bridegroom, with his well-trimmed moustache—he always strikes me as a bit of a fop. (I really don't know what the bride sees in him!)

And a pensive Mary: Who is this really? . . . My son, yet not mine.

Some other quick notes: there is no Crucifixion window. We move from the agony in the garden to the Resurrection. Is that because the Stations of the Cross focus our attention so dramatically upon Christ's Passion and death? Finally, the two last windows bring the New Testament into the Catholicism of the early twentieth century: Christ giving the keys to Peter, as St. Peter's Basilica appears behind them perched on a hill in Galilee. And, in the last, the Sacred Heart appears to Saint Margaret Mary. One of the fruits of that apparition is our own lovely church. Notice when you pause here the extended wings of the angels that begin in gold and unfold in swirling blue.

"How lovely is your dwelling place, O Lord of Hosts."

3. But there is another feature of the windows that is less noticed, more hidden, yet even more important, because it speaks of the faith and generosity that inspired them: their dedications.

So the first window is given by Mrs. Bridget (Roach) O'Connell "In Memory of her Mother and Father." (A number were given in loving memory of parents.)

And the seventh is the gift of Hannah Horgan "In Memory of her Sister and Brothers."

Perhaps, most poignantly, the twelfth window is given by Robert and Elizabeth Levi (a Catholic-Jewish marriage?) "In Memory of their Children."

In memory of their children: what a world of grief and hope contained in those few words!

On a joyful note, the ninth window shows Jesus with the children (today's Gospel). It is, appropriately, the gift of the Sunday School children. One can imagine the pennies and nickels that were diligently collected week after week to pay for the window. (I'm certain those children could never have imagined spending $4 for an ice cream cone at J.P. Licks!)

The last window, the Sacred Heart window, is the gift, as the inscription informs us, of the Reverend Dennis Wholey, first rector of this church (1891–1908).

Having overseen the foundation of the parish and the building of this church, Father Wholey was then dispatched to other pastoral responsibilities. As the Gospel of John reminds us: "One sows and another reaps" (4:37).

I have no idea whether Father Wholey was pleased at being transferred. But if you ask Peg Miller to show you the oil painting of Father Wholey in the rectory, you will be impressed by his authoritative brow and no-nonsense nose. That nose doesn't seem at all out of joint because of his reassignment. No record survives of an appeal to Rome. Standing before his portrait, one can picture him saying, "I too am a man subject to authority" (Matt. 8:9).

(On that same trip to the rectory be sure to ask Peg to show you the framed photo of Father John Connelly, by far our longest-serving pastor. To my eye he seems rather bemused at his placement near Cardinals Spellman and Cushing! He seems to be saying, Sure, you guys got the red hat, but I have a handsomely inscribed bench in Our Lady's Garden.)

"How lovely is your dwelling place, O Lord of Hosts."

4. For however lovely this building, these windows, the Lord's true dwelling place is in the hearts, minds, and bodies of his priestly people: they form a holy temple, the very Body of Christ. *We* form a holy temple, the very Body of Christ.

It is our faith, our generosity, our hoping against hope—all in Christ—that is the true beauty that shines so splendidly.

Of course, sin tarnishes the beauty—today, as it did when this church was built. Each of the inscriptions on the windows is not only a testament of love but also of regret, not only of loss but of failure: of things done or left undone.

They and we are Christ's Body bearing witness to God's love and mercy in Christ, not only in our wholeness but also in our brokenness: ordained priests and priestly people together.

The names today may be different. The faces are certainly more diverse and colorful. But the faith, hope, and love are the same. For "Jesus Christ is the same yesterday, today, and forever" (Heb. 13:8).

We, priests and people, are irrevocably united in the one Body of Christ. For the ordained priest is a baptized Christian anointed and consecrated to serve the priestly life of his brothers and sisters in the Lord.

Our priestly service, gathered around the altar, is to unite, through the ordained priest, our personal offering of praise and thanksgiving to the one perfect sacrifice of Jesus, the true Priest of the New Covenant between God and his people.

This Eucharistic meal we share is made possible by the sacrifice Jesus offered two thousand years ago on Calvary but present now both in heaven before the Father and on earth on every altar where Christ's sacrifice is remembered/re-presented.

So, I rejoice today in gratitude to the Lord and to those who have gone before us and who have handed the faith on to us. But also in deep gratitude to you who continue to bear generous witness to that faith. And I echo the words of the author of the Letter to the Hebrews, who exclaims,

> Therefore, since we are surrounded by so great a cloud of witnesses [past and present], let us lay aside every weight and sin which clings so closely, and let us run with perseverance the race that lies before us, looking always to Jesus, the pioneer and perfecter of faith, who for the joy set before him, endured the cross and is now seated at the right hand of the throne of God. (Heb. 12:1–2)

"How lovely is your dwelling place, O Lord of Hosts."

BIBLIOGRAPHY

Anatolios, Khaled. "A Patristic Reflection on the Nature and Method of Theology in the New Evangelization." *Nova et Vetera* 14, no. 4 (Fall 2016): 1067–81.

—. *Retrieving Nicaea: The Development and Meaning of Trinitarian Doctrine*. Grand Rapids, MI: Baker Academic, 2011.

Augustine. *Confessions*. Translated by F.J. Sheed. Park Ridge, IL: Word on Fire Classics, 2017.

—. *Tractatus in epistolam Ioannis ad Parthos*. In *Patrologia cursus completus*, series Latina, edited by J.-P. Migne, 35: 1977–2062. Paris, 1877.

Bailie, Gil. "Making Peace through the Blood of his Cross." *Communio* 45, no. 3–4 (Fall–Winter 2018): 471–93.

Balthasar, Hans Urs von. *The Glory of the Lord*. Edited by John Riches. Translated by Andrew Louth, John Saward, Martin Simon, and Rowan Williams. Vol. 3, *Studies in Theological Style: Lay Styles*. San Francisco: Ignatius, 1986.

Barron, Robert. *And Now I See: A Theology of Transformation*. 2nd ed. Park Ridge, IL: Word on Fire Academic, 2021.

—. "The Metaphysics of Co-Inherence: A Meditation on the Essence of the Christian Message." In *Handing on the Faith: The Church's Mission and Challenge*, edited by Robert P. Imbelli, 77–90. New York: Crossroad, 2006.

—. *The Priority of Christ: Toward a Postliberal Catholicism*. Grand Rapids, MI: Brazos, 2007.

Beaumont, Keith. *Blessed John Henry Newman: Theologian and Spiritual Guide for Our Times*. San Francisco: Ignatius, 2010.

Becker, Ernest. *The Denial of Death*. New York: Free Press, 1973.

Benedict of Nursia. *The Rule of St. Benedict in English*. Translated by Timothy Fry. Collegeville, MN: Liturgical, 1980.

Benedict XVI, Pope. *Deus Caritas Est*. Encyclical letter. December 25, 2005. Vatican.va.

———. "Homily for the Imposition of the Sacred Pallium on Metropolitan Archbishops." June 29, 2011. Vatican.va.

———. "Homily on the Solemnity of the Epiphany." January 6, 2006. Vatican.va.

———. "Homily for the Opening of the Year of Faith." October 11, 2012. Vatican.va.

———. *Jesus of Nazareth: From the Baptism in the Jordan to the Transfiguration*. Translated by Adrian J. Walker. New York: Doubleday, 2007.

———. *Jesus of Nazareth: Holy Week: From the Entrance into Jerusalem to the Resurrection*. Translated by Philip J. Whitmore. San Francisco: Ignatius, 2011.

———. *Sacramentum Caritatis*. Apostolic exhortation. February 22, 2007. Vatican.va.

———. *Spe Salvi*. Encyclical letter. November 30, 2007. Vatican.va.

Bernard of Clairvaux. *On the Song of Songs*. Translated by Kilian Walsh. Vol. 1. Collegeville, MN: Cistercian, 1971.

———. *On the Song of Songs*. Translated by Irene Edmonds. Vol. 4. Collegeville, MN: Cistercian, 1980.

Bonaventure. *The Journey of the Mind to God*. In *The Works of Bonaventure*, vol. 1, *Mystical Opuscula*, translated by José de Vinck, 1–59. Patterson, NJ: St. Anthony Guild, 1960.

Bonhoeffer, Dietrich. *Letters and Papers from Prison*. Edited by Eberhard Bethge. Translated by H. Fuller. London: SCM, 1953.

Bouyer, Louis. *The Memoirs of Louis Bouyer*. Translated by John Pepino. Kettering, OH: Angelico, 2015.

———. *Newman's Vision of Faith: A Theology for Times of General Apostasy*. San Francisco: Ignatius, 1986.

Bouyer, Louis. *The Paschal Mystery*. Translated by Sister Mary Benoit. Chicago: Regnery, 1950.

Boyle, Nicholas. *Sacred and Secular Scriptures: A Catholic Approach to Literature*. Notre Dame, IN: University of Notre Dame Press, 2005.

Cabasilas, Nicholas. *The Life in Christ*. Translated by Carmino J. DeCatanzaro. Crestwood, NY: St. Vladimir's, 1974.

Calvin, John. *The Epistle of Paul the Apostle to the Hebrews and The First and Second Epistles of St. Peter*. Translated by William B. Johnston. Grand Rapids, MI: Eerdmans, 1963.

Cavadini, John. "Christian Conviction Doesn't Shut Down Dialogue." *Church Life Journal*, March 17, 2021. churchlifejournal.nd.edu.

Christiansen, Keith. "The Bounty of Caravaggio's Glorious Exile." *New York Times*, December 12, 2004. Nytimes.com.

Coda, Piero, and Vincenzo Di Pilato, eds. *Teologia "in" Gesù*. Rome: Città Nuova, 2012.

Compendium to the Catechism of the Catholic Church. Washington, DC: United States Conference of Catholic Bishops, 2006.

Congar, Yves. *Vraie et Fausse Réforme dans l'Eglise*. Paris: Cerf, 1950.

———. *The Word and the Spirit*. Translated by David Smith. San Francisco: Harper & Row, 1986.

Congregation for Catholic Education. *Instruction on the Study of the Fathers of the Church in the Formation of Priests*. Washington, DC: United States Conference of Catholic Bishops, 1989.

Congregation for the Doctrine of the Faith. *Placuit Deo*. February 22, 2018. Vatican.va.

Corbon, Jean. *The Wellspring of Worship*. Translated by Matthew J. O'Connell. Mahwah, NJ: Paulist, 1988.

Cottingham, John. *The Spiritual Dimension: Religion, Philosophy, and Human Value*. Cambridge: Cambridge University Press, 2005.

Crosby, John F. *The Personalism of John Henry Newman*. Washington, DC: The Catholic University of America Press, 2014.

Daley, Brian E. "The Church Fathers." In *The Cambridge Companion to John Henry Newman*, edited by Terrence Merrigan and Ian Ker, 29–46. Cambridge: Cambridge University Press, 2009.

Dante Alighieri. *The Divine Comedy of Dante Alighieri*. Translated and edited by Robert M. Durling. Vol. 3, *Paradiso*. Oxford: Oxford University Press, 2011.

———. *Paradiso*. Translated by Robert Hollander and Jean Hollander. New York: Anchor, 2008.

De Lubac, Henri. *Catholicism: Christ and the Common Destiny of Man*. Translated by Lancelot C. Sheppard and Elizabeth Englund. San Francisco: Ignatius, 1988.

———. *Theological Fragments*. Translated by Rebecca Howell Balinski. San Francisco: Ignatius, 1989.

Dive, Bernard. *John Henry Newman and the Imagination*. London: T&T Clark, 2018.

Driscoll, Jeremy. "Reviewing and Recovering *Sacrosanctum Concilium*." *Origins* 43, no. 29 (December 19, 2013): 479–87.

Dulles, Avery. *The Craft of Theology: From Symbol to System*. New York: Crossroad, 1995.

———. *Evangelization for the Third Millennium*. New York: Paulist, 2009.

Durand, Emmanuel. *L'Offre universelle du salut en Christ*. Paris: Cerf, 2007.

Eagleton, Terry. *Culture and the Death of God*. New Haven: Yale University Press, 2014.

Ellis, John Tracy. "The Eucharist in the Life of Cardinal Newman." *Communio* 4, no. 4 (Winter 1977): 320–40.

Ellsberg, Margaret ed. *The Gospel in Gerard Manley Hopkins*. Walden, NY: Plough, 2017.

Farrow, Douglas. *Ascension Theology*. London: T&T Clark, 2011.

Fiorenza, Francis Schüssler. "Method in Theology." In *The Cambridge Companion to Karl Rahner*, edited by Declan Marmion and Mary E. Hines, 65–82. Cambridge: Cambridge University Press, 2005.

Francis, Pope. *Evangelii Gaudium*. Apostolic exhortation. November 24, 2013. Vatican.va.

———. *Laudato Si'*. Encyclical letter. May 24, 2015. Vatican.va.

———. Mass with the Cardinal Electors. March 14, 2013. Vatican.va.

Gallagher, Michael. *Faith Maps*. Mahwah, NJ: Paulist, 2010.

Gardiner, John Eliot. Introduction to "Cantatas Nos 34, 59, 68, 74, 172, 173 & 174." Hyperion Records. Hyperion-records. co.uk.

Gaventa, Beverly Roberts, and Richard Hays, eds. *Seeking the Identity of Jesus : A Pilgrimage*. Grand Rapids, MI: Eerdmans, 2008.

Granados, José. "The Synergy of Doctrine and Life." *Communio* 43, no. 1 (Spring 2016): 104–22.

Griffiths, Paul J. *Christian Flesh*. Stanford, CA: Stanford University Press, 2018.

Guarino, Thomas. *The Disputed Teachings of Vatican II: Continuity and Reversal in Catholic Doctrine*. Grand Rapids, MI: Eerdmans, 2018.

Haddad, Jordan. "Kneeling Theology: Believing in Order to See Scripture." *Church Life Journal*, October 17, 2018. churchlifejournal.nd.edu.

Hanvey, James. "*Quo Vadis*: Reflections on the Shape of the Church to Come." *America*, March 18, 2013.

Hart, David Bentley. *The Beauty of the Infinite: The Aesthetics of Christian Truth*. Grand Rapids, MI: Eerdmans, 2003.

Hawkins, Peter. *Dante: A Brief History*. Malden, MA: Blackwell, 2006.

Healy, Jr., Nicholas J. "Henri de Lubac on the Development of Doctrine." *Communio* 44, no. 4 (Winter 2017): 667–89.

Hemmerle, Klaus. *Theses Towards a Trinitarian Ontology*. Translated by Stephen Churchyard. Brooklyn, NY: Angelico, 2020.

Hopkins, Gerard Manley. "As Kingfishers Catch Fire." Poetry Foundation. Poetryfoundation.org.

———. "Carrion Comfort." Poetry Foundation. Poetryfoundation.org.

———. "Duns Scotus's Oxford." Poetry Foundation. Poetryfoundation.org.

———. "God's Grandeur." Poetry Foundation. Poetryfoundation.org.

———. "'No worst, there is none. Pitched past pitch of grief.'" Poetry Foundation. Poetryfoundation.org.

———. "That Nature Is a Heraclitean Fire and of the Comfort of the Resurrection." Poetry Foundation. Poetryfoundation.org.

———. "'Thou art indeed just, Lord, if I contend.'" Poetry Foundation. Poetryfoundation.org.

———. "The Wreck of the Deutschland." Poetry Foundation. Poetryfoundation.org.

Ignatius of Antioch. *Letter to the Trallians*. In *The Apostolic Fathers*, translated by Michael W. Holmes, 214–223. Grand Rapids, MI: Baker Academic, 2007.

Imbelli, Robert P. "Do This in Memory of Me: Vatican II Calls Us to a Renewed Realization of the Primacy of Christ." *America*, April 22, 2013.

Imbelli, Robert P. "The Holy Spirit." In *The New Dictionary of Theology*, edited by Joseph Komonchak, Mary Collins, and Dermot Lane, 474–89. Wilmington, DE: Michael Glazier, 1987.

———."Joseph Ratzinger's 'Spiritual Christology.'" In *Gift to the Church and World: Fifty Years of Joseph Ratzinger's "Introduction to Christianity*," edited by John C. Cavadini and Donald Wallenfang, 189–212. Eugene, OR: Pickwick, 2021.

———. "The New Adam and Life-Giving Spirit: The Paschal Pattern of Spirit Christology." *Communio* 25, no. 2 (Summer 1998):

———. "No Decapitated Body." *Nova et Vetera* 18, no. 3 (2020): 757–75.

———. "The Reaffirmation of the Christic Center." In *Sic et Non: Encountering Dominus Iesus*, edited by Stephen J. Pope and Charles Hefling, 96–106. Maryknoll, NY: Orbis, 2002.

———. *Rekindling the Christic Imagination: Theological Meditations for the New Evangelization*. Collegeville, MN: Liturgical, 2014.

———. "*Sursum Corda*: Ascension Theology and Spirituality." In *Sufficit Gratia Mea*, edited by Manlio Sodi. Vatican City: Libreria Editrice Vaticana, 2019.

International Theological Commission. "Theology Today: Perspectives, Principles, and Criteria." November 29, 2011. Vatican.va.

Irenaeus of Lyons, *Adversus Haereses*. In *Patrologia cursus completus*, series Graeca, edited by J.-P. Migne, 7:433–1225. Paris, 1857.

John of the Cross. *The Spiritual Canticle*. In *The Collected Works of St. John of the Cross*, translated by Kieran Kavanaugh and Otilio Rodriguez, 461–632. Washington, DC: ICS Publications, 1979.

Johnson, Elizabeth A. *Truly Our Sister: A Theology of Mary in the Communion of Saints.* New York: Continuum, 2003.

Johnson, Luke Timothy. "On Taking the Creed Seriously." In *Handing on the Faith: The Church's Mission and Challenge,* edited by Robert P. Imbelli, 63–76. New York: Crossroad, 2006.

———. *The Writings of the New Testament: An Interpretation.* Philadelphia: Fortress, 1986.

Kelly, Anthony. "'The Body of Christ: Amen!' The Expanding Incarnation." *Theological Studies* 71, no. 4 (2010): 792–816.

———. *Upward: Faith, Church, and the Ascension of Christ.* Collegeville, MN: Liturgical, 2014.

Ladaria, Luis. *The Living and True God: The Mystery of the Trinity.* Translated by Maria Isabel Reyna and Liam Kelly. Miami, FL: Convivium Press, 2010.

Langevin, Dominic M. *From Passion to Paschal Mystery.* Fribourg: Academic Press, 2015.

Lash, Nicholas. *The Beginning and the End of "Religion."* Cambridge: Cambridge University Press, 1996.

———. *Theology for Pilgrims.* Notre Dame, IN: University of Notre Dame Press, 2008.

Lemna, Keith. *The Apocalypse of Wisdom: Louis Bouyer's Theological Recovery of the Cosmos.* Brooklyn, NY: Angelico Press, 2019.

Levering, Matthew. *An Introduction to Vatican II as an Ongoing Theological Event.* Washington, DC: The Catholic University of America Press, 2017.

———. *Newman on Doctrinal Corruption.* Park Ridge, IL: Word on Fire Academic, 2022.

Lohfink, Gerhard. *Jesus of Nazareth: What He Wanted, Who He Was.* Translated by Linda M. Maloney. Collegeville, MN: Liturgical, 2012.

Lonergan, Bernard. *Method in Theology.* New York: Herder, 1972.

Mariani, Paul. *A Usable Past: Essays on Modern and Contemporary Poetry*. Amherst, MA: University of Massachusetts Press, 1984.

Marmion, Declan, and Mary Hines, eds. *The Cambridge Companion to Karl Rahner*. Cambridge: Cambridge University Press, 2005.

Marshall, Bruce. *Trinity and Truth*. Cambridge: Cambridge University Press, 2000.

McElroy, Robert W. "Cardinal McElroy on 'Radical Inclusion' for L.G.B.T. People, Women and Others in the Catholic Church." *America*, January 24, 2023. Americamagazine.org.

McGregor, Peter John. *Heart to Heart: The Spiritual Christology of Joseph Ratzinger*. Eugene, OR: Pickwick, 2016.

McIntosh, Mark A. *The Divine Ideas Tradition in Christian Mystical Theology*. Oxford: Oxford University Press, 2021.

Meconi, David Vincent. *The One Christ: St. Augustine's Theology of Deification*. Washington, DC: The Catholic University of America Press, 2013.

Merrigan, Terrence. "Revelation." In *The Cambridge Companion to John Henry Newman*, edited by Terrence Merrigan and Ian Ker, 47–72. Cambridge: Cambridge University Press, 2009.

Meszaros, Andrew. "Christocentrism in Theology and Evangelization in the Thought of Robert P. Imbelli." In *The Center Is Jesus Christ Himself*, edited by Andrew Meszaros, 1–25. Washington, DC: The Catholic University of America Press, 2021.

Miłosz, Czesław. "Creating the World." *The New Yorker*, February 26, 1990.

Moo, Douglas. *The Letters to the Colossians and to Philemon*. Grand Rapids, MI: Eerdmans, 2008.

Mühlen, Heribert. *Una Mystica Persona*. München: Schöning, 1964.

Murray, Paul. *Aquinas at Prayer: The Bible, Mysticism and Poetry.* London: Bloomsbury, 2013.

Murray, Placid, ed. *Newman the Oratorian.* Dublin: Gill & Macmillan, 1969.

Nellas, Panayiotis. *Deification in Christ.* Crestwood, NY: St. Vladimir's, 1987.

Newman, John Henry. *Apologia Pro Vita Sua.* London: Longmans, 1913.

———. "Biglietto Speech, Rome." In *Addresses to Cardinal Newman with His Replies,* edited by W.P. Neville, 61–70. London: Longmans, 1905. Newmanreader.org.

———. *An Essay in Aid of a Grammar of Assent.* Notre Dame: University of Notre Dame Press, 1979.

———. *An Essay in Aid of a Grammar of Assent.* Edited by I.T. Ker. Oxford: Clarendon, 1985.

———. *Lectures on the Doctrine of Justification.* London: Longmans, 1914.

———. *Letters and Diaries of John Henry Newman.* Vol. 11. Edited by Charles Stephen Dessain. Edinburgh: Thomas Nelson, 1961.

———. *Fifteen Sermons Preached before the University of Oxford.* 3rd ed. New York: Scribner, 1872.

———. *Parochial and Plain Sermons.* San Francisco: Ignatius, 1997.

———. *Prayers, Verses, and Devotions.* San Francisco: Ignatius, 1989.

———. *Selected Sermons.* Edited by Ian Ker. New York: Paulist, 1994.

———. *Spiritual Writings.* Maryknoll, NY: Orbis, 2012.

Nicholls, Guy. *Unearthly Beauty: The Aesthetic of St John Henry Newman.* Leominster, UK: Gracewing, 2019.

Nichols, Aidan. *A Key to Balthasar.* Grand Rapids, MI: Baker Academic, 2011.

O'Collins, Gerald. *Believing in the Resurrection: The Meaning and Promise of the Risen Jesus*. New York: Paulist, 2012.

O'Collins, Gerald. *A Christology of Religions*. Maryknoll, NY: Orbis, 2018.

O'Malley, John W. *What Happened at Vatican II*. Cambridge MA: Harvard University Press, 2008.

O'Regan, Cyril. *The Anatomy of Misremembering: Von Balthasar's Response to Philosophical Modernity*. Vol. 1, *Hegel*. New York: Crossroad, 2014.

———. "Newman and von Balthasar: The Christological Contexting of the Numinous." *Eglise et Théologie* 26 (1995): 165–202.

Paul VI, Pope. *Evangelii Nuntiandi*. Apostolic exhortation. December 8, 1975. Vatican.va

Peppard, Michael. "Testing the Boundaries." *Commonweal*, April 12, 2013.

Percy, Walker. *Lost in the Cosmos: The Last Self-Help Book*. New York: Farrar, 1983.

Prosperi, Paolo. "The Birth of *Sources Chrétiennes* and the Return to the Fathers." *Communio* 39, no. 4 (Winter 2012): 643–44.

Rahner, Karl. *The Love of Jesus and the Love of Neighbor*. Translated by Robert Barr. New York: Crossroad, 1983.

———. *Sacramentum Mundi: Encyclopedia of Theology*. Vol. 6. New York: Herder, 1970.

———. "Christian Living Formerly and Today." In *Theological Investigations*, vol. 7, *Further Theology of the Spiritual Life*, translated by David Bourke, 3–24. New York: Herder, 1971.

Rahner, Karl, and Joseph Ratzinger. *Revelation and Tradition*. Translated by W.J. O'Hara. New York: Herder, 1966.

Rathey, Markus. *Bach's Major Vocal Works: Music, Drama, Liturgy*. New Haven, CT: Yale University Press, 2016.

Ratzinger, Joseph. *Behold the Pierced One: An Approach to a Spiritual Christology.* Translated by Graham Harrison. San Francisco: Ignatius, 1986.

——. *Collected Works: Theology of the Liturgy.* San Francisco: Ignatius, 2014.

——. "*Communio*: A Program." *Communio* 19, no. 3 (Fall 1992): 436–49.

——. *Dogma and Preaching: Applying Christian Doctrine to Daily Life.* Translated by Michael J. Miller and Matthew J. O'Connell. San Francisco: Ignatius, 2011.

——. *Eschatology: Death and Eternal Life.* Translated by Michael Waldstein. Washington, DC: The Catholic University of America Press, 1988.

——. *God Is Near Us: The Eucharist, the Heart of Life.* Translated by Henry Taylor. San Francisco: Ignatius, 2003.

——. "Homily at the Mass 'Pro Eligendo Romano Pontifice.'" April 18, 2005. Vatican.va.

——. *Introduction to Christianity.* Translated by J.R. Foster. San Francisco: Ignatius, 2004.

——. *Milestones: Memoirs 1927–77.* Translated by Erasmo Leiva-Merikakis. San Francisco: Ignatius, 1998.

——. *Ministers of Your Joy.* Translated by Robert Nowell. London: St. Paul's, 1989.

——. *The Nature and Mission of Theology: Essays to Orient Theology in Today's Debates.* Translated by Adrian Walker. San Francisco: Ignatius, 1995.

——. *On the Way to Jesus Christ.* Translated by Michael J. Miller. San Francisco: Ignatius, 2005.

——. *Pilgrim Fellowship of Faith: The Church as Communion.* Translated by Henry Taylor. San Francisco: Ignatius, 2005.

——. *The Ratzinger Report.* Translated by Salvator Attanasio and Graham Harrison. San Francisco: Ignatius, 1985.

Ratzinger, Joseph. "*Sources Chrétiennes* and the One Unique Source." *Communio* 44, no. 2 (Summer 2017): 383–88.

———. *The Spirit of the Liturgy*. Translated by John Saward. San Francisco: Ignatius, 2000.

Ray, Richard. "'Clarity' in Honeck's New Brahms Recording Makes It a 2021 Standout." CPR Classical, November 19, 2021. Cpr.org.

Raymo, Chet. "It's Darker Than We Thought." Review of *The Fifth Essence: The Search for Dark Matter in the Universe*, by Lawrence M. Krauss. *Commonweal* 117, no. 4 (February 23, 1990): 118–19.

Robinson, Denis. "Preaching." In *The Cambridge Companion to John Henry Newman*, edited by Terrence Merrigan and Ian Ker, 241–54. Cambridge: Cambridge University Press, 2009.

Ross, Alex. "The Pittsburgh Symphony's Savage Precision." *The New Yorker*, February 10, 2020.

Royal, Robert. *A Deeper Vision: The Catholic Intellectual Tradition in the Twentieth Century*. San Francisco: Ignatius, 2015.

Rush, Ormond. "Toward a Comprehensive Interpretation of the Council and its Documents." *Theological Studies* 73, No. 3 (September 2012): 547–69.

Rutledge, Fleming. *The Crucifixion: Understanding the Death of Jesus Christ*. Grand Rapids, MI: Eerdmans, 2015.

Schmemann, Alexander. *For the Life of the World: Sacraments and Orthodoxy*. Crestwood, NY: St. Vladimir's, 1973.

Scarafoni, Paolo, ed. *Cristocentrismo: Riflessione Teologica*. Rome: Città Nuova, 2002.

Scruton, Roger. *The Face of God*. London: Bloomsbury, 2012.

Smart, Christopher. *Jubilate Agno*. Edited by W.H. Bond. New York: Greenwood, 1969.

———. *Poems*. Edited by Robert Brittain. Princeton: Princeton University Press, 1950.

Steinberg, Leo. *Michelangelo's Painting.* Edited by Sheila Schwartz. Chicago: University of Chicago Press, 2019.

Steiner, George. *Real Presences.* Chicago: University of Chicago Press, 1989.

Strange, Roderick. *Newman and the Gospel of Christ.* Oxford: Oxford University Press, 1981.

———. *Newman: The Heart of Holiness.* London: Hodder & Stoughton, 2019.

Sullivan, Andrew. "I Used to Be a Human Being." *New York Magazine*, September 19, 2016. Nymag.com.

Sumner, George R. *The First and the Last: The Claim of Jesus Christ and the Claims of Other Religious Traditions.* Grand Rapids, MI: Eerdmans, 2004.

Taylor, Charles. *A Secular Age.* Cambridge: Belknap, 2007.

Thomas Aquinas. *Quaestiones Disputatae.* Edited by Raymundi Spiazzi, Paulus Pession, Mannes Calcaterra, Tito S. Centi, Pio Bazzi, and Egidio Odetto. Vol. 1, *De Veritate.* Turin, IT: Marietti, 1949.

———. *Summa contra Gentiles.* Editio Manualis Leonina. Rome: Marietti, 1946.

Torrell, Jean-Pierre. *Le Christ en ses mystères: la vie et l'oeuvre de Jésus selon saint Thomas d'Aquin.* Vol. 2. Paris: Desclée, 1999.

———. *Pour nous les hommes et pour notre salut.* Paris: Cerf, 2014.

———. *Saint Thomas Aquinas.* Translated by Robert Royal. Vol. 1, *The Person and His Work.* Washington, DC: The Catholic University of America Press, 1996.

———. *Saint Thomas Aquinas.* Translated by Robert Royal. Vol. 2, *Spiritual Master.* Washington, DC: The Catholic University of America Press, 2003.

Tück, Jan-Heiner. *A Gift of Presence: The Theology and Poetry of the Eucharist in Thomas Aquinas*. Translated by Scott G. Hefelfinger. Washington, DC: The Catholic University of America Press, 2018.

Van Beeck, Franz Jozef. *God Encountered: A Contemporary Catholic Systematic Theology*. Vol. 1. Collegeville, MN: Liturgical, 1989.

Vatican Council II. *Dei Verbum: Dogmatic Constitution on the Church*. In *The Word on Fire Vatican II Collection*, 13–42. Edited by Matthew Levering. Park Ridge, IL: Word on Fire Institute, 2021.

————. *Gaudium et Spes: Pastoral Constitution on the Church in the Modern World*. In *The Word on Fire Vatican II Collection*, 211–337. Edited by Matthew Levering. Park Ridge, IL: Word on Fire Institute, 2021.

————. *Sacrosanctum Concilium: Constitution on the Sacred Liturgy*. In *The Word on Fire Vatican II Constitution*, 151–209. Edited by Matthew Levering. Park Ridge, IL: Word on Fire Institute, 2021.

————. *Optatam Totius: Decree on Priestly Training*. In *The Word on Fire Vatican II Collection: Declarations and Decrees*, 239–72. Edited by Matthew Levering. Elk Grove Village, IL: Word on Fire Institute, 2023.

Volf, Miroslav. *Free of Charge: Giving and Forgiving in a Culture Stripped of Grace*. Grand Rapids, MI: Zondervan, 2005.

Wallace, David Foster. "This Is Water." Commencement speech at Kenyon College, May 21, 2005. https://web.ics.purdue.edu/~drkelly/DFWKenyonAddress2005.pdf.

Wells, Harold. *The Christic Center*. Maryknoll, NY: Orbis, 2004.

Wicks, Jared. *Investigating Vatican II*. Washington, DC: The Catholic University of America Press, 2018.

Williams, Rowan. *Being Christian*. London: SPCK, 2014.

Williams, Rowan. *Christ: The Heart of Creation*. London: Bloomsbury, 2018.

———. *The Dwelling of the Light: Praying with Icons of Christ*. Grand Rapids, MI: Eerdmans, 2004.

Wilken, Robert Louis. *The Spirit of Early Christian Thought: Seeking the Face of God*. New Haven: Yale University Press, 2003.

Wiman, Christian. *My Bright Abyss: Meditation of a Modern Believer*. New York: Farrar, 2014.

Wright, N.T. *Paul: A Biography*. New York: HarperOne, 2018.

INDEX

Adam, xxiii, 39–40, 50, 73, 109, 121, 130, 234, 241, 245

admirabile commercium, 165

ad orientem, 92–93

Advent, 284–90, 294–96

Adversus Haereses (Irenaeus), xxi, 230

aggiornamento, x, 4, 18, 20, 62, 68, 108, 247–48, 252

Anatolios, Khaled, 23–24, 118, 132

Anselm, 22, 101, 103, 216

apophatic theology, 128–29, 248

apostasy, x, 54, 236, 246

Apostles' Creed, 68–72, 252

Ascension
  in Augustine, 144–45
  and continuing presence of Christ, 13–14, 44–45, 52–53, 76, 80, 144, 154–56, 171–73
  and divinization, 14, 129, 145, 173
  and Eucharist, 13–14, 80, 154–56, 171–73
  and headship of Christ, 143–56, 173
  and heaven, 12–13, 76–77
  and Incarnation, 12, 129, 153
  in liturgy, 9, 14–15
  and new creation, xxii, 13, 15, 76–77, 90, 132, 153–54
  in Newman, 44–45, 49
  and Paschal Mystery, 8–9, 12, 15, 76, 87, 90, 153–54, 172
  in Ratzinger, 12–13, 72–78

Ascension (*continued*)
  and Transfiguration, 12, 132, 154
  and transfigured humanity, xi–xii, 14–15, 49–52, 116, 129, 145–46, 152, 173

Augustine
  on Ascension, 144–45
  on Eucharist, 88, 173
  on headship of Christ, 144–46, 231–32, 304
  on memory, 280–81
  on new creation, 231, 304
  on Psalms, 231–32
  in Ratzinger, 64, 71, 84, 86, 88, 173
  and *totus Christus*, 15–17, 73, 88, 145–46, 231, 304

Bach, Johann Sebastian, 113, 158, 184, 256, 287–90, 301–2

Bach's Major Vocal Works (Rathey), 290

Baglione, Giovanni, 272

Balthasar, Hans Urs von, 71n35, 115, 124, 127–28

Baptism
  of Jesus, 262–63
  new life through, 90, 161, 232, 234
  as participation in Christ, xxii–xxiii, 41, 46–47, 71, 90, 161, 218, 232, 234, 238, 259
  and Paschal Mystery, 218, 224